The War Room

Past Kudos and Brickbats for Warren Kinsella

"Subtlety and restraint are not Mr. Kinsella's strengths; speed and a taste for the jugular are."
— Paul Wells, *Maclean's*

"... the Alliance's slide into oblivion hit the point of no return when the toe of Warren Kinsella's shoe made contact with Stockwell Day's rump."
— Jonathan Kay, *National Post*

"[Warren] Kinsella is passionate, opinionated and loyal ... people in important positions value his opinion. His blog is must-read stuff for political pundits ... [and] he's a colourful, feisty backroom boy doing his best to stir the pot in the grand tradition of Canadian politics."
— *Kingston Whig-Standard*

"[Warren Kinsella] is tiresome and biased ... vengeful ... fevered and sniping commentary ..."
— Gilles Gherson, former editor-in-chief, *Toronto Star*

"Warren Kinsella: Sound! Bite!"
— *National Post*

"[Warren Kinsella] represents the sleazy side to Ottawa politics that traffics in unverified innuendo and self-serving rumour ..."
— Tony Burman, former editor-in-chief, *CBC News*

"An inexperienced political staffer."
— Justice John Gomery

"Kinsella is a punk."
— *Globe and Mail*

"A cult figure for young Liberals."
— *The Financial Post*

The War Room

Political Strategies for Business, NGOs,
and Anyone Who Wants to Win

Warren Kinsella

Foreword by the Right Honourable Jean Chrétien

THE DUNDURN GROUP
TORONTO

Editor: Michael Carroll
Copy-editor: Andrea Waters
Design: Alison Carr
Printer: Marquis

Library and Archives Canada Cataloguing in Publication

Kinsella, Warren, 1960-
    The war room : political strategies for business, NGOs, and anyone who wants to win / Warren Kinsella.

ISBN 978-1-55002-746-4

    1. Campaign management--Canada. 2. Spin doctors--Canada.
3. Politics, Practical--Canada. 4. Political participation--Canada.
5. Liberal Party of Canada--Elections. 6. Campaign management--
United States. I. Title.

JL193.K55 2007   324.971   C2007-904655-X

1   2   3   4   5   11   10   09   08   07

We acknowledge the support of **The Canada Council for the Arts** and the **Ontario Arts Council** for our publishing program. We also acknowledge the financial support of the **Government of Canada** through the **Book Publishing Industry Development Program** and **The Association for the Export of Canadian Books**, and the **Government of Ontario** through the **Ontario Book Publishers Tax Credit** program, and the **Ontario Media Development Corporation**.

Care has been taken to trace the ownership of copyright material used in this book. The author and the publisher welcome any information enabling them to rectify any references or credits in subsequent editions.

                                                                              J. Kirk Howard, President

Printed and bound in Canada.
Printed on recycled paper.

www.dundurn.com

Dundurn Press	Gazelle Book Services Limited	Dundurn Press
3 Church Street, Suite 500	White Cross Mills	2250 Military Road
Toronto, Ontario, Canada	High Town, Lancaster, England	Tonawanda, NY
M5E 1M2	LA1 4XS	U.S.A. 14150

To my mom …

… who has been so brave
(and my dad knows it, too)

Contents

9 | Foreword by the Right Honourable Jean Chrétien

11 | Acknowledgements

17 | INTRODUCTION: Welcome to the War Room

41 | LESSON ONE: Let's Get Started!

63 | LESSON TWO: Get Spinning!

83 | LESSON THREE: Get Your Message Out (For Free)!

105 | LESSON FOUR: Get Your Message Out (For Money)!

135 | LESSON FIVE: Get Creative!

155 | LESSON SIX: Get Tough!

183 | LESSON SEVEN: Get the Facts and Numbers!

213 | LESSON EIGHT: Get the Handle Scandal Manual!

249 | LESSON NINE: Get Modern!

279 | LESSON TEN: Get Fighting!

289 | Bibliography

Foreword

I AM DELIGHTED that people have bought Warren Kinsella's new book, but I would be more delighted, and so would they, if they bought mine.

In all seriousness, I can reveal that Warren is passionate, loyal, and a good guy to have on your side in a political fight. When he worked for me, and afterwards, he never hesitated to fight the good fight.

His book is about how war rooms can help you to win. I encourage everyone to read it.

The Right Honourable Jean Chrétien
August 2007
Ottawa, Ontario

Acknowledgements

S OME WAG ONCE NOTED THAT political people read books differently from others. It's true. Whereas normal people read books from front to back, political folks do it the other way around. That's because they always check the index (or the acknowledgements page) to see if they, or anyone they know, is in the book. Only then do they buy it.

Consequently, I intend to thank everyone who was interviewed for this book, or anyone who has ever offered me their political insights in the past. That way, I not only get to offer them my sincere thanks, but I potentially get them to buy it, too. (Some folks named below, undoubtedly, may not want to be thanked, but they only have themselves to blame. They shouldn't have talked to me.) So here goes, starting from the left, where I got my political start.

In the Far West, I learned from the likes of Gary Collins, Gord Campbell, Clark Roberts, Greg Lyle, Stew Braddick, Ted Olnyk, Luigi Perna, John Eisenstat, Irv Epstein, Raymond Chan, Paul Fyssas, Ross Fitzpatrick, May Brown, John Kenney (RIP), Don Williams, George

Taylor, Royce Frith, July Kirk, Gord Robson, Steve Kukucha, Bill Brooks, Patrick Wong, Celso Boscariol, Kent Scarborough, Dave Wizinsky, Jay Straith, David Plewes, Heather Dunsford, Alan Shuster, Herb Dhaliwal, Diana Hutchinson, Alex Pannu, Dennis Prouse, Murray Dykeman, Pam McDonald, Fraser Randall, Andre Gerolymatos, Tim Morrison, Martin MacLachlan, Svend Robinson, Mike McDonald, Dirk Ricker, Jen Reid, Stuart Pelly, Jonathan Ross, Ed Barnes, Jim Sullivan, Lorne Burns, Chuck Strahl, Greg Walker, Don Millar, Renate Bublick, Christy Clark and Mark Marissen, Mike Brooks, Adam Korbin, Prem Vinning, Angus Reid, John Nuraney, Stan Winfield, Ted Nebbeling, and Neil Sweeney. Special thanks go to Brad McTavish, Mark Brady, and Naina Sloan. And I am immensely grateful to Toby Ward, the Canadian politico who interviewed Haley Barbour for this book, for his judgment, his loyalty, and his friendship, all of which I value a great deal.

In the Nearer West, my home, I was enlightened by Nick Taylor, John Cordeau, Steve MacAdam (RIP), Colin MacDonald, Joyce Fairbairn, Sheldon Chumir (RIP), Lloyd Axworthy, Derek Raymaker and family, Raj Chahal, David Asper and his dad Izzy (RIP), John Harvard, Ginny May, Elliott Poll, Ron Duhamel (RIP), Ken Boessenkool, David MacInnis, Cos Gabriele, Hugh McFadyen, Martin Egan, Lee Hill, Rey Pagtakhan, Ethel Blondin-Andrew, Catherine Lappe, Dan Nearing, Jim Keelaghan, and Bob Haslam. Always standing by me when I was battling western separatists and/or kooky right-wingers were my parents, Lorna and Doug; my brothers, Lorne and Kevin; and the two guys who have been allies the longest, Alan Macdonald and Pierre Schenk.

In Godless Central Canada, where my brood and I currently reside, there are about a million people to thank, and to whom I owe much, whether they know it or not. The list will only be partial, for which I offer *mea maxima culpa* in advance. There is Barb "Babs" Joy, Bob Lopinski, James Villeneuve, Jen Norman and Dave Pryce, Tom Allison, Gordie Brown, Rick Anderson, John and Peter Wilkinson, Beth Clarkson, Eugene Bellemare, Jack Fleischman, Andy Stein, Sen. David Smith, Wendy Iwai, Don Millar, Matt Maychak, Ben Chin, Steve Dyck, Gordon Prieur, Jeff Ryan, Jo Reath, Richard Patten, Percy Downe, Angelo Persichilli, Sheila Copps, Jane Taber, Pierre Marc Johnson, John Hayter, Benoit Chiquette, Malcolm Lester, John Hinds, Michelle Bishop, Anne and Rob Morash, Joan Bryden, Gordon Ashworth, the McGuinty family, Justin Trudeau, Laura Miller, Dave Gene, Jim Peterson, Herb Gray, Chris Sweeney, Emond and Heather Chiasson, David Peterson, Robert Houle, Dennis Mills, Rob Toole, Dale Lastman, Aaron Lazarus, Andrew Steele, Dwight Duncan, Chris Benner, John Rae, Manuel Prutschi, Mark Quinn, David Gourlay, Jeff Steiner, Patti Munce, Shannon Deegan, Marc Laframboise, Gabor Apor, Hugh Segal, Christine McMillan and the Fearless McGuinty War Room '07, Charlie Angelakos, Zoe Amos, David Zussman, Bob Murdoch, Mark Poole, Jack Warren, Bruce Drysdale, Stevie Cameron, Eric Maldoff, Beatrice Raffoul, Adrian Montgomery, Phyllis Bruce, Paul Godfrey, Gary Clement, Duncan Dee, Ian MacLeod, Val Poulin, Dan Dunlop, Sharon Smith, Randy and Luba Pettipas, Dominic Agostino (RIP), Greg Wong, Mark Stokes, Peter Gregg, Bob Nault, Kaz Flinn, Taras Zalusky, Stan and Bernie Farber, Eric Johnson, Nick Nelson, Alice Willems, Jonathan Goldbloom, Isabel Metcalfe, Grant Kippen, Doug Wotherspoon, Greg Schmidt, Pat Neri, Monique Bondar, Sean O'Connor, Oliver Carroll, Sheila Ward, Aaron Dobbin, David Caplan, Laurel Broten, Doug Melville, Greg Tsang, Tony Knill, Kevin Lee, Murray Campbell, Cal and Darryl Bricker, Jerry Yanover, Chethan Lakshman, Paul de Zara, Nathalie Gauthier, Helen Burstyn, Claudette Levesque, John Chenier, Johanne Senecal, Joe Belfontaine, Krista Scaldwell, Earl Stuart, Gerald Butts, Dominic LeBlanc, Ron Drews, Jean Pelletier, Jen Nicholson, Phillip Gigantes (RIP), Priya Suagh, John Parisella, Deb Roberts, Christine Hampson, Titch Dharamsi, Tenio Evangelista, John Wright, Jack Siegal, Mike Marzolini, Rob Ritter, Hugh Scott, Don Boudria, Mike Pearson, Joan Lajeunesse, Tim Barber, Peter Lauwers, Alister Campbell, "Marc the Ninja," Eme Onuoha, Dan Rogers, Kevin McGuire, Dan Hays, Pete Tuinema, Jonathan Kay and John Turley-Ewart and Doug Kelly and everyone at the *National Post*, Leo Guilbault, Bill Fisch, Sheila Finestone, Denise Costello, Ezra Levant, Dan Rath, Bob Lay, Len Kuchar, Bill Fox, Don Guy, Hugh Blakeney, Lisa Raitt, Chris Clark, George Smitherman, Scott Sheppard, Peter Cathcart, Paul Pellegrini, Mary-Ellen Kenny, Steve Kelly, Jim Anderson, Shimon Fogel, Christine Albee, Patrick Muttart, Debbie Gowling, Julienne Racicot, Con Di Nino, Bob Chant, Heather Armstrong, Louise Harris, Maryse Harvey, Lina Bigoni, Dan Miles, Kevin Bosch, Keith and Ian and

Catherine Davey, Dan Cook, Ray Heard, Cindy Boucher, Derek "Deeks" Kent, Gen LeBlanc, Karim "Special K" Bardeesy, Ralph Palumbo, George Young, Herb Metcalfe, Phil Dewan, Christine Hampson, Claudette Brown, the Abbotts, Craig and Susan Wright, Diane Gemus, Jim Munson, Mark Cameron, Bruce and Deb Davis, Ron Atkey, Steve Janke, Sandra Pupatello, Patrick Parisot, Dan McCarthy, Rob Steiner, Nicole Lovell, Heather Bradley, Rusty Baird, Greg King, Paul Genest, Nicki Holland, Michael Bryant, Paul Wells, Megan McGillicuddy, Jason Cherniak, Mike McAdoo, Kassandra McMicking, Rarihokwats, Adam Radwanski, Greg Boyd Bell, Rick and Angie Bartolucci, Sergio Marchi, Jean Carle, Greg Owen, Stephen Taylor, Fred Gaspar, Peter Milliken, Dan Tisch, Tracey Sobers, Rick Smith, Monte Kwinter, Stephen Rouse, David and Chris Collenette, Alf Apps, Scott Sellers, Tony Genco, Christina Blizzard, John Harding, Chris Fleck, Randi Rahamin, Michael Meighen, Maurizio Bevilacqua, Leslie Noble, Kate Malloy, John Duffy, Johnny Z., John Manley, Eddie Francis, Jimmy Warren, Richard Cleroux, Monte Solberg, Andre Ouellet, Tony Macerollo, Duncan Fulton, Yves Gougoux, Nick Parker, Natasha Hassan, Dan Hayward, Keith Sharp, Sean Plummer, Martin Cauchon, Carole Coté, Conrad Winn, Ajay Chopra, Phil Goodwin, Pierre Tremblay (RIP), the Calgary Grit, Mike Duffy, Jerry Grafstein, Rudy Griffiths, Chaviva Hosek, Joan Fraser, Sonia Clement, and countless others. Special thanks go to Graham Scott for his support and informed insight; Canada's best libel lawyer, Brian Shiller; my other friend and lawyer, Clay Ruby; Jim Watson, for many years of support and "shameless" photo-mongering; Bruce Hartley and Randy McCauley, for political smarts far beyond their collective years; my blogging co-conspirators and regulars; my pal Bob Richardson, who is one of the sharpest political strategists around; and my partners and colleagues at the Daisy Consulting Group, Cameron Summers, Declan Doyle, Omar Soliman, Katherine Stoneman, Emily Hill, Sandra Leffler, and Megan Harris.

In the Far East, I have learned much from the likes of Tony Blom, Shona Kinley, Kirk Cox, Allison MacNeil, Paul Sparkes, Tim Powers, Brian Tobin, Kevin Fram, Willy Moore, Steve MacKinnon, Jean Lepine, Greg MacEachern, Lawrence Macaulay, Al Graham, Meredith Naylor, and Carl Gillis, whom we all miss so much still. Most of all, I have had the privilege to have learned at the knee of the great Roméo LeBlanc, one of the most decent men ever to set foot on Parliament Hill.

Beyond our borders, I am grateful to James Carville, John Rowley, Betsey Wright, Haley Barbour, Rod Shealy, Phil Noble, Lynda Kaid, Tony Schwartz, Dick Morris, Lucianne Goldberg, Tobe Berkovitz, Pippa Norris, Mark Mellman, Dane Strother, Scott Howell, and many others.

For those who went above and beyond the call of duty to get this book in your hands, I offer the most sincere thanks of which I am capable. Included in this small group are Grace Tsakas and Jackie Roach, my former assistants, for overseeing interview transcripts and keeping me organized. There is also Prime Minister Jean Chrétien and his wife, Aline, who have stood by me when many others would not.

Thanks, too, to my agent, Helen Heller. She's the best there is. (If the book wasn't a good idea, you can blame her, too.) My publisher and editor, meanwhile, are Kirk Howard and Michael Carroll, respectively. They are both patient and smart, which publishers/editors need to be with the likes of me. I would also like to thank my copy-editor, Andrea Waters.

Most of all, thanks and love to Suzanne, for giving me the support I needed to get this one done, and to our little army of future cabinet ministers (and prime ministers!): Emma, Ben, Sam, and Jake.

Thanks to one and all.

Welcome to the War Room

My world changed one sunny day in the middle of August 1992, when Republicans were gathering in Houston's Astrodome to confirm George Bush Sr. as their presidential nominee. At the time I was far away, sitting on a bench on the Sparks Street Mall in Ottawa, eating a hot dog, grinning.

The mall itself was not much to look at. It ran from the Bank of Canada building in the west to the War Memorial in the east. In between, there were a handful of banks, a Zellers, a Marks and Spencer, and more than a few shuttered shops. Along the way, there were also government offices — lots of government offices. In buildings of all shapes and sizes, the government of Canada played landlord to members of Parliament, senators, political assistants, parliamentary employees, and, most notably, journalists. Hundreds of journalists and editors and media technicians.

The Sparks Street Mall, as a result, was much more than a place to grab a hot dog. It was also a place to obtain, disseminate, or (more than occasionally) manufacture political gossip. During the lunch hour, journalists and political staffers could be seen here and there, leisurely sharing tidbits about who was up and who was down. Sparks Street was no Downing Street or Pennsylvania Avenue, but it had its uses.

I was vaguely aware that the way in which political information was then being dispensed — through a daily newspaper story, on a nightly TV newscast, in a unhurried chat at a place like the Sparks Street Mall — was, well, rather sluggish. Between the *happening* of an event (say, a speech at the nearby Château Laurier hotel) and the *communication* of that event (say, a columnist's analysis of the speech), an entire day could go by. Hell, sometimes even two or three days. That seemed awfully slow to me.

At the time, however, I didn't preoccupy myself overmuch with the slowness of summertime in Ottawa or in other political capitals around the world. I was thirty-two years old and special assistant to Liberal Party Leader Jean Chrétien. My job description was pretty imprecise. I wrote speeches and helped prepare members of Parliament for the daily Question Period ritual. Other things I did included approving letters for the Liberal leader's signature, keeping an eye on the direct-mail efforts of the Liberal Party, and just generally stirring up trouble for the Progressive Conservative government. I loved working for Chrétien. There was nothing more satisfying than getting under a political opponent's skin. I would have done it for free.

So there I sat, eating a hot dog, drinking a Diet Coke, and reading the *New York Times*. During the Republican convention, there was plenty to read. The Republicans usually bested the Democrats in presidential races. Most years, they were better funded and better organized. In August 1992, the Republicans were about twenty points behind the Democrats, but most of them were professing not to be worried. Four years earlier, George Bush had been about twenty points behind Michael Dukakis, too, but he went on to decisively beat the Democratic candidate. The Republicans claimed that they felt confident. Bill Clinton's "zipper problem" was well known, as were revelations about his past drug use. In fact, Mary Matalin, Bush's political director and Democrat advisor James Carville's then-girlfriend, had referred to Clinton, on-air, as a "philandering, pot-smoking draft dodger." Meanwhile, the GOP was readying itself to appoint U.S. Secretary of State James A. Baker, a pretty accomplished politico, to the post of campaign manager.

Tucked in the middle of all of the *Times*' Republican convention coverage was a little item about the Democrats. The piece noted, with some amusement, that the Democrats were at the convention, somehow, and were faxing reporters information about the GOP's missteps. In one case, the Democrats were actually responding to Republican speakers *while* they were onstage. *While* they were speaking to the assembled delegates.

That minuscule reference jolted me, like sticking my finger in a wall socket. (It transformed the way I looked at politics, in fact.) I read it, then read it again. The Democrats were hitting back at the Republicans before the Republicans could complete their sentences. Nobody had ever done anything like that before. The Democrats, led by James Carville, as things turned out, were taking the political game to an entirely different level. I hurried back to the office to learn more.

The Internet didn't really exist in those days, so there would be no research done in a few seconds. The Library of Parliament, which is an extraordinary resource available to members of Parliament, senators, and their political staff, was no help at all. With my eyes gleaming, I spoke to the librarians about "quick response" and "opposition research"— phrases mentioned in the *Times* story — and they looked at me as if I was crazy, which I arguably am. So I had to scrabble together bits of information from my reading of the *New York Times* and other U.S. media. Who *were* these Democrats? What were they *doing*?

A piece from the *Los Angeles Times*, written the week before the Republican convention, revealed that the "quick response" effort was being directed out of Little Rock, Arkansas, where Bill Clinton's campaign was headquartered. The quick response people had a magical name for their headquarters: "the War Room." I read on. The story talked about how "Clinton responded to a criticism of his health care plan by Bush before the President had levelled it." And how the War Room operated twenty-four hours a day, seven days a week, with dozens of people scanning wire copy, monitoring satellite feeds, and speaking to field operatives about their political adversaries. And how, as James Carville told the *L.A. Times* reporter, if a charge is left unanswered for even one day, it cannot be effectively answered.

Another story, from the *Boston Globe*, published just before the convention, was just as fascinating. Headlined "Attack and counter-attack: Clinton team masters striking back, and hard," the story revealed how the War Room was hammering back at Republican criticisms, up to half a dozen times a day, "sometimes within minutes of the charge, always within hours." Another War Room representative, communications director George Stephanopoulos, explained that the quick response team drew upon other parts of the Clinton campaign to do what it did — opposition researchers, press people, and field workers scattered across the United States. From what I could glean from my distant perch on Parliament Hill, Carville and his colleagues seemed to have somehow welded opposition research to quick response, creating one hell of a political machine. As far as I knew, no one had done it that way before; certainly, no one had done it as *well*.

Over the next few weeks, I learned that a group of Democratic operatives had indeed gained admittance to the Astrodome, where the Republican convention was taking place. The group, called "the SWAT team," was led in part by Democratic National Committee chairman Ron Brown, who, as commerce secretary four years later, would die in a tragic plane crash in Bosnia. Also leading the SWAT team effort was Betsey Wright, Clinton's chain-smoking Arkansas chief of staff from 1983 to 1990. Wright was the person with the best knowledge of the former governor's record and is credited with conjuring up the phrase "bimbo eruptions," which referred to the not-infrequent appearance of women claiming to have been bedded by the libidinous Clinton. (In the movie *Primary Colors*, the fictional account of Clinton's 1992 campaign, Wright is played by a pistol-packing Kathy Bates, but Wright insists that she is not *that* crazy.) Brown and Wright's luckiest break in Houston came when they were handed an embargoed copy of George Bush's acceptance speech by a careless Republican campaign worker. The War Room's opposition research team picked through the speech and produced critiques of virtually every line, backed up with facts. The opposition research was then faxed back to Brown and Wright in Houston, who used it to torment Bush and his team during what should have been the convention's most important moment — the acceptance speech.

"We were defending Bill Clinton against the charges of our opponents," says Wright, who went on to live a quieter life in the little town of Rogers, Arkansas. Her reputation is that of a fierce political warrior who sacrificed a great deal to assist her friends the Clintons. She doesn't give many interviews. Speaking with an easy Southerner's twang, her pet bird cheeping in the background, Wright says being on the ground at the GOP convention in Houston was vital to the Democrats' effort to get Clinton to the White House. "I took two or three people with me and we went down to Houston in order to answer immediately the allegations they would make about Bill Clinton. And we did that."

Every morning during the convention, Wright and her team would gather before journalists at a restaurant not far from the Astrodome to respond to Republican attacks against Clinton and to take a few swipes of their own. Every evening, she would appear on news talk shows to do the same thing. When the GOP's bosses saw how much coverage Wright's team was getting, they dispatched frat boy Young Republicans to try to disrupt the press briefings, often by banging on the restaurant's plate glass windows. "It was scary, some days," recalls Wright.

In the summer of 1992, there were plenty of Democrats who were skeptical about Carville, Brown, and Wright's operation. To the doubters, it seemed too reactive, too defensive. Why not simply wait to see which Republican charges stuck, and then deal with those? Why respond to an allegation that the media, or the public, would ultimately ignore? "My operation was purely a defensive operation," recalls Wright. "There were just all kinds of scurrilous attacks being made on the state of Arkansas, on the Clinton record as governor, and on his personal character. Those were my responsibility to respond to and to defend. *You have to respond.* And you have to respond *immediately*, because of the rapid and massive and immediate media situation that exists in the world today. That's just the way it is," Wright says. "And that's what we did in Houston!"

AND THAT'S THE WAY IT'S DONE everywhere else now, too. In Houston, in Washington, in Ottawa, in London, everywhere. Wherever a campaign is being run these days — wherever political people gather to ply their dark trade — you can reasonably expect to hear that a war room is at the centre of the campaign. It's ubiquitous, this war room stuff. So what is it?

Physically, a war room is usually just an airless, windowless little hole in the wall. It reeks of sweat and old pizza boxes. Huddled around tables and battered old desks is a small group of people basically doing three things. One, they're putting together information — information that is as factual and as error-free as the circumstances permit. Two, they're doing it really, really fast, because, as Betsey Wright observes, that's the environment in which the media now operate. And, three, they're being creative and aggressive in order to capture the attention of the media and, through the media, the public. That's it: that's a war room. Nothing fancy, but — if done right — potentially lethal.

What my federal Liberal friends and I did in 1992 and 1993 wasn't particularly original. Not at all. We simply copied the war room James Carville, George Stephanopolous, and Betsey Wright had built to counter the Republicans. But, being good Canadians, we made sure it wasn't a carbon copy. There were some differences.

As a regular reader of the *Times* and an amateur watcher of the news media, I had observed a few trends, none of them particularly promising for aspiring young journalists, but theoretically quite helpful to political hacks like me.

First, it was clear that people were receiving their news from many more sources than they used to. In the United States, the all-news channel calling itself CNN was becoming increasingly important for those wishing to communicate something politically. In Canada, since 1989, CBC Television's Newsworld network had been doing likewise. Newspapers, once the dominant source of in-depth political news, were fading. TV, meanwhile, was in ascendancy, particularly the cable TV offerings.

Second, TV was a whole lot faster than newspapers. Papers basically come out just once a day. TV broadcasts, thanks to the folks at CNN and Newsworld, were starting to happen hourly, 7 days a week, 365 days a year. The leisurely old way of doing things — call up a reporter, take him or her to lunch for a good-natured spin session, head back to the legislative office for a nap — was fading fast. For politicos, TV was making clear the need for speed. If you weren't fast, you were going to be politically obsolete.

Third, penny-pinching media barons had started to notice that they didn't need as many reporters to fill news pages and news broadcasts. A series of early-1990s media strikes and lockouts made that apparent to everyone. A reporter who once was relied upon to write a story or two a day was now being asked to file three, four, or five stories. With cross-media ownership — that is, a big newspaper buying a TV station, or vice versa — reporters were expected to provide content for more than one media outlet, too. Increasingly, reporters were overworked and under-compensated.

"What does it all mean?" Jean Chrétien asked me. As I spoke to him about the need for a Liberal Party war room in the 1993 federal election campaign, I sensed that Chrétien already knew the answer to his own question. "Boss," I said to him (because that's what those of us who worked for him called him), "I think the whole news paradigm thing is shifting. Everything's changing. TV is killing newspapers for political coverage, and that means everything is speeding up. The news cycle has shrunk from a day to an hour. And there are a lot fewer reporters and editors being asked to put out a lot more stuff."

"So?" he said. "Why do we need one of these war room things?"

"Because it can help us *win*," I said. "If we have something like that, we can sort of become *part* of the news media. If they sense that we have a group of people who can provide them with reliable, factual, no-bullshit information on a rapid basis — if we can help them do their job, in effect, and we aren't running around and taking credit for it — then they'll rely on us more and more. And then they'll write the stuff we want them to write."

Chrétien regarded me for a moment. "Okay," he said, finally. "Go do it."

So we did. We built a war room at the centre of the 1993 Liberal election campaign — a news operation attached to a political party. Folks told us no one had ever done anything like that before in Canada, and I don't know if that is true. But I do know that a few folks told us that our little war room helped out, and I tend to think that part might actually be the case. After all, as James Carville later told me, we Liberals ended up winning the election, didn't we?

And that's still what matters most, in every campaign. Like the great California Democrat Dianne Feinstein says, "Winning may not be every-thing … but losing has little to recommend it."

SATURATION PLAZA, AS IT WAS KNOWN, was a long, narrow room tucked away in a corner of the 1993 national Liberal campaign headquarters on Laurier Avenue in Ottawa. On folding tables lining the cluttered perimeter, a battery of computers permitted the room's occupants — the Task Force, they called us, so that we would sound as benign as possible to outsiders — to track electronic broadcasts, and even reporters' unedited news footage, transmitted by satellite dishes located in different parts of the country. Widespread use of the Internet was still some years away, but we denizens of Saturation Plaza had even contracted with a small Ottawa-based company to supply digitized clips of election coverage within hours of broadcast.

Tacked to a large board on one wall, near maps of Canada, Task Force members had collected dozens of unflattering photographs and cartoons of Kim Campbell, the leader of the Progressive Conservatives. Every morning, someone would be sent to a nearby convenience store to anonymously fax one of these photographs to the national Conservative campaign office, just a few blocks to the west. Usually, an embarrassing quotation or unhelpful poll result would be appended to the fax, to render the Tory troops as dispirited as possible.

Against another wall, occupying every inch of available space, were large filing cabinets containing every published statement Campbell had ever made. Each of these quotations had been entered into a huge database, along with its source and date of publication. The database allowed Task Force members to quickly access embarrassing or contradictory comments made by the Conservative leader. When printed off, the quotations could be faxed to reporters. Sometimes, the faxes were sent anonymously; most often, the reporter knew who was sending them but agreed to keep the Liberals' identities confidential. Whenever a reporter's published story used a quote taken from the Task Force database, it too would be clipped, copied, and filed. The unhelpful quotations would be used in no less than three books published about the newly minted Tory leader in the spring of 1993.

Perched precariously on the tops of the filing cabinets were three large televisions equipped with built-in videocassette recorders. One of the televisions was permanently tuned to CBC Newsworld. Task

Force members watched Newsworld a lot, from about 5:00 a.m., when the first of them entered the office, to approximately 3:00 a.m., when local news coverage of British Columbia candidates had been broadcast and dissected.

The room's windows looked down on Laurier and were mirrored. In this way, visitors to Saturation Plaza could not be photographed from one of the buildings on the other side of the street. For weeks, curious journalists had been attempting to learn who made up the Task Force and what they did. But the members of the Task Force did not give interviews. Anyone who did would immediately be fired. In the view of those who ran the national Liberal election effort, talking about the campaign's inner workings — "process" stuff, as political consultants call it — was *verboten*. Voters want to hear about issues, the Grit campaign managers believed, not minutiae about the inner workings of a political office.

As I mentioned earlier, our Task Force was modelled on the group that James Carville and George Stephanopoulos had led on behalf of U.S. presidential candidate Bill Clinton. Like the Democrats' group, it was designed to do two things before and during the election: one, respond promptly to opponents' partisan attacks; and, two, promptly initiate partisan attacks when needed. Attack and defend, attack and defend. Unlike Carville and Stephanopoulos's group, however, the Canadian effort was comparatively small, made up of less than a dozen people.

With one exception, all of the members were assistants to Liberal members of Parliament or senators; all but two (regrettably) were males, in their twenties or thirties. Among these were people who would go on to be legislative and executive assistants to the future Liberal prime minister, one who would become his press secretary, and others who would take up senior positions throughout government. The most notable person in the war room was Roméo LeBlanc, the leader of the Task Force, who would eventually become Canada's governor general. (I'm not sure if he became the viceregal representative because he oversaw the war room. But it probably didn't hurt.)

The Task Force did not show up on any flow charts depicting the 1993 federal Liberal Party campaign. Members did not attend public meetings. They did not speak to reporters, unless all agreed that the journalist in question could be counted upon to keep his or her mouth shut. Within the campaign itself, Task Force members interacted with only a handful of people — campaign bosses John Rae and Gordon Ashworth and select pollsters and advertising executives. Only one of the Task Force operatives, Bruce Hartley, communicated directly with the leader's campaign tour as it criss-crossed Canada.

In later election campaigns, some war room operatives (like me) became well known in the media. But in 1993, when the concept was relatively new, and therefore controversial, we preferred to keep the whole thing quiet. So we did.

Saturation Plaza got its name from the title of an album by the rock group Urge Overkill, which was a favourite of mine at the time. All of us Task Force members agreed that the name accurately described what we did: saturate the media, directly or indirectly, with messages that buttressed the Liberal campaign themes, while simultaneously depicting the Conservative government as tired, inept, and callous. Our little gang of political assassins had been engaged in guerrilla warfare for many months, since late 1992, attacking our Tory opponents with a barrage of leaks, stunts, and advertising. The way I looked at it, our job wasn't dirty tricks or smears or that sort of thing; our job was to dominate the communications landscape, leaving no room for our opponents to breathe. If, at the end of every day, the Tories and the New Democrats were utterly and completely miserable, I was happy. I know that probably isn't very nice, but it's true.

As such, around the office I was known as the Prince of Darkness.

As near as I can tell, the first person to call me the Prince of Darkness (to my face) was Alex Pannu. Pannu is a bright Conservative lawyer from Vancouver who, way back when, was an assistant to the former minister of national defence, Kim Campbell. In the spring of 1993, I was working as a political assistant to Jean Chrétien, leader of Her Majesty's Loyal Opposition. At the time, Campbell was running for the leadership of the governing Progressive Conservative Party, which she was almost certain to win. That spring, we were doing our utmost to make life unlivable for Campbell, attempting to link her to assorted scandals, battering her reputation in the House of Commons, and generally depicting her in the most unflattering light possible. It was a lot of fun.

As we settled ourselves in some chairs at a committee room in the East Block, waiting for Campbell to come and speak to the parliamentary committee on defence about yet another mess at the department, Pannu approached me. "You know what we're calling you, don't you?" he said, grinning. "We're calling you the Prince of Darkness." After Pannu retreated to his side of the room, one of the young Liberals working with me leaned over and whispered, "Wow! The Prince of Darkness! Is that cool or what?"

It was better than some of the other things Tories were calling me back then, most of which are unprintable in a family-friendly book like this one. But I admit that it made me laugh. Political people are like that: they think take-no-prisoners politicking — the kind you would expect a Prince of Darkness to practise — is, indeed, cool. When appearing on televised pundit panels, or when being quoted by the print media, they know that it is not a good idea to sound too enthusiastic about hardball politics, however. So they will make soothing noises about the need to "do politics differently" and to avoid "the old politics" (or what has been called "the politics of personal destruction"). They make these disclaimers because they know it is what the voting public wants to hear (even if it isn't what the voting public necessarily believes, but more on that later). Watching them, you would think such politicos would seldom utter a discouraging word about anyone.

But that's a pile of crap. Political people love duking it out with their adversaries, and people who vote love to watch. And that, partly, is what this book is about: it argues that the accelerated, aggressive, around-the-clock stuff done by war roomers helps to win campaigns. And not just political campaigns, either.

Now, before I became the Prince of Darkness, I was a University of Calgary law student and a part-time newspaper reporter on the police beat. On weekends, I earned a few extra dollars at the *Calgary Herald*. Most of the time, I sat in the newsroom and listened to the police radio. Whenever a drugstore was robbed or someone was murdered, I would hop in my battered old Gremlin and speed out onto Calgary's freeways to learn more. If the car crashes I heard about over the police band were sufficiently spectacular, I would also file stories about them, and my news editor would almost always assign a photographer to take pictures. When there wasn't very much else going on in the news world, we would run photos of the car crashes.

Whenever we did that, I was reminded of two things. First, you could publish a fistful of photographs of African children starving to death, corpses floating alongside an overloaded Indian ferry, or the bombed-out wreckage of someone's home in a war zone, and no one would call in to complain. If they cared, they sure weren't saying anything about it to us.

Second, if you ran a photo of a car crash involving locals — without bodies, of course — you'd better make darn sure you had someone around the newsroom to handle the calls of complaint, because you'd get plenty. Subscribers would call in to declare, loudly, that we were insensitive, ghoulish, and beneath contempt. They would call to cancel their subscriptions. But here's the funny thing: whenever I was out at those accident scenes, scribbling away in my notepad, I noticed that everyone making their way past the orange pylons and the traffic cops — and I mean *everyone* — would slow down to take a long, hard look. Every once in a while, I'd see them fumbling for a camera so that they could take some pictures, too.

Later on, when I got involved in full-time politics, I remembered this car crash thing. When a microphone is pointed in their direction, folks will insist they do not like it when political parties, or newspapers, involve themselves with life's unpleasantness. They will tell pollsters they disapprove of those sorts of things. They will heap opprobrium on the perceived wrongdoers. But, believe me, ten times out of ten (and when they think no one is looking), *they will slow down and take a look*. Political consultants — the smart ones, anyway — know that. To mangle a phrase used by Dick Morris, one of the smarter political strategists around, it's a mutually reinforcing deceit. Political types say they don't like doing the tough stuff — but they do. And voters say they aren't influenced by tough stuff — but they are.

Ask a war roomer. They'll tell you.

BEFORE I PASS ALONG what I've learned in political war rooms over the years, I figure I should relate how politics became a big part of my day job.

I was, I think, nine years old the first time I got involved in a political campaign. A neighbour of ours in Kingston, Ontario, was running for reeve, so I created some handmade lawn signs for him. I even wore one of his buttons to class; I don't recall if my Grade 3 classmates at Our Lady of Lourdes Elementary School thought I was weird for doing that, but I forgive them if they did. It *was* kind of weird.

My dad was a doctor, and he spent a lot of time doing medical research, so we lived all over the place. As a grade school kid in Texas, I knew, and still remember, the Pledge of Allegiance. In Quebec, as a youngish teenager, I was transfixed by the debate over sovereignty. Later on, in Alberta, where my family settled for more than a quarter of a century, I typed out letters to the editor, castigating Western separatists and anti-bilingualism nutbars. It wasn't until 1989, however, that I decided to get involved in politics as a full-time thing. In Ottawa, the seat of government, so to speak.

In that year, a debate was raging about the Meech Lake Accord, a package of constitutional amendments conjured up by Prime Minister Brian Mulroney and the provincial premiers. Lots of people were enthusiastic about the accord, but I wasn't one of them. I thought it stunk. As a young lawyer, toiling as a litigator at a smallish Ottawa Valley firm, I thought the notion of sticking a phrase like "distinct society" into the constitution of Canada was just plain wrong. Nobody in a position of power seemed to know what it meant, but they were certainly ready to move heaven and earth to get it in there. I was suspicious when they refused to get the phrase defined in advance by the Supreme Court of Canada. That suggestion was deemed un-Canadian, and would needlessly humiliate Quebec, I read somewhere.

To hell with that, thought I. So I started combing through the classifieds to find a politician to represent my point of view.

I didn't have far to look. In the very next office tower, at another Ottawa Valley firm, Jean Chrétien, formerly a senior Liberal cabinet minister, was also practising law. He wasn't wild about the Meech Lake Accord, either. Every once in a while, I would see him lined up at the sandwich bar located between our respective buildings. He didn't send out his secretary to get his lunch; he'd just stand there, along with me and the other lesser mortals. When he paid for his sandwich, he'd sit at a table on his own, eating it. I liked that. Like most voters, I am not partial to snobs or elitists, and Jean Chrétien wasn't a snob. He wasn't a member of the elite, either, but, as I later learned, he knew how to get them to do what he wanted.

When it looked as though Chrétien was going to seek the leadership of the Liberal Party of Canada, I called up one of his advisors. I told this fellow that I could write a little and that I wanted to volunteer. He was knocking at my door before I had a chance to hang up the phone.

Throughout 1990, while I continued to practise law, I helped out on different things for Jean Chrétien's leadership bid — speech writing, letter writing, policy-making, you name it. It was a hoot. Sometimes, Chrétien would ask me to sit in on meetings he had with various Liberal members of Parliament. They would discuss the Meech Lake Accord, or free trade, or taxation, or whatever was hot. I was always too nervous to say anything, but I sure did plenty of listening.

I came out of those meetings with a lot of respect, and a lot of loyalty, for Jean Chrétien. In politics, as in life, I value loyalty: I give it, and I expect it. I "bleed it," as one Tory friend told me, and I guess that is true — I tend to stick with my chosen candidate, even when the cause is hopeless. If someone violates my trust, I never forget it or forgive it. If someone takes a swipe at someone on my side, I hit back. It's how I am with all of the politicians I am proud to have supported.

Some people in the media have called my loyalty to Jean Chrétien a lot of wild-eyed fanaticism, but that's fine with me. They didn't sit in on those meetings in his law offices and see what a truly remarkable guy he is. The former Liberal leader has an intimidating grasp of political strategy, and he held most of the major portfolios in government, but you will never hear about any of that from him. Chrétien taught all of us who worked for him one rule: undersell and overperform. In politics, it's one of the rules worth remembering.

Now, it's not as if I was his buddy or anything. I was, in truth, an employee. But over the years, the Little Guy from Shawinigan tends to grow on you. I've learned plenty from him, too.

After he won the Liberal Party leadership in June 1990, Chrétien used the oldest line in the world to get me to work for him. "You can be a lawyer anytime," he said, "but how many chances do you get to work on Parliament Hill and have some fun?" I became his special assistant, which meant I wrote speeches, helped out on the daily Question Period ritual, and did whatever needed doing. And what needed doing, most days, was digging up the goods on the government of Brian Mulroney.

Back when I was a reporter at the *Calgary Herald* and the *Ottawa Citizen*, I loved investigative journalism. To me, poking through stacks of documents for something sensational, or spending weeks trying to get someone to speak to me, was a lot more interesting than attending a press conference and typing up what everybody else did. In my investigative days, I staked out cemeteries at midnight to spy on satanic cults, had neo-Nazis stick rifles in my chest, and chased Libyan terrorists around Washington. When I went over to the political side, I simply carried on doing investigative work, but I had a different publisher. I continued to sift through documents; I continued to try to learn everything I could about Chrétien's opponents. If I found out something that the media had missed — something that was unhelpful to the political fortunes of the Mulroney Tories — I would make certain that the media found out. That was my job, pretty much.

And that was how I came to be on the Sparks Street Mall in August 1992, eating a hot dog and reading the *New York Times* about something the Americans were calling a "war room."

LIKE A WEDDING DRESS, *The War Room* contains something old, something new, something borrowed, and something blue. Sort of.

There is nothing in it that is blue, actually. But *The War Room* certainly contains plenty of new stuff. And some of it is older, too, and has been borrowed from my weblog (www.warrenkinsella.com), columns I have written over the years at the *National Post*, and a book called *Kicking Ass in Canadian Politics*. After it was released, *Kicking Ass* showed up on a couple of bestseller lists, but it didn't do all that well. I partly attribute that to the fact that it was released on September 11, 2001, a day on which all of us would understandably come to be preoccupied with more important things. As conservative columnist Mark Steyn put it, correctly, in early October 2001: "Books like *Kicking Ass*, whatever its merits might have been in early September, now seem like artefacts of a lost age." True enough.

But *Kicking Ass*, improbably, still seemed to be stubbornly popular among people who work in politics, or people who follow politics. In the intervening years, and just about every day, I would get an email from someone, somewhere, who wanted to buy it. It is out of print, I'd tell these folks. Sorry. When a few people recently told me that they would pay me for a used copy of *Kicking Ass*, I suggested they buy it on-line somewhere. They then sent me links to on-line book resellers, noting that used copies of *Kicking Ass* are going for hundreds of dollars. In U.S. currency, no less!

Perhaps, thought I, something like *Kicking Ass* is worth doing. Not *Kicking Ass*, exactly, but something like it. Lots had changed, in half a decade: technology, political players, the media itself.

In the intervening years, something else had happened, too. As a lawyer, as a journalist, and as a political consultant, I started to notice that I was being approached by people — in the form of associations, non-profit agencies, corporations, unions, and so on — who wanted my help in setting up a war room for them. For an advocacy campaign, for a membership drive, to promote an idea, to defend against a hostile take-over: people were suggesting to me that a war room was what they were looking for, albeit in a non-political context. Soon enough, I was running more non-political war rooms than political war rooms. So I quit the Bay Street law firm where I was a partner, left the too-Conservative consultancy I was aligned with, and started up a firm — called the Daisy Group, for reasons that will eventually become apparent — that was based upon war room–style communications. Hitting hard, hitting fast, and hitting for the back fence.

So that's where the idea for *The War Room* came from. That, and beating circus monkeys. In the 2000 election campaign, you see, one of the guys in the Liberal war room summed up the war room job in this way: "Beat them like circus monkeys."

That line never failed to get a laugh with us — and it still does in every political war room in which I have toiled. (They say political people are twisted: guilty as charged.) The joke, however, inadvertently raises a valid question: what possible use is a war room outside of the context of a political campaign? I mean, *sure*: in politics, that testosterone-charged stuff — with stick-swinging, bench-clearing brawls being a daily occurrence, and epithets and *ad hominem* attacks being commonplace, and circus monkeys being assaulted with glee — nastiness and speed is probably useful. It probably attracts the attention of the news media, and is therefore arguably useful in attracting the affections of voters. But in the real world? What possible interest would a company or a non-profit association or a coalition have in beating an opponent, to wit, like a circus monkey? Isn't that kind of stuff a bad idea for non-politicians?

Well, yes and no. If you've got a message to get out, beat *it* — not your *opponent* — like the proverbial circus monkey. Tell your story the right way — with media stories, with advertising, with polling, with creativity and speed and aggression. Most of the time, your most formidable adversary is *not* the other name on the ballot, or the guy on the opposite side of the debate. No, your enemy is more powerful than that. In the new media environment, you are competing for the attention of folks (journalists, consumers, voters) who generally don't give a damn what you have to say (because they're bored, because they're busy, because they're skeptical). That is why God — or in this case, James Carville — invented war rooms. Because *the audience*, not your enemy, has changed.

Herein, then, ten war room lessons that you can clip and save and post on the fridge door — lessons that describe how to survive, and how to win, in a super-crowded, super-aggressive, super-fast communications environment. With regular folks being bombarded by literally millions of words and images every day, with news becoming increasingly fractured, and with the Internet (and the Internet's bastard children, like blogs and YouTube and social networking websites) making it nearly impossible to figure out what is important anymore, Joe and Jane Frontporch deserve to be courted. And that's what the best war rooms do: they attract attention, they reach inside people's hearts and heads, and they change outcomes. That's what *The War Room* is all about.

The War Room will profile and analyze some of the best war roomers and spinners around. Since I am (thankfully) neither an academic nor a historian, I promise you that it will not be an academic or a historical treatise. Relying upon the experiences of war room veterans who are a lot smarter than me — and, here and there, some of my own experiences in campaigns for prime ministers, premiers, and sundry other politicians — I will talk about spin and war rooms.

Why? Because big challenges don't simply happen to political parties and politicians anymore — they hit almost every company, non-governmental organization, or group eventually. *Disaster* (n.): a big scandal, a big misquote, a big mistake that lands one (and one's organization) on the front pages of the nation. In a bad, bad way.

If there is one thing that political people understand above all else, it is the exquisite loneliness of lying awake at 4:00 a.m., waiting for the morning paper to thud against the front door, containing shrieking headlines about tax dollars misspent, or a press scrum that went terribly awry. Containing a crisis that will consume, and sometimes destroy, careers.

Through long, hard experience, canny political veterans have learned how to survive such disasters — and how, sometimes, to even benefit from the experience. They've got the scars to prove it.

The War Room will offer up ten lessons, described below, about how to tell a story and how to get people's attention. About how to get past a crisis and how to end up in a happier place. About how to deal with hostile media and a disbelieving public. It will tell some fun behind-the-scenes stories of political war rooms of every political stripe, and will offer common sense advice about how to survive big challenges and how to win.

Lesson One is all about getting organized. In any campaign — in any advocacy effort — organization counts. When facing a crisis, or when rushing to capitalize on an opportunity, the winner is almost always the one who attends to the basic stuff first: hammer out the key messages; build a team; identify the best spokesperson; and find the resources to get the message heard by the right audience. (And if your message isn't part of the same news cycle that gave rise to the crisis, you're typically done like dinner.) This chapter will explain what a war room really is, how it works, and how it can work in a non-political environment. Work according to a plan, I always say. Don't just plan to work.

Lesson Two focuses on the importance of getting the right story. In politics, and ever since Jesus was a little fella, some of the best storytellers have been essentially honest, passionate, and smart men and women with a desire to persuade the largest number of people to embrace their point of view. Political storytellers have stories — which, in essence, are just words and pictures. Facts tell, stories sell: this chapter will describe how to tell your story.

Lesson Three is about how to get your story out for free. That is, with earned media — getting your story covered by reporters. Right off the top, I confess: not only have I committed the mortal sin of journalism, I have even taught the skill to unwitting youngsters. Forgive me, Lord. In this chapter, I'll suggest that reporters are wired differently than other human beings, and that misery, failure, and disaster are what arouse them the most. For them, it is bad news that makes the best headlines. This chapter will provide tips, along with real-life examples, about how to avoid becoming a bad headline in tomorrow's newspaper.

Lesson Four is about getting your message out by paying for it. When telling one's story to the so-called unpaid, or earned, media — that is, ink-stained wretches, *supra* — is ineffective, or unwise, political campaigners turn to paid media. That is, advertising. On TV, on radio, in newspapers, on the Internet. This chapter will discuss when it's a good idea to advertise, when it isn't, and what kind of advertising captures people's attention and changes minds.

Lesson Five is about getting creative. No matter how well funded, no matter how well staffed, no matter how cautious and risk-averse, boring campaigns are, well … *boring*. They don't work — or they don't work as well as they could. This chapter takes the position that creativity, ideas, and stunts are at the centre of every successful campaign, large or small. Do they entail risk? Certainly. But voters, consumers, and regular folks know when a campaign is playing it safe — and they tune out. Simplicity, repetition, and volume work. Risk-taking and creativity, too.

Lesson Six is about the necessity of, sometimes, getting tough. Any of these sound familiar? *No comment. None of this happened. Maybe it happened, but we didn't know about it. Let's have a committee investigate what we did know. We can't do anything until the committee reports …* This chapter will offer an alternative approach, most notably popularized by Johnson and Johnson in the early 1980s: take care of the problem right away, and the victims, too. Notify your team, and always aim to respond quickly. Above all, tell the truth — and fight back. This chapter tells how, with real-life examples from political and non-political campaigns. I argue that hitting back — fast and with facts — is not only fair, it's the right thing to do. In democratic contests for high public office, voters are entitled to know about dumb votes and quotes taken from a politician's public record. The same applies in a non-political context: hit back, hard. Or lose, badly.

Lesson Seven is about why it's vital to get the facts and numbers. These are the central objective in what political operatives call opposition research. "Oppo," as it's also known, is dark, mysterious, arcane, and misunderstood. But in political campaigns, knowing everything there is to know about one's opponent — as well as one's own candidate — is vital. No war room can function without good oppo. (The same goes for campaigns in the profit and not-for-profit realms.) And while relying entirely on gut instinct is sometimes a good barometer of public opinion, it's perhaps not the best way to manage a multi-million-dollar campaign. This chapter also argues, therefore, that good public opinion research is a key component of any winning campaign. Research counts. Facts, too.

Lesson Eight is what to do when the shit hits the fan — and how to get your hands on the Handle Scandal Manual. Too many politicians and media people over-hype "scandals," real or perceived. The public, as a result, have become exceedingly wary of demands to oust public figures over scandal allegations. They've seen too many baseless charges levelled too many times, and they (often rightly) suspect partisanship and/or grudges are at work. The key is to *politicize* differences with one's opponents — don't *criminalize* them. Play the vitriol and bluster of one's opponent against the tolerance of the public, and, by all means, don't overreact.

Lesson Nine is about getting modern — about using the Internet, and its progeny, to ensure that your war room is a winning war room. Increasingly, the web is the way in which people get political information — and other kinds of information, too. Given that I have been blogging about politics and other stuff for years, I acknowledge that I am biased in favour of web-based communications. But plenty of other folks now feel as I do — and right across the ideological spectrum, too. The Internet permits you to do what has never been possible before: communicate with potentially millions of people, instantaneously, and for pennies.

Lesson Ten is about getting campaigning. Campaigns, after all, are designed to highlight choices. In election campaigns, they highlight the differences between candidates, or between issues. In other kinds of campaigns, the burning issue may only be about building a new hockey rink in your neighbourhood or putting it somewhere else. But the choices almost always have a real impact on people's lives and are consequently very important to those people. This chapter describes how to set up and run a winning campaign with information and motivation. Because at the end of the day — and at the end of the book — a winning campaign, and a winning war room, is what you want the most.

In the communications-crowded world in which we all live, there is a fierce competition for the public's attention. With simplicity, repetition, and volume — with lessons learned from the political war room, in fact — individuals, companies, and associations can survive and succeed. They can *win*. This chapter will tell a few fun war stories, ones that bring together the book's main themes and that (hopefully) validate its essential thesis: namely, that war roomers know how to communicate and how to capture the attention of the folks you need to win.

In relating these stories about what a war room *is*, my hope is that I'll also be able to clear up what a war room *isn't*.

It isn't what some media folks often say it is: you know, a place where horrible, soulless Machiavellian types propagate dirty tricks and negative politics and smears and innuendo and blah blah blah. Contrary to what a few addled journalists claim, a war room isn't a backroom where political operatives scheme and plot to destroy people. That's not how to win. It doesn't work now, and I doubt it ever did.

What a war room is, truly, is a recognition that the world has changed. People are a lot busier. They're working their tails off, they're ferrying their kids to ballet lessons or hockey practice, they're catching up on a few hours of sleep; to get their attention these days, you have to work a lot harder. Journalists are busier, too, as I mentioned earlier, with fewer reporters doing more, and the media atom has split a hundred times, with zillions of websites and blogs and podcasts and downloads competing for the eyeballs and eardrums of every Earthling. On top of all of that, technology has made everything a lot faster. There's nothing — not a book, not a song, not a picture, not a newspaper, not a broadcast — that you can't now get in a matter of seconds.

That's why smarter political parties, corporations, unions, and associations all put together war rooms: because if they don't, nobody is going to pay much attention to what they have to say. Because there are many, many more people in on the conversation these days, and they're all pretty impatient. Their day-to-day lives, the speed of technology, the explosion in the number of media choices: all of those things have made war rooms more than advisable. They've made war rooms absolutely *essential*.

So, to anyone who says that the inhabitants of war rooms are nothing more than a collection of character assassins, dirty tricksters, and drive-by smear artists, I offer you one of my favourite war room war stories. The one about evil reptilian kitten eaters.

It was around noon on September 12, 2003, and a sunny Indian summer kind of day. Don Guy — my friend, and the scary-smart manager of the Ontario Liberal Party campaign effort, then underway — cupped the phone and looked at me. "They just called us evil reptilian kitten eaters," he said, grinning. I was in Don's office to talk about the day's "announce-ables," as we called them — on that day, the things Ontario Liberal Party Leader Dalton McGuinty was saying about health care. Long before the Liberal campaign (which we had branded "Choose Change") got started, we had identified September 12 as one of our health care days. And then the evil reptilian kitten eater thing happened. So much for announce-ables about health care.

I still did not fully comprehend what Don was saying, but I would soon enough. In an e-mailed press release, the geniuses at the Conservative campaign had called Dalton — then three weeks away from leading his party to a massive majority win — an "evil reptilian kitten eater." It wasn't an accident, it wasn't a prank. The leading minds of the Conservative Party of Ontario's war room had actually issued a press release calling their main opponent an evil reptilian kitten eater. It was the stupidest thing I had seen a war room do in years — as stupid, almost, as the federal Conservative war room attacking Jean Chrétien's facial paralysis in a television ad, almost exactly ten years earlier. (It involved some of the same people, interestingly enough.)

Within a matter of minutes, I was on the phone to reporters, suggesting that the Tory campaign had "just swallowed an enormous furball." With a matter of hours, our war room had made up T-shirts for our partisans to wear at a rally that night, proclaiming, "Call Me an Evil Reptilian Kitten Eater … But I Want Change."

"Evil reptilian kitten eater" was not a turning point in the campaign, per se, as the Tories were already well along the road to defeat. But it was, as some journalists wrote at the time, a defining moment in the 2003 Ontario election campaign. Later on, we surmised that the kitten eater epithet was an obscure reference to an episode of *Buffy the Vampire Slayer*. That same week, Dalton had written on his campaign weblog that he enjoyed the now-defunct TV series. The Tories had been trying to make a joke at Dalton's expense, but the joke was decidedly on them. We Ontario Liberals pounded them on election day, taking three times as many seats as the Conservatives and ten times as many seats as the New Democrats.

"Evil reptilian kitten eater" has now entered the pantheon of Really, Really, Really Big Campaign Mistakes. There is no one on the planet, and certainly no one in the Conservative Party of Ontario, who will now try to make the case that puerile, personal, poisonous attacks are what an effective war room should ever do. A war room should be funny, fair, fast, and factual. But calling the other guy something like an evil reptilian kitten eater? Um, no.

Growl, agrees the Evil Reptilian Kitten Eater — which is Evil Reptilian Kitten Eater–speak for "And so begin the Ten Lessons of the War Room."

Let's Get Started!

IT'S 1896 IN THE UNITED STATES of America: there is a bitter recession, massive joblessness, worker and farmer unrest, and the U.S. Supreme Court has upheld segregation of the races. It is a profoundly unhappy time.

For President Grover Cleveland, things are bad enough to persuade the Democrat to abandon his plans for a third term in the White House. Delighted, the Republicans select William McKinley — a likeable former Ohio governor and congressman — as their presidential candidate. The Democrats, meanwhile, settle on a youngish Nebraskan, William Jennings Bryan. They are pleasantly surprised: Bryan turns out to be an outstanding speaker and a commanding political presence. Right away, he puts his oratorical skills to work. Bryan travels to twenty-six states and speaks before an estimated 5 million voters — and, in so doing, he successfully distances himself from Cleveland's unpopular policies. Bryan becomes the champion of "the common man," as he puts it. Voters like him, and in increasing numbers, too.

McKinley is worried. The Republicans are suddenly facing a tight race where they had expected none, and they are uncertain about how to recapture the momentum they have lost to Bryan. To make matters worse, McKinley cannot stump for votes: his wife is an invalid, and no one — including the Republican presidential candidate — believes he can match the Democrat's rhetorical prowess. Anxious, McKinley turns to his friend and fellow Ohioan, Marcus Alonzo Hanna.

MARK HANNA, AS HE WAS AND IS MORE WIDELY KNOWN, was a politician, a wealthy industrialist, and (as things turned out) the first bona fide campaign strategist. More than a century later, he is considered by some American political gurus — among them George W. Bush's fabled muse, Karl Rove — to be the best there was.

Before Hanna, American political campaigns had been haphazard, unscientific, romantic affairs. Unlike today, there was no polling, no saturation advertising campaigns, and certainly no agreement on the need for campaign strategy, organization, and tactics. Hanna changed all of that. He profoundly changed the way in which political campaigns would be done, in fact.

Hanna was not much to look at, and he was sometimes caricatured as "Dollar Mark," an obese thug, by the newspapers of William Randolph Hearst, who despised him. But Hanna was a complex man, one who (as a shipper and broker) had been considered a friend of the working class and who arguably (as a Republican leader) championed comparatively moderate policies towards labour. He "always heard patiently, and considered fairly, what [employees and labourers] had to say," wrote his biographer.

Once approached by his friend McKinley, Hanna did not waste any time. He immediately kicked off a massive Republican fundraising effort focused on New York and Chicago, and he raised some $3.5 million in the process, more than any political campaign had ever raised before. Nor would anyone raise that much money for a presidential race until nearly a generation later.

It is as a campaign strategist, however, that Mark Hanna is remembered best. Using the millions he raised, Hanna hired fourteen hundred people and set about building the first modern campaign organization. He wrote his plan down, and he said that it followed business principles, although that is not altogether true.

What *is* true is that Hanna did things that no one had ever done before in a political campaign. For instance, he created bureaus within the McKinley campaign to appeal to key constituencies, such as Germans, wheelmen, merchants, and even disenfranchised blacks and women. He printed campaign literature in foreign languages and targeted ethnic groups within certain key neighbourhoods. One hundred years later, Hanna's approach — called narrowcasting— is well-known, and is used in every political campaign, large or small. Back in 1896, it was unprecedented.

Despite his innovations, Hanna had one big, big problem: his candidate could not travel. The Democrat candidate, William Bryan, could — and he was accordingly reaching millions of pairs of ears, in every corner of the United States. Like all of the best politicos, Hanna made a virtue out of necessity. He could not bring McKinley to the campaign, so he brought the campaign to McKinley.

Hanna's written campaign plan has not survived the years, but accounts of his organizational triumph certainly have. Hanna sought, and received, the assistance of Republican railway moguls, obtaining passes for the curious to travel, free of charge, to William McKinley's front porch in Canton, Ohio. One million people made these "pilgrimages," as they were called, and McKinley made more than three hundred speeches from his front steps. Hanna meticulously orchestrated every pilgrimage — ensuring the media were present to record the encounters, asking Mrs. McKinley to serve lemonade to the crowds, and even carefully scrutinizing the remarks of those who were to introduce the Republican candidate so that the campaign's key themes (the gold standard, high tariffs, high wages, and prosperity) were emphasized.

Did it work? Well, the *New York Tribune's* Francis Loomis offered this assessment: "The desire to come to Canton has reached the point of mania." Over the course of the summer and fall of 1896, the "mania" was such that visitors carried away stones, grass, twigs, and pieces of the McKinleys' fence as souvenirs.

William McKinley, once expected to lose badly to William Jennings

Bryan, took 51 percent of the vote. That year, Election Day witnessed one of the largest voter turnouts in the history of the United States. Hanna would go on to a successful career in the U.S. Senate — selecting the route for the Panama Canal, becoming chairman of the Republican National Committee, and successfully bringing many labour unions into the Republican fold. But it was as a campaign strategist — the first to recognize the importance of strategy, organization, and discipline — that Marcus Alonzo Hanna is remembered. He was the first, and he forever changed the way in which politics is done.

"CAMPAIGN," I LIKE TO SAY, "is another word for 'Something is going to go dramatically wrong today.'"

Imposing order on chaos is the main task of every campaign manager — and every war room occupant, of course. That's axiomatic. But it's a challenge, truly, to put into words how thoroughly, how completely, how jaw-droppingly *chaotic* a political campaign can be. Some days, whatever can go wrong, will. It is as inevitable as sunset.

Misstatements? Poorly attended rallies? Hostile media treatment? *Pshaw.* That kind of stuff barely registers. It's routine. How about working on campaigns — two of them — where the candidate puts his hands, publicly and inappropriately, on the body parts of women he is not married to? How about a campaign wherein the candidate appears, and probably is, drunk half the time? How about a big-city mayoralty campaign where I told the candidate that, if he didn't sign a letter asking the police to investigate a bribe offer allegedly made by one of his senior campaign staffers to an opponent, the rest of his senior campaign staff would quit en masse? I've worked on campaigns where all of those things happened. (All of them were losing campaigns, in case you are wondering. Which you are.)

Campaigns contain too many unhelpful variables — inexperienced candidates, wonky policy, bullheaded fundraisers, overeager volunteers, unstrategic advertising, nasty journalists, unrealistic deadlines — for one person, or one war room team, to fully control. Campaigns are a mishmash of emotions and egos and ambitions that are sometimes too big, and budgets and resources and timetables that are usually too small. When you have worked at the centre of a political campaign, what is extraordinary is not that things go wrong. What is extraordinary is that *more* things don't go wrong.

Thus, the need for organization: a comprehensive, detailed, written-down plan, or blueprint, about how to win. Hard work and good intentions won't suffice. As Daniel M. Shea wrote in his valuable book *Campaign Craft*, "Neil Armstrong could never have reached the moon simply by pointing the rocket."

The plan that lies at the centre of every winning campaign and that guides the efforts of every smart war room determines what the campaign is all about and what the key messages are; who should be doing what job and who makes up the audience the campaign wants to win over; when certain important things will happen and where; and how and why support will be won and kept. The campaign plan doesn't need to be engraved in granite, obviously, because no one knows for sure what is going to happen tomorrow. Tactics (the way in which a strategy is carried out) change; a strategy (the goal of your campaign) should not. And keep in mind that no sane person will ever consider donating time or money to a campaign that lacks a campaign plan.

The campaign plan is going to vary depending upon the candidate, the cause, the consultant, and the context. Because I am a Liberal and a liberal, I typically tend to agree with these rules, laid out by Dick Morris, a former senior advisor to Bill Clinton: "Message is more important than money. Issues are more central than image. Strategy matters more than tactics. Positives work better than negatives. Substance is more salient than scandal." (Why do I see those as "liberal" choices? Because, in recent years, it has been conservatives who have generally favoured multi-million-dollar campaigns that are relentlessly tactical, frequently negative, and too preoccupied with image and trumped-up scandals. Liberals tend to lose when they try to steal a page or two from this conservative campaign manual.)

In my experience, you need to address ten things in your campaign plan. Number one, money. Two, a campaign structure, identifying who does what. Three, a campaign calendar. Four, everything there is to know about your candidate — particularly what he or she believes in, and why.

Five, everything there is to know about the opposition — and how those things make the opposition an inferior choice. Six, what the target audience believes about your policies and plans and about the policies and plans of your opponent. Seven, the key messages, and how to communicate them to the media and through your advertising campaign. Eight, the campaign context — just a fancy way of describing the other things that are going on in the world, which may or may not have an impact on what you hope to do. Nine, the geographic outlines of the place where the campaign will be fought, and everything you need to know about that battleground. Ten, the campaign strategic theme — that is, the front step pitch. As in, your targeted supporter has opened his door to you, you've told him who you are, and now you need to tell him what you stand for: "Hi there. I'm running because I want every little girl to have a pony, and because I favour ballistic missile defence systems." (It's not much of a campaign theme, admittedly, but it's something.)

First off — and as Mark Hanna made clear more than a century ago — you really can't run an effective campaign without money. It pays for the advertising, it pays for full-time staff, it pays for all of the travelling that needs to be done, it pays to keep the lights on, it pays for all of the bad food you'll consume. You need it.

To give money, people generally need to know the candidate or the person who is the face of the campaign. They may agree with what the campaign and the candidate seek to do. They may back the political brand with which the candidate is associated. They may want to beat the other side. Or — and I say this as a guy who has written many a mass-fundraising letter, and because I know this one is more important than a lot of people realize — they may give you money because they feel it helps democracy. And it does.

(Sometimes, people will give money in the hope that it will help them to exert influence over the candidate. If you sense that is the case, don't take the money. It isn't worth it.)

The second element in a good campaign plan is the campaign structure; you need to start hammering together one that lays out who are the big bosses in the campaign. In any successful campaign that I've been associated with, there has been the campaign manager–type person; the top media person; the head policy wonk; the fundraiser; the tour boss —

that is, the person who ensures that the candidate is getting to where he or she needs to be on time; the coordinator of volunteers and staff and the office; and — of course! — the war room director.

To populate one's campaign and war room — and to motivate the people you put there — you certainly need dough, as I admitted a few paragraphs ago. But, in my experience, ideas and beliefs count way, way more with the best people. If your campaign seeks to change the world in a way that they do, too, they will sleep on smelly couches for you, eat stale pizza, and go without sleep for days. Money, while inarguably important for certain necessities of life, is not the prime motivator of the best campaigners and war roomers. Those people don't get involved to get rich — they do it *to make things better*.

For me, the best war room recruits are the younger ones. They tend to be hungrier, they tend to be more driven, and they are always a lot less cynical than the old farts, *comme moi*. What they lack in experience, as the cliché goes, they more than make up for in their willingness to jump onto live hand grenades to protect the candidate and the team. (Don't attempt jumping on live hand grenades at home, folks!)

The third element in the campaign blueprint is the calendar. Unlike plans put together by ad executives to market soap or cars or whatnot — plans that are often wrongly likened to political campaigns by those same ad people, who almost always know diddly-squat about politics — a political/issue campaign has a very defined time frame. It has a start, a middle, and an end (usually voting day). Each moment of the campaign needs to buttress the overall campaign theme, and the calendar should lay out the events planned for each day. On every campaign calendar, however, things inevitably change — you never know when an opponent is going to call you a "reptilian kitten eater," for instance, and throw you off your plan for a day or two — so how it looks at the start isn't typically how it looks at the end. But you need to have one.

The fourth element is knowing your candidate. The campaign team needs to sit down with the candidate and identify — clearly and comprehensively — what he or she believes. That may sound pretty simple, but you'd be amazed how many campaigns don't ever get around to doing that. Liberal Prime Minister Paul Martin, for example, was legendary for having dozens of "priorities," to the point that it became a national joke. So in the 2006 federal election campaign, the Conservatives issued a funny press release titled "Paul Martin — All Things To All People." The release then went on to list fifty-six "priorities" Martin had identified for his government, along with dates on which he made the statements. The press release concluded by saying, "If you have 40 priorities, you don't have any." (The source of the statement? Paul Martin.)

It's vital, therefore, that a campaign have a clear sense of the candidate's beliefs, well before the campaign gets underway. It's not necessary that the policies always oppose what the opposing candidate plans to say. (And, in fact, it's risky to highlight only the stuff that is adversarial. It makes you look, well, too adversarial.) In a democracy, it's okay to occasionally agree with an opponent. Just don't forget your obligation to remind everyone that *you* have a plan to achieve the shared goal, and your opponent *doesn't!*

Jean Chrétien was always really good at that kind of approach, which some folks call triangulation. When he was leader of the Opposition, for example, he knew the ruling Tories wanted to depict him as a free trade–hating, loony-left nutbar. So he gave a speech in November 1991 — one I helped to write, as I recall — wherein he said, "Protectionism is not left wing or right wing. It is simply passé. Globalization is not right wing or left wing. It is simply a fact of life." That speech naturally enraged some of the anti-free-traders in the Liberal caucus. But Chrétien also made certain to say that, while he favoured liberalized trade, he wouldn't go about it the heartless, favour-the-rich way the Conservatives had. Said he, "What is important are policies that contribute to the well-being of all of our citizens."

The fifth element is a heck of a lot easier to say than it is to achieve: a detailed record of your opponent's every quote and vote, in detail, and going back as far as humanly possible. Opposition research is all about scrutinizing the public record of one's adversary and letting people know about things that he or she would prefer to keep off the front pages. (It doesn't mean prying into their personal life; if you do that, looking for dirt, it says more about you than it does about your opponent.) Most often, but not always, the oppo stuff is intended for your earned media campaign, and not for paid advertising. In a campaign, oppo teams scrutinize anything said or done by their main opponents and critically respond to it in a way that is both fast and factual. If they do a good job, an oppo team can inflict serious damage to an opponent's campaign.

When the conservative Canadian Alliance selected Stockwell Day to be their leader in 2000, for example, we Liberals started to see that his loony flat-tax idea, plus his law-and-order proposals — along with his youthful, athletic media image — were winning him some voter support, even among women. So those of us doing oppo in the Grit war room made certain that Canadians, particularly Canadian women, had all the facts. Such as the story in the *Edmonton Journal* in June 1995 in which Day had said, "Women who become pregnant through rape or incest should not qualify for government-funded abortions unless their pregnancy is life-threatening." Or a March 2000 story in the same newspaper, wherein Day likened Canadians who favour reproductive choice to child abusers: "The thinking is, if you can cut a child to pieces or burn them alive with salt solution while they're still in the womb, what's wrong with knocking them around a little when they're outside the womb?" I am happy to report that, when female voters read what Day had to say, they started deserting him in droves. He never recovered.

The sixth component in the campaign plan is research — as in, the facts and numbers. In any campaign (political or non-political) it's never a great idea to guess. It's better to know. That's why good polling firms, and good pollsters, are so dearly loved by political consultants, because both are inevitably needed to assist any political campaign in securing victory. For nearly two hundred years, politicians and their campaign teams have lusted after solid public opinion research. If it's done right, public opinion research helps to map out the campaign — where the candidate should be spending his or her time; who is part of the "gettable" vote that is needed to win; what messages will work and what won't; when voters are paying attention and when they aren't; why the candidate needs to be associated with certain values; and so on.

A few years back, for example, I was part of a war room that had been set up to beat back a hostile airline industry takeover by a respected business leader. This guy was a formidable adversary: he had lots of money, he was a philanthropist, he had shrewdly hired every lobbyist in Canada, and he was a red-blooded Canadian. I also happened to like him personally. It looked like he was going to beat us.

But war is war, so we commissioned a battery of polling and public opinion research to determine what folks thought of him and what
he wanted to do. While respondents didn't seem to be staying awake at
night, fretting about the impending buyout, we found — to our genuine
surprise — that they didn't like this man. Something about him rankled
them, big-time. We didn't agree with their assessment, but we weren't
about to argue, either.

So we made certain that everything we did — every speech, every
press statement, every leaflet, even every button airline employees wore
on their lapels — mentioned this fellow's name. We made certain that *he*
became the public face of the hostile takeover. His own pollsters eventually warned him about the problem, but by then it was too late. We had
won the battle of public opinion and, therefore, the support of the public
opinion–obsessed politicians who would be needed to okay the acquisi-
tion. We beat back the takeover bid. Moral of the story: if you can afford
it, always do solid public opinion research. It's worth it.

The seventh crucial element in a solid campaign plan is The Message.
In case you are wondering, I capitalized the "T" and the "M" to communicate a message of my own: a campaign can probably *survive* without
a smart, strategic, tested message. But without a smart, strategic, tested
message, it is a campaign that is never going to *win*. Ever.

Two entire chapters in this book are devoted to the importance of The
Message, so I won't belabour the point. But I will relate the story of Hebrew National, and how hot dogs — yes, hot dogs — should remind us all
of the importance of being relevant, being repetitive, and being unique.

Back in the 1960s, Oscar Mayer was one of the top-dog manufactur-
ers of hot dogs on the planet. Americans loved Oscar Mayer hot dogs,
and the company sold millions of them. Millions. Oscar Mayer's name
was so indelibly associated with hot dogs, in fact, that the company even
created a big hot dog–shaped vehicle it called the Wienermobile, and
people loved that, too. In 1963, it created a jingle for its hot dogs, and the
resulting song became an actual pop chart hit. And so on and so on. You
get the picture.

The folks at Hebrew National made hot dogs, too — the kosher way.
They didn't sell as many hot dogs. Fed up with being clobbered by Oscar
Mayer, Hebrew National came up with a brilliant ad campaign in 1975.

The TV ad, created by Scali, McCabe, Sloves, put a (famous) face on their message, and they repeated it over and over. It was relevant to consumers, because many moms and dads were increasingly concerned about what, exactly, was *in* the hot dogs being consumed by their kids. Most of all, the Hebrew National message was unique. It made a claim that Oscar Mayer could not.

To American advertising guru Drew Babb, it's one of the top one hundred ads of all time: "It's just a medium shot of Uncle Sam holding a hot dog. The voice-over rambles on about how Hebrew National could make their franks using lesser ingredients, etc. But they can't because, he intones, *We have to answer to a Higher Authority.* Camera pans up from Sam's stupid hat to the clouds in the sky. Translation: God is the client. Hokey, hokey, hokey. Good, good, good!"

The eighth element in a good campaign plan is the context. Is something else happening that you need to think about? Can some event — somewhere, somehow — throw you off your plan? Well, yes, Virginia, it can.

One hundred lifetimes ago, when I had more hair and (arguably) less sense, my family and I lived in North Vancouver, a prosperous, tidy federal electoral district situated between Lions Gate Bridge, Deep Cove, Burrard Inlet, and a bunch of mountains to the north. The most populous urban riding in Western Canada, it was blessed with natural beauty and a median income in excess of $60,000 per annum. Engineers and nurses abounded. Two children per. Dogs in abundance.

This was the riding in which I decided to take a stab for public office — a lawyer, writer, former political assistant in faraway Ottawa, and unreserved optimist about my political chances as the Liberal Party candidate in the June 1997 general election. No Grit had won the riding in some twenty-two years, but I was equipped with a sling filled with mildly favourable poll results and the latest demographic data from Statistics Canada.

At about the same time, Winnipeg experienced its worst disaster in 150 years. Water flowing from south of the border, along the Red River, flooded virtually all of southern Manitoba. Locally, it was being referred to as the "Flood of the Century," because it was. It caused $2 billion in damage and destroyed many lives.

You want *context*? Here's context. During a canvass of a North Vancouver neighbourhood, I went to the door of an elderly couple who, according to the helpful Liberal candidate sheet I carried everywhere I went, were lifelong Liberals. The door opened. I smiled and started my pitch. With a sweet smile, the elderly woman stopped me. "That's all right, dear," she said. "We know who you are."

"So I can count on your support, then?"

"No, dear, you can't," she said, smiling all the while. "We've been Liberals since well before you were born. And we think you and Mr. Chrétien should be ashamed of yourselves for calling an early election, and during that terrible flood in Manitoba, too." Pause. "Do I make myself clear?"

"Yes, ma'am," I said. The door closed. I shuffled down the hallway and called my wife. "Hey, babe," I said. "I have just received official word that I am going to lose, big-time." And I did — with the Reform Party incumbent capturing 26,000 votes, and me about 19,000. Beaten (mainly) by a flood, two provinces to the east: that's context. And that's why campaign context is so important.

Geography, the ninth element, doesn't require much explanation. You obviously need to figure out the exact geographic outlines of where your campaign will be contested. "All politics is local," Tip O'Neill remarked famously, and he was, of course, right. Well before the campaign gets underway, you must know where — and as precisely as possible — to focus your resources. You do not have enough time, money, and people to be everywhere at once. Fish where there's fish.

Finally, the tenth element in a well-thought-out campaign plan is the most important one: the campaign theme.

Plenty of politicians and politicos believe that The Message is the same thing as The Theme. But they're wrong. The former is derived from the latter, but never the other way around. To extend what I said a few paragraphs ago: you can't win without The Message. But neither can you win with The Message *alone*.

What you need, desperately, is the campaign theme.

Many campaigns are busy. They raise money, hire staff, and start printing up brochures. They do all of the things you'd expect they'd do. But a few campaigns — and quite a few more than you'd suspect — have no clear sense of what they want to accomplish. "They know they are trying to win," notes Joel Bradshaw, a Democratic political consultant, "but they never come to a resolution as to how they are going to win … they fail to define a strategy."

When that happens, get ready for a lot of seriously unhappy days on the election trail. With no strategy and no coherent, cohesive theme, you can fully expect to be tossed around like a piece of lint in a hurricane. To win, you will be depending on luck, or some unforeseen external event (like a flood in Manitoba, say), or a screw-up by your opponent. More than once, I've been in a smoke-free backroom, and some genius will say, "Just wait. You'll see. [Insert opponent's name here] will say something stupid. It'll happen." And it never, ever does.

A campaign strategy is like a great rock'n'roll song: it should take about a minute or so to sing, but it should take about a month or so to get down on paper. It should address the mood of voters, and it should make people sit up and take notice. Most of all, it's the same at the start as it is at the end: *tactics will change, but your strategy never does.* In its simplest form, the campaign's strategy should answer the following question, as posed by the candidate: who do I need to vote for me, and why should they vote for me?

Answering that question is never particularly easy. But once you ascertain the answer, it becomes a lot easier to articulate your campaign's theme: that is, the rationale for your win, and the rationale for the other side's defeat. One of my all-time favourite campaign themes was used by New Democrats to beat us British Columbia Liberals in 1996. Their campaign theme was stunningly simple, but undeniably brilliant: "On Your Side." With three simple words, the NDP spelled out the rationale for both *their* victory and *our* defeat. And it provided a comprehensible reason for voting that way, too: the New Democrats wanted the same things you, the voter, wanted. Simultaneously, it reminded you, the voter, that the B.C. Liberals were — almost certainly — meat-eating, Hummer-driving, tree-chopping, Bible-thumping, misogynistic crypto-fascists. And captive of interest groups. And kickers of puppies. And smelly.

We weren't, not at all, but it didn't matter. They had a way, way better campaign theme than we did. And I should know — I wrote ours, and it wasn't very good: "Taxpayers Deserve Better." Yuck.

So: after all of that stuff — after all of that fundraising and hiring and polling and researching and strategizing — once you've got your campaign plan in hand, then what?

Well, you go and talk to God, that's what.

IN THE DARK, mysterious, arcane, misunderstood world of war rooms and war roomers, James Carville is God.

During the 1993 Canadian federal election campaign, as related in the last chapter, the Liberal Party of Canada assembled its own small war room team. In the long room that served as the nerve centre for the Liberals' war roomers, atop a battery of televisions and video machines, was a photograph of James Carville. Below the photo, someone (me, actually) had inscribed, in big, black letters, "GOD."

Many years later, God — who is bald, lanky, and possessed of squinty eyes — sits in his office on South Washington Street in Alexandria, Virginia, a posh suburb of Washington, D.C. He laughs uproariously when he is told that a group of young Canadian politicos regarded him as their deity and shamelessly copied his formula for political success.

"Well, surely it wasn't a shameless copy," he says in a Louisiana drawl so thick he is barely understandable.

When I assured him that we Canadians stole as much as we possibly could, then brazenly claimed to have originated the idea, Carville lets loose with another whoop of laughter. "Well, fuck," he says. "If y'all had been original, you would've never gotten into politics, right?"

Right. Like the New Orleans rhythm and blues that he loves, which trades on a limited number of beats and a finite catalogue of chord progressions, James Carville knows that, in modern political campaigns, there aren't many original ideas. Empty chairs at all-candidates' debates, volunteers wearing chicken suits chasing around candidates, people waving colourful props on television, speakers using pop culture analogies in spin lines — all have been done to death. If a voter has the impression that he or she has seen something or heard something before, he or she usually has. Political campaigns are notable for many things, but new ideas are not typically among them.

James Carville, however, is not notable merely for his friendship with Bill Clinton, nor for his success in guiding political campaigns around the globe, nor even for the fact that his own wife, a Republican spinner of note named Mary Matalin, calls him "Serpenthead." He is not notable merely because he is, in his own words, a "pamphleteer, raconteur, and Democratic party animal." He is not notable merely because he refers to himself, on national television, as "the Ragin' Cajun" or "Corporal Cue Ball," the latter appellation referring to the fact that he is, to paraphrase the words of Joseph Conrad, not just bald, but impressively bald. No: James Carville is notable because, in 1992, he and a small group of other Democrat whiz kids elevated campaign strategy and campaign planning to an entirely new level. In that year, Carville used a smart plan to change history and to elect his candidate to the post of president of the United States — a candidate who, just a few months before, everyone except Carville had considered to be unelectable.

That, in a nutshell, is why scrappy political operatives around the planet regard him as God.

JAMES CARVILLE WAS BORN IN OCTOBER 1944, in, appropriately enough, Carville, Louisiana. It was, he says, a "one-stop-sign town," about a half-hour's drive from Baton Rouge, and it bore the name of his grandfather, who had once been its postmaster. Carville's father, also a postmaster, ran the local general store, while his mother, called Miss Nippy, sold World Book encyclopedias door to door so that she could put her eight children through college. Which she did — all of them. James, an altar boy, was the oldest.

While still a student at the all-boys Ascension Catholic High School in nearby Donaldsonville, young James Carville became involved with his first political campaign, for Price LeBlanc, a car dealer seeking a seat in the Louisiana state legislature. LeBlanc called himself "the Trading Country Boy," and his Elvis-inspired campaign slogan was the refreshingly honest "I Want You, I Need You, I'll Work for You." Along with passing out LeBlanc's pamphlets to locals, Carville would, like every young volunteer to every political campaign, put up his candidate's signs by day and tear down the opponent's signs by night. Carville recalls that he put his heart into that campaign, but Price LeBlanc still lost.

After high school, in 1962, Carville enrolled at Louisiana State University, where he flunked out. Having come from an all-boys Roman Catholic high school, Carville admits that he was much more preoccupied with his social life than with his studies. He spent very nearly every weekend hundreds of miles away from school, carousing with his buddies in the wild Texas border town of Laredo. The rest of the time he chased coeds. After he racked up too many Fs, LSU asked Carville to occupy himself elsewhere.

Being Catholic, and being accordingly guilt-stricken, Carville immediately sought to expiate his academic sins with a stint in the Marines. Given that the United States was then at war with Vietnam (and itself), Carville's decision to enlist could easily have been one of his last. But the young Louisiana Democrat remained stationed at Camp Pendleton in San Diego, toiling as a regimental food supply corporal, and thereby avoided combat in Vietnam. By 1968, he was out of the Marine Corps and back at Louisiana State University, where he took night courses to complete his undergraduate degree. Since he was a talker, he was talked into attending law school because, his relatives reasoned, lawyers get paid a lot to talk too much.

For a time, Carville laboured as a litigator with a Baton Rouge firm called McKernnan, Beychok, Screen and Pierson. He was there for six years. His mother, for one, says, "He was the worst lawyer in the world." During that time, Carville recalls that he was happiest when helping out on local and state-wide campaigns. He helped one of his firm's partners, Jerry McKernnan, in a race for a spot on the public service commission. Carville also helped another lawyer at the firm, Mary Olive Pierson, in a bid to become a judge. Both McKernnan and Pierson lost. His chosen candidate to become governor, "Bubba" Henry, lost too.

But James Carville had the bug — the political bug. In 1980, he quit the law, went to work for a political consulting firm, and finally racked up some wins, one in a congressional race and another in the Baton Rouge mayoralty race. He was happy, and he was starting to attract attention as a smart political operator.

By 1982, he was running a successful Democratic Senate campaign in Virginia, nursing a slender lead as the race entered its final days. And then he made a mistake. When his candidate committed a gaffe, essentially by saying that it was "too bad" if young Americans did not like providing Social Security support to older Americans, Carville chose to play it safe. Even though the Republican opponent seized on the blunder, Carville decided against responding or hitting back. On election day, his candidate lost to the Republican side by a single percentage point. It was a political lesson Carville would not soon forget, and the lesson was simple: never leave a charge unanswered.

In 1983, Carville headed farther north. For very little money, and for not very long, Carville toiled for U.S. Democratic presidential candidate Gary Hart in Washington, D.C. When the money ran out, Carville headed home to Louisiana and waited for his phone to ring. Eventually, it did: in the same year, Lloyd Doggett was seeking the Democratic Senate nomination in Texas, and he asked for Carville's help.

Doggett was far behind his two opponents in the nomination race — "about a gazillion points," Carville recalls. But the Ragin' Cajun, as Doggett's people came to call him, threw himself into the race; he developed a campaign plan that worked. When one of Doggett's opponents derisively referred to him as a "Little Leaguer," Carville leapt on the remark. He took Doggett to small towns across Texas, where he would hold press conferences on Little League baseball diamonds. As smiling youngsters in baseball uniforms crowded around him, Doggett would cheerfully admit to being a Little Leaguer, and then declare that the "Big League" insurance companies, banks, and utilities already had enough representation — in the form of Doggett's principal opponent.

Later on in the campaign, Carville discovered that the front-runner, a Texas state senator, had taken few, if any, firm positions on any public policy issue. He pounced again. The Doggett campaign's speech writer, Paul Begala (Carville's future business partner), produced a text stating that only Doggett had "the guts" to stand up against special interests, and for schoolchildren and civil rights. Carville suggested a change. Guts, he told Begala, was "gross" imagery. He said to use "backbone" instead.

The "backbone" theme proved as beneficial as the Little Leaguer stunt. Holding up a plastic replica of a human spinal column at every stump speech he delivered, Doggett declared, "This is what I have that my opponent doesn't have: a backbone. I'm going to take this backbone to Washington so I can stand up for the voters of Texas." Doggett went on to do what had been considered impossible: he beat the front-runner. That done, Carville and Doggett turned their attention to the runoff race for the Democratic nomination.

Doggett's next opponent, a congressman, was calling for beefed-up border patrols to keep out Mexicans seeking to enter the U.S. illegally. His position was a very popular one. When Doggett tried to oppose the congressman's policy using facts and logic, his opponent merely grew more popular. "We tried to argue emotion with intellect," Carville wrote later. "That didn't make a dent. The head has never beaten the gut in a political argument yet, and I doubt if it ever will."

Carville's strategy: he deployed his research staff to find out what the congressman had said about the issue on the floor of the House, and what bills he had introduced to toughen border patrols. After poring over stacks of paper, the opposition researchers had located precisely nothing. Carville, therefore, decided to hold a press conference.

Doggett stood beside an easel draped in velvet. "Now we are going to show you everything, every word, that my opponent has ever said about the question of immigration, until his pollster found it in a poll, about eight weeks ago." He dropped the veil to reveal a blank slate. "The truth of the matter," Doggett continued, "is that my opponent is a single-issue candidate on a single issue that he has never done a single thing about." Doggett beat his last remaining opponent and secured the nomination to become the Democratic candidate for senator. It was a huge, heady victory.

In the general election, Doggett faced off against a formidable foe — Republican Phil Gramm. It was 1984, at the height of Reagan-mania: Carville and everyone working for Lloyd Doggett knew they faced a gargantuan uphill climb, but they also knew that they had a fighting chance. And then disaster struck. The press learned that Doggett had attended a fundraiser at a San Antonio gay club featuring Frankie the Banana Queen and Mr. Gay Apollo. Doggett had accepted money — $354 in all — from those in attendance, thus attracting the attention of reporters around Texas and around the globe, and thus abruptly ending his dreams of a Senate seat. And James Carville returned to part-time lawyering and consulting in Louisiana.

In 1986, Carville got a break. A three-time loser, Bob Casey, was running for governor of Pennsylvania against William Scranton III, a moderate Republican with pro-choice views and scion of one of the state's most prominent families. Casey was a strong-willed anti-abortion Irishman, the son of a coal miner; Scranton practised transcendental meditation and had campaign money to burn. Being broke and unemployed, Carville did not hesitate to take the job Casey was offering, but this time he knew he had to win.

By October 1986, following six weeks of hard work, James Carville and the Casey campaign team had helped to narrow Scranton's lead with a lot of aggressive campaign messages and a smart strategy. For example, Scranton was the son of a popular former Pennsylvania governor, but Carville's team quickly established that he had a poor attendance record as lieutenant-governor. So Carville developed a take-no-prisoners tag line for their advertising: "We gave him the job because of his father's name. The least he could do is show up for work."

After a few weeks of back-and-forth nastiness, Scranton threw Carville and the Casey campaign a curve ball: he held a press conference to renounce all negative campaigning. No more attack ads, no more cheap shots, just sunshine and light. The trick had the desired result. Scranton was the beneficiary of lots of glowing press coverage and editorial commentary, while Casey looked like a crass practitioner of "old politics," digging around in the dirt with the help of his opposition researchers. Following a candidate's debate, where Scranton appeared modern and Casey appeared anything but, Casey lost eight points of support — in a single night. There were only nine days left until election day.

To the chagrin of voters everywhere, plenty of politicians make pledges that are promptly discarded after they secure office. By the time they are sworn in, politicians are beyond the voters' immediate reach. When one makes a promise in a campaign, however, it is axiomatic that the promise needs to be kept while the campaign is ongoing; electoral retribution, after all, can be immediate and decisive. William Scranton III forgot this rule.

Notwithstanding his solemn vow to reject anything smacking of negative campaigning, Scranton's Republican team sent out six hundred thousand letters describing Bob Casey as a crook. He threw around a few other insults, too, but "crook" caught everyone's attention — as a flagrant violation of Scranton's promise to avoid negative campaigning. Once he had a copy of the letter, Carville orchestrated day after day of press coverage hammering the front-runner for his flip-flop. Scranton's lead started to shrink. The weekend before voting day, Carville approved the development of a spot that remains infamous in Pennsylvania political lore — the unforgettable "guru ad." In the commercial, Scranton is quoted praising transcendental meditation, while viewers are shown a photograph of the Republican candidate in college, wearing hippie-style clothing and sporting a head full of scruffy hair. A sitar twangs in the background. Without explicitly mentioning drugs, the spot suggested to voters that Scranton was a meditating kook — and, if that were not enough, a druggie.

Carville took a lot of heat for the spot, but shrugs off the criticism. "Since time immemorial, there has been nothin' wrong with coating a tougher message with a bit of fun. You keep your blade in its scabbard, but you still get your point across." He laughs. "Yeah, that's a good skill to have — to demean an opponent in a nice, funny way, you know?"

Bob Casey's Pennsylvania gubernatorial campaign went from an eight-point deficit to a two-point lead in just over a week. Casey had broken into the big time — and so, finally, had James Carville.

ON ONE POINT, James Carville and Mark Hanna agree: every campaign, every war room, needs a plan. It needs to be organized. Says Carville, in one of his books: "If some campaigns founder because of lack of clear objectives, even more of them confuse strategy with tactics. Strategy is hard. Tactics are easy."

In 1992, the strategy Carville designed for Bill Clinton was the same from the start of the primaries to voting day in the general election for president. Clinton was the candidate of change — the new ideas Democrat who would fix the economy. It was always the same strategy, the same plan, from beginning to end.

"Our staff, however, was frequently distracted," Carville admits. So he put up a famous sign on the war room wall in Little Rock. Here's what it said:

> Change Versus More of the Same
> It's the Economy, Stupid
> And Don't Forget Health Care

Change, as James Carville recalls, was the message. Positioning Bill Clinton as the agent of change was the strategy. The message was heard; the strategy was a winner.

Get a plan. It worked for Mark Hanna, it worked for James Carville. It'll work for you.

Get Spinning!

Spin isn't bad. Spin — as practised by politicians, marketers, clerics, and anyone else engaged in the difficult task of persuading the masses about something or someone — is *good*. And spinners have been spinning for a long, long time. Throughout history, in fact.

Spin is hopeful persuasion (because it doesn't tell, it sells). It is inherently democratic (because dictators and autocrats have no need to persuade the masses). It is creative and compelling (because it has to be, to attract the attention of people who could just as easily be paying attention to something or someone else). It is enduring (because it can, and often does, have a lasting impact on the hearts and minds of entire generations).

Despite all of that, spin gets a bad rap. Because politicians have appropriated the word — and because they have substituted "spin" for what it is they are really doing, which is "lying" — too many people associate spin with dishonesty. They regard spin as sin.

It isn't. Throughout human history, some of the best spinners have been essentially honest, passionate, and smart men and women with a desire to persuade the largest number of people to embrace their point of view. They are storytellers. They do not possess millions for Madison Avenue advertising campaigns. They do not have access to the latest polling and focus group data. They do not have the power to impose their point of view on people with legislation or regulation or imperial fiat. Spinners have spin.

Jesus Christ — and his de facto press secretary, St. Paul — used words and good stories, and not much else, to change the world. Sergei Eisenstein, with a camera and his creativity, persuaded the Russian people (and beyond them, millions of other people) to embrace Bolshevism and thereby changed the world. The French and American revolutionaries — assisted, admittedly, by the occasional guillotine or musket — relied principally upon the power of the word to bring over masses of frightened people to their side. Famous criminals like Bonnie and Clyde or Jesse James wove spectacular stories about their criminal misadventures and became early pioneers in what communications consultants now call "reputation management."

Spinners include born-again Christians; balladeers and playwrights; Moses; the Jesuits, the Papacy's ecclesiastic ground troops; Cromwell; the creators of urban legends; Aristotle and some of the great Greek democratic philosophers; bloggers and pro-diversity web dissidents; penniless comic book writer Ron Hubbard, who created a religion, Scientology; and the best of the journalists, who know that a well-told story can have greater worldwide impact than any single army or TV ad campaign.

If you ask me — and you have, sort of, when you picked up this book — to qualify for inclusion in the august body of some of history's best spinners, certain ground rules should apply. Anyone proselytizing on behalf of anti-democratic movements (such as fascism or communism) should be unwelcome, because, as noted above, spin is only necessary and possible in a democracy. Similarly, proponents of discredited ideologies (again, such as fascism or communism) should be sent packing, because, ultimately, those ideologies were repudiated by history, and the best spin endures over the centuries. Any person or group possessing immense riches, and who is capable of financing a glossy propaganda campaign, should also be considered for exclusion, because the best spinners know how to effectively spin with the most meagre of resources. They know the power of stories.

Not all spin is good or democratic, but it stubbornly endures. Some spin is demonstrably — most notoriously, as with the anti-Semitic forgery called *The Protocols of the Learned Elders of Zion* — a foul, loathsome virus. But such evil spin is ultimately defeated by education and democracy and a thoughtful, engaged public. Similarly, while some of the best political spinners did so on behalf of democracy — in a memorable way, and with precious little in the bank account — they shouldn't be allowed to dominate the proceedings or claim most of the credit (as they are wont to do).

In this chapter, in this lesson, I want do a bit of a spin job myself: I want to rehabilitate the reputation of the word and reclaim it from the politicians. I want to promote the notion that spin and spinners can, and did, change the way the world works, and/or the way we regard the world. Spin is not an invention of modern electoral politics but, in fact, an important ingredient in history's march. Spin, and stories, have that much power.

Spin, ultimately, is (and has been) democratic, creative, positive, and very nearly eternal. It's good, mainly.

Here begins lesson two!

FACTS TELL, BUT STORIES SELL.

If there is any truth left in politics — if there is anything at all that any smart politician or war room soldier knows to be beyond dispute, beyond debate, that can never, ever be refuted, even by God — it is that. *Facts tell, stories sell.*

The other Big Truth is that you need to stick to your story, once you figure out what it is. But first, let me tell you what I mean when I (and others) proclaim that facts tell, stories sell.

The tidy tautology of that truism was made clear to me in the fall of 1993, during the federal election campaign. Michael Marzolini, a smart young guy from Toronto, was the Liberal Party's pollster. Nobody as young had ever been in a position like that before, but Marzolini didn't let us down. His ability to analyze the polling numbers and tell us what we needed to know, and not what we wanted to hear, was remarkable.

One day during the campaign, he said something that may have been total and complete bullshit. Even now, so many years afterwards, I don't know if Marzolini — who is the pollster I use, whom many of my clients use, and who is respected from coast to coast — was pulling our leg. But here's what he said: "Forty percent of Canadians don't know how many millions there are in a billion."

Inside my tiny, malformed, maladjusted skull, the clouds parted. A chorus of angels sang. A bright beam of light descended from the heavens and illuminated the path in front of me. All that was unknown became known, at the moment.

Everything that corporations and political parties have been saying to regular folks has been wrong, wrong, wrong, I said to myself, and possibly out loud. They have been speaking in tongues. No wonder consumers and voters are so pissed off! Praise the Lord! I understand now! Hallelujah!

Facts, figures, statistics, charts, graphs, decimal points, and sums of money — sums of money so enormous that no one can imagine themselves ever *seeing* that much money in one place, let alone *touching* it — are the things that corporations and the media and governments have traditionally used to communicate with millions of people. But the people weren't hearing what they had to say — either because the message was disconnected from the reality of their daily lives or because they didn't fully understand it. The public dialogue, which determines the public agenda, had become broken.

Now, I fully realize that I probably attached way too much importance to Michael Marzolini's perfectly innocent little bit of statistical conversation-making. But, for me, it was a political seismic shift. It provided the best possible explanation for quite a number of things, among them Ronald Reagan's presence in the White House. Reagan, to me and millions of other people, hadn't been the brightest light on the Christmas tree. Even his own son, Ron Reagan Jr., observed about the anticipated end of his father's administration: "It will be a relief, I think, for everyone." But President Reagan — like all of the greatest journalists — knew that the best way to grab peoples' hearts and minds was with *stories*. Not columns of figures and factoids. Reagan told stories, and that is why they called him the Great Communicator. It's how he got to be president of the United States, and how he got re-elected.

In October 1980, just a week before Election Day, Reagan won the keys to the Oval Office when he went toe-to-toe with the guy who was then still working there, Jimmy Carter. Carter was an amiable, decent man, but he was also completely unable to communicate in a simple, compelling way. He couldn't spin his way out of a wet paper bag, in fact. The United States had been going through an economic and post-Vietnam existential crisis, and the Democrat from Georgia appeared completely incapable of describing what needed to be done. Like many aspiring engineers I have met, Carter didn't think the devil was in the details — he thought *salvation* was in the details. So, during the second presidential debate, Reagan turned to the cameras and delivered the line that would bring an abrupt end to Carter's re-election hopes: "Are you better off than you were four years ago?" It was simple and (to some) simplistic, yes. But it did the trick.

Communicating in a deliberately uncomplicated, unsophisticated way is not condescending. It does not suggest that you think your audience are dummies, or slow, or poorly educated. Far from it: taking pains to ensure that your words reach the greatest number of ears — doing all that you can to ensure that you are understood — is the very essence of democracy. It is respectful. It acknowledges your obligation to win the support of the greatest number, and not just a select few. If voters and consumers have a problem in the new media environment, it is not that they are unintelligent. It is that they *lack the information* they feel they need to make an intelligent choice.

That's why the campaign narrative is so important: it provides information, and also the ideal environment in which people feel comfortable enough to make important choices. Your story — your spin, your message, call it what you will — can be expressed in just a few words, in a single sentence, or (sometimes) in a single paragraph. It can be communicated in all sorts of different ways: press releases, speeches, advertising, media interviews, letters to the editor, talking points, postings on websites or blogs, you name it. But no matter where you tell your story, and no matter how long it is, on one point all agree. As *Campaigns and Elections* magazine guru Ron Faucheux puts it: "It must be clear, consistent, understandable, and relevant to the … choice at hand." No facts and figures.

If your story is any good at all, it'll usually have four big advantages. One, it will say why you deserve to win and why your opponent doesn't. Two, it will magnify the differences between the choices. Three, on those days when the shit hits the fan — and, believe me, there are going to be days when the shit does just that — it will keep everyone calm and remind you about what you need to say to get back on track. Four, it'll keep you out of trouble. Why? Because if you are always repeating your "clear, consistent, understandable, and relevant" message — in the same way, with minor variations, over and over — you won't need to make things up, or speculate, or say something awful like "No comment." If you always tell the truth, in other words, you will never need to fib.

Ronald Reagan's October 28, 1980, question to voters — "Are you better off than you were four years ago?" — met all of the key requirements. It reminded voters why Jimmy Carter deserved to lose and why Reagan, by implication, deserved to win. It emphasized the perceived difference between the two men — one guy allegedly wanted you to make do with what you had, and the other guy apparently felt you deserved better. It impliedly addressed the concerns about Reagan's too-conservative nature by suggesting that, as bad things could be, they couldn't be as bad as they were with Carter. And it provided a narrative for everything that would happen thereafter in the 1980 presidential race. That is to say, Ronald Reagan's narrative. Story-based narratives — sans figures, graphs, charts, and the like — are really, really important.

Reagan was, as many have acknowledged, a master storyteller. Reagan acknowledged it, too. As the former president once said: "You've heard, I'm sure, that I like to tell an anecdote or two. Well, life not only begins at forty but so does lumbago and the tendency to tell the same stories over and over again."

To guys like me, Reagan was a bit of a far-right radical, obsessing about stuff like communism (even when it was dead), big government (which he made bigger), and big tax hikes (which he was unafraid to make). But because Reagan was able to leaven his criticisms with humour, it was hard to stay mad at him. One memorable example of this came in the next presidential debate, in 1984, against Democrat Walter Mondale, who was seventeen years younger than Reagan. Said the Republican candidate, "I will not make age an issue of this campaign. I am not going to exploit, for political purposes, my opponent's youth and inexperience."

Reagan honed his storytelling skills early on by announcing Chicago Cubs games, fleshing out what he saw on the sports ticker with imagination and spin. He told even more stories with a syndicated radio show in the late 1970s, weaving tales he wrote himself. He'd use stories to break the ice with people, to get a laugh, or — most often — to illustrate a political point. Reagan's tales were often embellished or exaggerated, and there was a widespread suspicion that he sometimes lacked the ability to distinguish between fact and fiction. But he knew how to captivate an audience and get them on his side.

To the astonishment of some, Reagan bent the truth in his very first inaugural speech. He spoke about the memorials to Abraham Lincoln and George Washington, and then said:

> Beyond those monuments to heroism is the Potomac River, and on the far shore the sloping hills of Arlington National Cemetery with its row upon row of simple white markers bearing crosses or Stars of David … Under one such marker lies a young man — Martin Treptow — who left his job in a small-town barbershop in 1917 to go to France with the famed Rainbow Division. There, on the Western front, he was killed trying to carry a message between battalions under heavy artillery fire. We're told that on his body was found a diary. On the flyleaf under the heading, "My Pledge," he had written these words: "America must win this war. Therefore, I will work, I will save, I will sacrifice, I will endure, I will fight cheerfully and do my utmost, as if the issue of the whole struggle depended on me alone."
>
> The crisis we are facing today does not require of us the kind of sacrifice that Martin Treptow and so many thousands of others were called upon to make. It does require, however, our best effort and our willingness to believe in ourselves and to believe in our capacity to

perform great deeds; to believe that together with God's help we can and will resolve the problems which now confront us.

Here's the problem: Martin Treptow was not buried in Arlington Cemetery. He was buried in Wisconsin. Reagan had made up a key fact, and in his very first speech as president, too. But when that key fact came out, nobody particularly cared. Reagan's storytelling ability — his desire to render America "a shining city upon a hill" once again — was more important to millions of Americans. To wit: *facts tell, stories sell.*

That's Big Truth number one. Here's Big Truth number two: make certain that the story that dominates the discussion is *your* story. Always. Here's why: no matter how nice your opponent looks — no matter how articulate, no matter how charming — he or she can't win if your message is the dominant theme of the campaign.

Televised leaders' debates — like the one in which Reagan clobbered Carter — show us all why this narrative stuff is so crucial. TV debates give candidates a chance to stress basic campaign themes, and in front of what is usually the biggest audience of the campaign. They also let candidates depict their opponents' campaign message in an unflattering way. Contrary to what some media pundits claim, debates are not about defining moments (although, admittedly, Reagan's "are you better off" line was certainly a defining moment). Debates are about ratifying your side's issues — and *the* issues in the campaign — and looking good at the same time. They're not about defeating the opposition's claims, proving something, or answering reporters' questions, either. They're about getting your story — your spin, your message — heard by as many people as possible. Full stop.

Now, keep in mind that a single night's debate is not going to change voters' minds about the key issues. To win, you first develop and then repeat your campaign's theme. That's it, pretty much. The most successful presidential and prime ministerial performers enter debates with a single clear message they wish to get across — and they use questions and interruptions to return to, or highlight, their single key message. As Dick Morris has noted, a simple way to measure success is to count the number of debate minutes devoted to your key messages (e.g., for a liberal like me, health or the environment) and not the opposition's (e.g., for a conservative, tax cuts or "getting tough on crime"). You win when your story has taken up the greatest number of minutes. Before they head off to bed, you want the people who tuned in to conclude that your guy or gal is humble, energetic, trustworthy, passionate, positive — and that he or she is "fighting for me."

Losing, on the other hand, is easy. If a liberal guy or gal performs well on an issue like "getting tough on crime," and the other side doesn't, it doesn't matter that the liberal did a fabulous job presenting his or her case and sounded like the best debater in the history of planet Earth. The "getting tough on crime" issue is *their issue*. The other side will *always* sound more credible when the subject matter is their issue.

During the 2000 Canadian election campaign, which saw Liberal Party Leader Jean Chrétien win more seats than he won in 1997, I was part of a little group that helped to prepare him for the TV debates. In the mock debates, I played the role of Canadian Alliance Leader Stockwell Day, which was quite amusing. Chrétien certainly thought it was.

I sat in on quite a few meetings of the debate preparation group, and I didn't find a lot of it particularly helpful. A couple of the people in the group were idiots. And a lot of the people gathered around the table and talked a lot about their theories on defining moments and so on, but I thought it was a lot of crap. To me, defining moments just happen, like when you win the lottery. You don't spend time planning a lottery win. Either you win it or you don't.

I was frustrated, so I wrote a little memo, and I gave it to Jean Chrétien. I told him that it was about telling people what his story was, telling the story, and then reminding people that he just told them his story. I also wrote another very brief memo, part of which read like this: "Our key message is about choosing between two messages, one of which is extreme. It is choice between a reasonable and reasoned Liberal alternative on taxes (big, and better for moderate and middle income Canadians) and Stockwell Day's extremist choice (tax cuts which are only better for a select few); between a Liberal alternative on health care (well-funded, national standards with all that implies, etc.) and Day's version (privatized, ten-tier, no national enforcement of standards, etc.); and other issues, as necessary."

Health care, education, and the environment were all good things to talk about, so that's what Chrétien did, even though the other party leaders were attacking him like a pack of crazed, rabid dogs. Chrétien, meanwhile, effectively avoided talking about things that were bad for him. Stockwell Day, however, persisted in going on and on and on about things that were unhelpful to his cause — to the point, even, of repeatedly holding up a little handmade sign in the English-language debates, to protest that he had been misunderstood about health care. "No Two Tier Health Care," it said. It looked like it had been written in crayon. At that point, there was only one way we Liberals could have managed the dialogue better, and that would have been to make up the little "Two Tier" sign ourselves and request that Day hold it up on TV.

Political storytelling — political spinning — requires some intestinal fortitude. It's important that one doesn't whine, and former Canadian Alliance leader Stockwell Day had a penchant for whining a lot. Politics is a nasty, unpleasant, mean-spirited business, which is presumably why some of us are drawn to it. (Many of us are nasty, unpleasant, and mean-spirited people.)

Stockwell Day had come from my home province of Alberta, which has been properly likened to a one-party state. Once on the national scene, he quickly distinguished himself as a youngster who could not take a punch without complaining about it to the school principal. (In that way, he resembled future Liberal leader Paul Martin, but with a great deal less formal education.) As we continued to try and ensure that our issues dominated the political discussion, a thought occurred to us: we were dealing with a great big, wet, bona fide fish here. So we kept putting interesting things at the end of our fishing line — things like health care, or pensions, or abortion, or referendums. And Stockwell Day, being a hungry little fish, could not resist taking the bait. He'd complain about all this, sure. He was being misconstrued and misquoted and misunderstood, he whined, by the worldwide Liberal conspiracy. It was unfair. It was mean.

"Call off your attack dogs, Mr. Chrétien," was one favourite headline — which we promptly enlarged and posted on the war room wall.

To the very end, however, Stockwell Day couldn't resist blathering on and on about his own negatives. And his negatives, of course, were our positives. That, as my mother likes to say, is how you get your ass kicked on election day. Stockwell Day helped us get a bigger share of the popular vote than we did in 1997. That isn't easy to do, but he did it.

To recap: facts tell, stories sell. And when you've got a winning story, stick to it. Don't talk about the other guy's story.

HARRINGTON LAKE HAS A FABLED NAME, but it does not look like much. It is a nice old wooden home — a cottage, really — with two storeys and an unobstructed view of one of the prettier lakes in Gatineau Park, north of Ottawa. Down the steps near the front door there is a small boathouse. It is a quiet retreat that could never be described as posh or extravagant.

In 1959, John Diefenbaker paid a visit to the place, at the urging of friends who thought it would serve him as an excellent country home. Believing that Diefenbaker needed some persuasion, his friends spoke to the property's caretaker and told him to ensure that Diefenbaker went fishing and, should he go fishing, also to ensure that he caught a trout. Diefenbaker did go fishing, and he caught a fish, too. Soon after, the federal government acquired Harrington Lake.

Since then, all of Canada's prime ministers (and the Queen, who rested her head there in the fall of 1977) have stayed at Harrington Lake. The one who was most taken with the place was Pierre Trudeau, who went there as often as he could with his three sons. In the woods to the south of the house, Trudeau and his children had a secret spot where, some speculate, they buried a bottle containing a poem. Not long before his son Michel tragically died in an avalanche in British Columbia in 1998, Trudeau and his boys returned there for a last time, to hike through the woods and find their secret cache.

Even now, with the exception of the presence of the Royal Canadian Mounted Police (RCMP) at a roadblock a few minutes' drive from the house, and also in a clapboard building near the estate's small parking lot, there is little about Harrington Lake to suggest it is a prime ministerial residence.

It is for that reason, partly, that thirty or so people descend on this retreat one autumn Sunday in October 2000: it is a quiet place to prepare some political spots without having to worry about nosy journalists.

Anyone who tries to get near, after all, must first get past the Mounties. The Liberal Party of Canada has rented the estate for the shooting of the commercials, with the approval of the bureaucrats who maintain official residences and whatnot.

The election call is just a few days away. Most of those present are technicians, brought there by Vickers and Benson (V&B), the Toronto advertising agency that has prepared political spots for the Liberal Party of Canada for as long as anyone can remember. Representing V&B are its president, John Hayter, and its chairman, Terry O'Malley.

Also gathered at Harrington Lake, loitering outside, taking in the view, are a number of Chrétien political loyalists, me among them. Most notably, for this story about political stories, there is a young adman from Western Canada, Don Millar. Millar is a professional storyteller.

Of all of those present, Millar is the least known, which is how he prefers it. Wearing a borrowed sweater (he forgot how cold Ottawa can get), a pair of chinos, and a bemused expression, Millar hangs at the edges of the V&B people or the Chrétien people. Everyone is waiting for shooting to begin. Millar occasionally scribbles in a notebook or squints through his dusty glasses at a monitor the technicians have set up in a mud room. He does not say much, but when he does, he has the undivided attention of those who are directing the day's events.

Despite his youth (he is still in his thirties) and the fact that he is largely unknown to the tightly knit Chrétien crowd (apart from me, who recommended him to various senior Liberals a few months earlier), Don Millar is unique in Canada: he is an adman, a spinner, a purveyor of stories who understands politics. In the United States, the species is comparatively commonplace, but Canada doesn't have many people like Don Millar. Here, there are plenty of advertising people who think they understand politics, but they decidedly do not. There are also far too many political people who believe they know how to do advertising, but do not. Millar has attracted the attention of the people who help to run one of the most successful political franchises in the world. That is not easy to do.

The political advertising work done by Millar's agency, which operates in both Canada and the United States, is recognized as some of the best around. In the U.S., he takes on only Democrats as clients; in Canada, only Liberals. Like most politicos, he knows that clients do not make use of consultants who represent both sides of the ideological divide; consultants are generally only liberal, or only conservative, and they must stick with their team.

The trade magazine of political consultants, *Campaigns and Elections*, gave an award to Millar's firm for the best political TV commercials. The *Chicago Tribune* has called his work creative, while the *Washington Post* has declared that voters love the spots Millar and his colleagues produce. In the United States, his clients have included mayors, judges, congressmen, senators, the Democratic National Committee, and the Bill Clinton and Al Gore campaign of 1996.

Millar was born in Alberta in 1961. He will not say much about his family, other than to mention that they still live in Western Canada and that "they still vote Liberal." In his youth, he was that rarest of political commodities — a Grit who lived in the West. By the time he was in his twenties, Millar was doing advertising in the United States. He was good at writing ad copy, but he was interested in doing more. "I was in advertising," he says, "but I had always been tremendously interested in politics. That's what I wanted to do." Millar could tell stories. He could render complex, confusing policy stuff understandable. He was smart, too.

Before he established his own firm with a well-known U.S. media consultant, Millar had been a senior strategist and producer with a huge political communications outfit in Washington, D.C. The firm is one of the U.S. capital's oldest political Democratic communications firms, representing senators Paul Simon and Bill Bradley, Congresswoman Geraldine Ferraro, and a number of high-profile lobby groups. Following his move to the United States, Millar counted a number of prominent U.S. politicians among his clients, including senators Dianne Feinstein and Bob Kerrey, as well as Congressman Dick Gephardt.

Millar is passionate about political storytelling and about what it can mean to people's lives. He reacts angrily to suggestions, often made by his colleagues in the advertising world, that political issues can be sold in the same manner as soap or toothpaste. "The difference between a decision about the future of your country, or your state, or your province, and what you are going to have for breakfast is obvious," he says. "Some people may say political advertising is like selling soap, but it's not. That's a crazy, insulting suggestion. Political advertising is about making important choices."

What Don Millar is good at — very, very good at — is depicting those choices through advertising, through stories, in tough terms. That's not negative, it's informative. It's dishing out criticism where it's deserved. And informed criticism is what election politics is all about.

THE MORNING AIR IS CRISP AND CLEAR, and the scenery is beautiful, so Millar, the Chrétien people, and the senior V&B creative team stand outside the house, waiting. On the driveway, there is a large white eighteen-wheeler containing klieg lights, cameras, and recording equipment. Over some of the ground-floor windows, technicians have affixed screens to make the sunlight seem more diffuse inside. Before long, there is a commotion: word has been received that Chrétien and his RCMP escort will be arriving in a few minutes. The advertising and political people move quickly into the house and assume their positions.

Moments later, Chrétien steps out of his car, wearing a Gap shirt, a sweater, and a pair of slacks. A big guy with an easy manner, he waves at familiar faces. After a bit of glad-handing, he heads into the house to get to work. While a woman applies makeup to the prime ministerial face, Chrétien chats about the recent polls with an aide. The campaign director brings Don Millar into the room, and Chrétien reaches over to shake Millar's hand. "Hello there, young man," he says. "Thank you for your help. What do you think of our chances?"

Don Millar gives a toothy smile. "Oh, I think they are very, very good, Prime Minister."

Some time later, Millar sits on a chair in the cramped garage at Harrington Lake, writing. His desk is a few planks laid atop a pair of large boxes. He is oblivious to the RCMP officers and staff buzzing around him as he squints at a sheaf of spot scripts. The text for one, called "Canada," is on a single sheet, in large print. It reads:

Canada is a great nation. Built on Liberal values. Freedom ... justice ... sharing ... tolerance. Today, Canada can be a leader in a new world. What is most important for me, Jean Chrétien, is that each and every Canadian can take their place in this new world ... without ever losing sight of our fundamental values. We have a bright future. It is up to us to achieve it.

The spot script is for what is referred to as a "thirty" — as in, a thirty-second-long advertisement. In political advertising, the early days of a campaign are made up of a lot of thirties, so that a candidate may present one or two ideas or issues. (Some candidates with a lot of money, like Ross Perot in the 1992 U.S. presidential election campaign, may even employ sixty-second spots.) Once the campaign is up and running, it is possible to run a cluster of "fifteens" on single issues that are important in the race.

Millar scowls at the text, which has not been written by him. Repeating some of the phrases aloud, he extracts a pen from his jacket and starts scratching out words and sentences. The first to go is "nation"— the word is one that Americans use, but English Canadians do not, explains Millar. It is also a word favoured by Quebec separatists to describe their province, and he knows that no one in Canada wishes to discuss the Quebec issue for a long, long time. So "nation" becomes "country."

The sentence fragment about "Liberal values" is the next to go. That phrase sounds like Liberals believe the country can only be defined in the context of their own value system. "Arrogance" is a word the opposition and the media are throwing around a lot to describe the Liberal decision to call an election before the end of its four-year electoral mandate. So "Liberal values" is also excised, and becomes "Because of the values we all hold — freedom, justice, tolerance, sharing."

The next sentence, about Canada being "a leader in a new world," sounds too ephemeral, too vague. He writes, "In today's world, we must be even more of a leader. But we have to do it together." He chews on the end of his pen and looks disapprovingly at what he has written. "New world," he says. "What the fuck is that, new world?" He sighs. The

"together" sentence is important. One of the key messages of the anticipated Liberal election campaign is inclusion; it is a strong but subtle way
of distinguishing itself from the right-wingers. Millar and others want
to depict the Canadian Alliance challenger as an extremist group with a
hidden agenda — an agenda that includes fat tax breaks for millionaires
but little for middle-class or moderate-income Canadians.

The next section, too, ends up completely rewritten. "We can never
make a choice that says some Canadians are more important than the
rest. Every Canadian must take their place in this new world. If we stay
true to our values, then we ensure that every Canadian wins." Millar
squints at this last part, reads it aloud to a couple of political people
standing nearby. The changes he has made are the product of his own
experience about what works, and what does not, in political advertising. Most of all, however, the changes reflect the results obtained in focus
groups held in different Canadian cities just a few days earlier. Each one
of the phrases and concepts has been rigorously tested because, as Millar knows, the writer of the spot may find a phrase funny or powerful or
somehow effective, but the viewer — a potential voter — may hate it. So
testing an ad, both before and after production, is essential. Before the
Liberal leader sees the text, later in the day, Millar will have changed it
again.

All day will be spent with Jean Chrétien, rehearsing half a dozen
spots like "Canada." The text will be run over a transparent teleprompter,
placed directly over the camera's lens so that the prime minister will not
be looking off-screen when he speaks. On that day, and in the days that
follow, Don Millar's pen will fall on some other scripts, too — these ones
much tougher than those being filmed at Harrington Lake. One spot,
also filmed with Chrétien facing the camera and called "Not A Toy," was
never broadcast. It reads:

> Stockwell Day and his Reform Alliance party want to
> do something very dangerous for this country of ours.
> Mr. Day wants to take your federal government out of
> your health care. He wants to give control of it to the
> provinces. This could lead to a have and have-not health
> care system in which some Canadians simply could not

afford to get sick. This is totally unacceptable to me and to the Liberal Party. On election day, tell Stockwell Day that your health care system is not a toy to be played with. In our Canada, everybody must win.

Originally, all of the critical scripts referred to the Liberal's principal adversaries as the Canadian Alliance. By doing that, however, we were effectively going along with the opposition's attempt to re-brand itself as something kinder and gentler. Millar and I therefore lobbied for the name that was ultimately used: the Reform Alliance. Our adversaries' former name, the Reform Party, recalled their past, which, many Canadians felt, was characterized by policies that were intolerant and mean (for example, opposing Sikhs wearing religious symbols in the RCMP, or preventing changes to Canada's ethnic culture). Thereafter, in Liberal circles, the party became and remained the Reform Alliance.

The spot also focused on what Millar and others felt was a major tactical error by Stockwell Day: a few weeks earlier, the Reform Alliance leader had sent a strangely worded letter to the provincial premiers. The letter's tortuous structure permitted an interpretation that Day favoured a wholesale withdrawal from health care by the federal government. It would be a theme the Liberal campaign would return to many times in the fall election.

Another toughly worded thirty-second spot, written for shooting at Harrington Lake, was called "Not That Difficult." Again featuring the prime minister, the script read:

> Stockwell Day and I see the issue of tax relief in this country very differently. With his proposed flat tax, Mr. Day would have a country in which the interests of a few take priority over the well-being of the many. I see another option. I see a country in which tax relief benefits you and your friends and your neighbours. I see a tax relief program where everyone is better off. If that is more like the Canada you see, vote Liberal on election day. In our Canada, everybody must win.

The notion that Day and his Reform Alliance were proposing a flat tax — which, as every economist knows, disproportionately benefits the rich — is one that a few of us had been propagating for many weeks. At their glitzy policy platform launch a few weeks earlier at Conestoga College in Kitchener-Waterloo, Day had gone to great lengths to emphasize that his party had abandoned its previous single-tax-rate stance. It now had two marginal tax rates, he said. While some might have felt it unfair to continue labelling his tax plan a "flat tax," Millar and I were of the view that we were not in the fairness business. Judges dispense fairness; in a political campaign, we told little stories that we hoped would say a lot of good things about our side and a lot of bad things about the other side. Day could call his plan whatever he liked, but we would continue to call it a flat tax that favoured the rich. And we did. The spot, as written, did not make it to television, but its basic theme was used in other Grit campaign communications that fall.

There were other such tough spots, some of which were filmed, some of which never made it past the ideas stage. One of Don Millar's very best spots never made it to television. I had found out that in 1994 Stockwell Day had purchased a revolver at an auction to protest the Liberal government's plans to introduce a gun registry and better gun control laws. When I told him this, Millar's eyes lit up. He got to work. The spot he quickly wrote was called "Example." Alongside a photo of a handgun like the one Day bought, and alongside newspaper headlines documenting that Day had, in fact, done what we said he did, Millar found an actor to read his script, as ominous-sounding music played in the background.

> While Canada's Liberal government was protecting our families with gun registration, Stockwell Day had a different idea. He bought a handgun. In fact, the Reform Alliance wants to scrap gun registration altogether. No wonder the gun lobby is working so hard to end gun controls and elect them. What kind of an example is that? Ask yourself: does Stockwell Day's Reform Alliance speak for you?

Despite the fact that the spot was not used by the Liberal Party's campaign, Don Millar's devastating tag line — "Does Stockwell Day's Reform Alliance speak for you?"— was repeated hundreds of times, at the conclusion of other spots about health care and gay rights.

Those spots — that story, that bit of spin — helped the Liberal government win re-election. We won more seats than we did in 1997, our share of the popular vote grew more than 10 percent, and 5,252,031 Canadians voted for us — 2 million more votes than Stockwell Day got. Not bad.

Moral of the story? Get a winning story, and stick to it.

Get Your Message Out (For Free)!

THERE ARE PROBABLY A ZILLION things said every week to describe the news media. Most of them aren't very nice. For example, one of the greatest men who ever lived, Mahatma Gandhi, had this to say: "I believe in equality for everyone, except reporters and photographers." Gandhi said that! Gandhi, the guy who said we should love everyone! Gandhi, the peace-loving non-violence guy! Kind of makes you wonder what Jesus Christ or the prophet Mohammed would say about Rush Limbaugh, doesn't it?

Anyway. If you ask a politician or a campaign manager or the occupant of a war room about the media, you will often hear a lot of analogies to other living creatures. Reporters and editors are "jackals" or "snakes" or "mangy dogs" or "intensely evil bottom feeders." Not nice.

Having been a reporter myself, I think these analogies aren't very accurate, either. If you want to compare reporters to something, compare them to the boards at a hockey rink. It's a way better analogy.

We have four kids, you see, and they all love hockey. On weekends during hockey season, we spend all of our waking hours huddled on cold benches in hockey rinks. It gives you a lot of time to think about things as you sit there, freezing your ass off. I do some of my best political strategizing in hockey rinks, and (I suspect) so does Canadian Prime Minister Stephen Harper. More on him later.

So there I was, early one Saturday morning, experiencing no sensation whatsoever in my hindquarters, thinking about zero-sum game theory, when I heard this: "The boards are your friends!"

It was one of the loud parents. They're meek and mild employees of the financial services sector during the week, but on the weekend at the hockey rink they turn into screaming, scary sociopaths. They all think their kids will play in the National Hockey League one day if they yell a lot, so it can get pretty noisy out at the old neighbourhood hockey rink. I, meanwhile, focus on the lack of feeling in my arse, think up mean things to say about political adversaries, and don't talk very much.

"*The boards are your friends!*" one of the bank management maniacs hollered again at their kid, who is never going to play in the NHL. That's when it occurred to me.

The reason coaches and hockey parents say "the boards are your friends" to the kids is because it's true. When you've got the puck and you're whizzing towards the other side's blue line, and there's a wall of kids in front of you — kids who are experiencing puberty early and are about three times your size, too — bounce the puck against the boards to get past them. Then you or one of your teammates can grab it and pop it in the net. It works.

I would think the brilliance of my hockey rink analogy should be crystal clear by now, but if it isn't, let me get out the hand puppets for you. There are three reasons why the news media are like the boards at a hockey rink. First, like the boards, journalists set the parameters on what's going on. They delineate the outlines of the public discourse, mostly. No single group — not the politicians, and not the public itself — has as much agenda-setting power. Contrary to what some politicians (cf. Mr. Harper, *supra*) think, however, you can't play the game up in the stands. You can't completely sidestep the news media with blogs and obscurantist partisan websites and whatnot. You just can't. Most of the game is played down on the ice, and if you want to win, you have to play where everyone else is playing.

Second, the boards at hockey rinks are hard. They are made out of wood and metal and whatnot. If you slam into the boards at about seventy miles an hour, you're not going to be playing a lot of hockey games for the foreseeable future. Same with the news media: you may not like them very much — you may agree with Gandhi, for example, and consider reporters and editors a lesser species — but in a head-on collision, the media will always be the ones who are going to be left there, unhurt. You, meanwhile, will be the one left wearing Depends and eating your meals through a straw.

The third reason the news media are like the boards at a hockey rink, as per my stupendously brilliant above-noted analogy, is this: the media — like the boards — can often be helpful. During your campaign, be it for a candidate or for a cause, you are going to encounter multiple obstacles. Funds will run short, advertising will go awry, volunteers will quit, the public will be uninterested, mistakes will get made. There is no shortage of problems in any campaign. So, when you get the metaphorical puck and you're skating towards a wall of scary-looking mesomorphs, bounce the metaphorical puck off the metaphorical boards. Bounce it off the news media. With the right shot — with the right spin, the right play, the right speed — you will get past the big obstacle, get the puck again, and shoot. Maybe you'll score, and maybe you'll win.

So, now that I've beaten that sports analogy to death, now that you will never again look at a hockey rink in the same way, you may ask: Should I consider the news media to be my new best friends, Warren? Should I hang out with them all the time and tell them my innermost secrets?

Um, no. No, no, no. That would be totally crazy.

Journalists who write about politics — and I write this as someone who has been one, and as someone who has even taught *unsuspecting youngsters* how to be one — are regarded by most politicians as duplicitous, lazy, amoral confidence artists. They are seen as cynical, soulless sophists, to a one. If Jesus Christ himself were one of their confidential sources, they would burn him in a New York minute, just to get the scoop on his resurrection.

That's not what I think, having been a journalist. But when the majority of political consultants, regardless of party affiliation, age, race, gender, or place of origin, are asked about reporters, their eyes will start to look for the nearest exit. When pressed, they will mumble something about how they have plenty of friends who are political journalists, or that there are some reporters who they trust, or that they understand that the media are "professionals" and have a job to do. But put away the tape recorder, get a few beers into them, and the truth will eventually tumble out. Political consultants (and, usually, the politicians they represent) hate political journalists. Hate 'em.

In the past couple of decades or so, relationships between politicos and hacks — never easy to begin with — have deteriorated rather dramatically. Statistics do not lie, generally, and the statistics tell the story. In their 2000 Brookings Institution study called *Campaign Warriors: Political Consultants in Elections*, American University professors James Thurber and Candice Nelson reveal the results of a survey that was, in part, about consultants and reporters. Thurber and Nelson conducted two hundred in-depth interviews in 1997 and 1998 with the principals in a number of major U.S. political consulting firms, and found that political activists are "full of negativity" about the news media.

Nearly 70 percent of political consultants, for example, rated the job that journalists do as "poor" or no better than "fair." It did not matter what party the consultants were affiliated with, the vast majority regarded reporters as stinkers. Only 1.5 percent described journalists as "excellent." (This works out to be approximately three of the two hundred consultants interviewed, in case you are wondering.)

The older the consultant, the worse his or her views of the fourth estate. Wrote Thurber and Nelson, "Political consultants who have been around longer develop more concrete attitudes toward the media. The experiences or run-ins they have had over the years may have reinforced their beliefs about journalists." Reporters and editors in search of a silver lining in this statistical storm cloud may point to one statistic: Thurber and Nelson found that only 30 percent of the consultants polled had actually worked for a media organization. Ipso facto, most political flak catchers cannot be expected to understand the doings of political hacks. But not so fast. Employing awkward sentence structure, the pair of academics note, "Not only were the consultants who had worked in the media not more likely to rate political journalists more favourably, they actually gave more *negative* ratings. Seventy-five per cent of those consultants who had worked for the news media, compared to 65 per cent of all other consultants, rated today's political journalists as fair or poor." Of all of the consultants consulted, 50 percent said journalists were, in fact, getting worse.

Concluded Thurber and Nelson, "Considering the evidence … the results are striking. Political consultants dislike the media … [They] do not like political journalists." Political consultants must, however, accept one immutable law of nature. They are bound together with media people in perpetuity, metaphorical groom and bride in a diabolic marriage without end. One cannot properly exist without the other. Political consultants need reporters to tell nice stories about the candidates they wish to elect and, naturally enough, unpleasant stories about their electoral opponents. Political reporters, meanwhile, need consultants to provide them with the stories that sell newspapers and boost ratings.

Disliking journalists is a waste of time, in my opinion. I think most journalists are professionals, and — most of the time — they do a very good job. You need them, and they need you. And, even if you can't bring yourself to *pretend* to like ink-stained wretches — as in the case of Prime Minister Harper, who clearly would choose serial root canals over a press conference — consider this: the news media save you money. Lots of money.

If you've got a story to tell, the news media can help you tell it. That's why every war room must have two media plans. One plan needs to address paid media, meaning advertising to get one's message out to the widest possible audience, on TV, on radio, on the Internet, in newspapers, on billboards, on buses, you name it. The other needs to address earned media, obtaining positive coverage in the news media for free. It's possible to win without advertising. But in my experience, you can't ever win without an effective earned media plan.

Rich conservatives politicians don't generally hesitate to spend tons of dough to "go over the heads" of the media, whom they consider to be willing tools of the secular humanist, One World Government, black helicopter conspiracy. Remember Delaware Governor Pete DuPont in 1986, yappy Texas billionaire H. Ross Perot in 1988, and nerdy gazillionaire publisher Steve Forbes in 1994? They spent millions and millions to advance their presidential aspirations. Often, rich guys do this sort of thing because they consider the media to be hostile, and because they hate the fact that the media exercise so much control over the public agenda. Does it work? Well, in a multi-million-dollar ad campaign, you certainly have complete control over how and when your story is told. That much is true. But all of that control is costing you multi-millions of dollars — and not everyone is as wealthy as DuPont, Perot, and Forbes. Getting your message out through the news media, on the other hand, costs basically nothing. If you develop an intelligent media plan and you follow it, you can save your campaign a fortune and still tell your story to Joe and Jane Frontporch.

That all said, there are indeed risks associated with chasing earned media coverage, and not just for rich conservative politicians, either. Ask Gary Hart. In May 1987, when he was seeking the Democratic presidential nomination for the second time, rumours were rampant that the handsome former Colorado senator was a philanderer and was following his little soldier into battle too often. The *New York Times* asked him about the rumours. Said Hart, "Follow me around. I don't care. I'm serious. If anybody wants to put a tail on me, go ahead. They'll be bored."

Not quite. Boring Gary was not!

As luck would have it, two reporters from the *Miami Herald* were already tailing Hart, and they had staked out his Washington, D.C. townhouse. In the wee hours of the very day Hart had dared the *New York Times* to tail him, the two *Herald* reporters spotted a pretty young woman named Donna Rice slipping out a side door at night. Not to put too fine a point on it, Donna Rice was not Gary Hart's wife. A couple of days later, the *Herald* received photos of Hart on a boat with Ms. Rice, not Mrs. Hart, in his lap. The boat was called — this is the best part, everyone subsequently agreed — *Monkey Business*. (You can't make this stuff up, folks.) Hart gave a celebrated press conference in which he attacked the news media, which was almost as dumb as daring them to follow him around in the first place. A few months later, he pulled out of the race. He now practises law, and he probably reflects — every now and then — on if it all could have been different.

Well, yes, Gary. It could have been quite different, if only (a) you had stayed away from leggy former models and yachts, and (b) you had heeded the Twelve Handy and Immutable Media Rules.

As much as some politicians would like to rule in perpetuity, and as much as they would like to avoid ever being asked a tough question, neither is ever going to happen. The fact is this: the media are eternal, like death and bad sitcoms. They are here to stay, so deal with it. All politicos and war room lurkers have accordingly developed a few rules about how to survive encounters with the news media. As a public service, here are mine, *gratis*. You're welcome.

The Twelve Handy and Immutable Media Rules

The Press Is the Enemy, Sort Of

President Richard M. Nixon was a crook, as everyone knows. But he wasn't totally incapable of insight. Nixon, God rest his grimy soul, once declared that "the press is the enemy," and, on this single occasion, he was sort of right. For any political consultant hoping to remain one, it is essential to recall that reporters are different from the rest of us. Their stock-in-trade is misfortune, conflict, and an unkillable distrust of political success. As U.S. television host and former Democratic political staffer Chris Matthews puts it in his bestselling book *Hardball*: "Their mission is to produce a good story, and in their business it's generally the bad news that makes the best headlines. Failure, misery, disaster — that's what makes the bells go off in a journalist's nervous system: the kind of story where somebody gets hurt."

Keep in mind, accordingly, that the reporter with whom you are currently sharing an intimate bottle of Cherry Jack is not your best friend. Reporters, all evidence to the contrary, are professionals who have an obligation to report on interesting stuff. If, upon finishing the bottle of Cherry Jack, you are moved to blurt something really interesting — say, that your candidate has a criminal record no one knows about and that he dates a stripper named Kitten — you are about to learn a painful, but valuable, lesson. The media aren't necessarily the enemy, but they certainly aren't your friend. If you want a new friend during a campaign, get a dog.

Leave No Charge Unanswered

It's James Carville's rule, and it applies to the words of both political journalists and political opponents, and it has become particularly crucial since the advent of a twenty-four-hour, seven-day-a-week news cycle. Any critical statement offered up by a reporter or the other side, no matter how imbecilic or nonsensical it may seem at first blush, must be taken seriously, and pronto. If the charge appears to be getting ready to blast off into the political stratosphere, fight back. Says Carville, "Make sure you go on the offensive right away. Rush the passer. Blitz. Send in the linebackers, send in the cornerbacks. Send the punter in from the sidelines." There are a lot of sports analogies going on there — political hacks love sports analogies (cf. the hockey boards stuff, *supra*) — but Carville's point is a gospel truth. Hit back or lose. In politics, it is fatal to simply shrug off a criticism that may initially seem minuscule or ridiculous, or to wait too long to reply.

How can one know which attack is going to get media coverage and which isn't? You can't, and it's dangerous to start guessing in the middle of a hotly contested campaign or controversy. In my experience, the super-competitive nature of the news business now means you need to take every allegation seriously, even the nutty ones. In January 1998, for instance, *ABC News* repeated a rumour that there had been a witness to an amorous encounter between President Bill Clinton and White House intern Monica Lewinsky. The *Dallas Morning News* decided to put the rumour on its front page, citing *ABC News* as its source. Within minutes of the Dallas paper hitting the streets, Associated Press was reporting it nationwide as fact. It wasn't. It was completely false: there was no witness. The *Dallas Morning News* fessed up to its error, and the Associated Press issued "kill" notices, but for those still interested in the truth it was too late. With the advent of twenty-four-hour news channels and the Internet, the media are more terrified than ever about being scooped. So they are rushing stuff into print, or on air, that isn't ready.

That means you and your campaign now need to be ready to respond quickly and effectively to reports that are wildly inaccurate. It means leaving no charge unanswered.

Nothing Is Off the Record

Put down your pen. That's what some of us were taught in journalism school, anyway. When the intended subject of an interview says that what he or she has to say is off the record, then that's the end of the interview, pretty much. The reporter in question should put down his or her pen and turn off any and all recording devices. No reporting of what is said. Period. If a reporter is interested in hearing about the background to a decision, or needs help in understanding something, off-the-record sessions have some value, one supposes. But mostly, I side with the admonition published on the Canadian Association of Journalists (CAJ) website: "There is not much point in knowing something if it can't be reported, so this undertaking should be used sparingly, if at all." And, as the CAJ notes, "off the record" is truly a contract-like undertaking given by the reporter to another person. In some places, like the United States, journalists have actually been sued for breach of contract for breaking the "off the record" rule. As a Minnesota court ruled in 1988, reporters have a moral commitment to keep their sources confidential when promised.

So what, then, are we to make of stories like the one published in *Maclean's* magazine in January 2007, about Pierre Trudeau's son Justin (who is, I freely disclose, a friend of mine)? Headlined "His Secret's Out," and written by a guy named Nicholas Kohler, the story described Justin's rumoured interest in electoral politics (later in 2007, he took the plunge, too). Midway through the two-page report, a friend of Justin Trudeau's was named, in full, and quoted: "Off the record, I think [Trudeau's] pretty much there." It wasn't a paraphrase. It was a quote, with quotation marks around it, and that's exactly what it said: "Off the record."

I spoke to the source, whom I know well (and whom I will not burn by naming here). He told me he laid out the ground rules in advance, like you're supposed to. But he got sent to the political burn unit anyway.

This, folks, is bad, bad journalism. "Off the record" should mean just that. No reporting, in any way, shape, or form. No exceptions. There are some variations on the "off the record" interview format, however. "Not for attribution" means the information supplied may be published, but not the source's name. Depending on the agreement reached at the outset, a general description of the source's occupation may be possible. "On background" is often confused with "off the record," but it's different. As the CAJ defines it, "we may use the thrust of the statements and generally describe the source, but we may not use direct quotes."

So, all these rules aside, what should you do when deciding whether or not to blab? Well, in my view, if you say something is off the record, you are typically right to assume that the journalist will not print or broadcast your identity somewhere. You are wrong to assume that the journalist will not tell a few dozen friends the identity of his or her source later that night at Hooters. And here's another thing to keep in mind: before you step forward to play the role of someone's Deep Throat, it is worth remembering that, sooner or later, you will be outed. Despite all evidence to the contrary, political parties are filled with smart people, and some of them are very good at figuring out the name of a particular reporter's "anonymous source."

Proceed with caution!

Politics Is War

That's what journalists think, anyway. Notwithstanding the reality — and the reality is that voters say they are fed up to the teeth with stories about politicians' endless squabbling — political reporters cannot resist battle-field rhetoric. To them, mortality itself is at stake. Take, for example, some of the verbiage that flew around at the time of the 1992 New Hampshire primary. From CNN on February 13: "[Paul] Tsongas knew when he took the lead, they'd be gunning for him. Tom Harkin was the first to open fire … The stream of salvos into the Tsongas camp may only be light artillery compared to what's ahead." From NBC the next day: "[Clinton's] opponents are like sharks with blood in the water." From *Newsweek* on February 10: "[Clinton] will slowly bleed to death, die of a thousand cuts in the Summer and Fall." You get the picture. Every smart political consultant knows that defeats are never as final, or their causes as definitive, as reporters think. But if one's campaign ever hopes to get coverage, describing differences in apocalyptic terminology is never a bad idea. So come out with guns a-blazing, as it were. The media will lap it up.

Keep It Simple, Stupid

The KISS rule existed long before Carville tacked a version of it on the wall of Bill Clinton's War Room in Little Rock. There are two reasons why consultants need to always ensure their communications are really, really, really simple. First, an overwhelming majority of voters are rushing kids to hockey games or ballet classes, or trying to get to work on time. They do not have enough hours in the day (or night) to sleep, let alone research party platforms. Voters want to know what they want to know fast, and in simple terms (which is another reason negative political ads work with them: they contain a single digestible fact). Second, political reporters are divisible into two categories: they are either lazy or busy. Either way, reporters have neither the time nor the inclination to analyze and synthesize reams of policy documents. Keeping one's message simple does not imply that voters or reporters lack the grey matter to understand; it merely acknowledges that they lack the *time*.

A smart American guy named David Shenk came up with a phrase to describe what any war room — any campaign — is up against here: data smog. That is, average folks are bombarded with hundreds of thousands of words and images every single day. They are barraged by complexity and factoids, and it creates a fog that makes it difficult out what, exactly, is going on in the world. Says Shenk in what he calls his first rule of data smog: "Information, once rare and cherished like caviar, is now plentiful and taken for granted like potatoes." Amen to that. To ensure that your bit of information penetrates the data smog, keep it simple. Don't take two hours to say what can be said in two minutes (or less). Like Confucius said: "Life is really simple, but we insist on making it complicated." We shouldn't.

Get It Right the First Time

Political reporters, as evil as they may seem to consultants, are — to me, at least — dedicated professionals. The majority are fair and decent. They can and will forgive a candidate's unwitting minor errors, as long as the flubs aren't happening every other minute. But God help the politician who makes an error of fact that is, well, funny. Reporters love to laugh at politicians, and so do voters. So press accounts of Dan Quayle's June 1992 visit to an elementary school in Trenton, New Jersey, should be required reading for anyone seeking public office.

Sitting next to twelve-year-old William Figueroa to help him with his studies — while a horde of television cameras recorded the exchange

— the U.S. vice-president made a horrifying and historic error of fact. Young William had gone to the board to spell the word "potato," which he did, correctly. Young Dan instructed William to add the letter "e" to the end of the word. Published accounts note that the assembled press in the classroom grew very, very quiet, somewhat like hunters do just before they are about to shoot some lumbering beast in the woods. The next day, William Figueroa threw more dirt on Quayle's figurative coffin at a press conference, when the grade-schooler soberly pointed out that the vice-president "needs to study more."

Indeed.

Swords Are for Falling On

During the year 2000 federal election campaign, former Canadian Alliance leader Stockwell Day (who, it should be noted, bears more than a passing resemblance to Dan Quayle) decided to use Niagara Falls as a backdrop to a campaign announcement. Standing at the falls' edge, Day attempted to draw an analogy between the flow of Lake Erie from north to south and the "brain drain" from Canada to the United States. A reporter from the area pointed out to Day that, in fact, the relevant body of water drained from south to north. Missing a golden opportunity to poke fun at himself, and thereby seem as human as the rest of us, Day darkly warned that he would "check the record, and if someone has wrongly informed me about the flow of this particular water, I'll be having a pretty interesting discussion with them." Not only did Day succeed in making himself *look* like a dummy, he also came across *sounding* like a dummy who couldn't take responsibility for his own mistakes.

Some of these mistakes can have profound consequences, if you don't deal with them quickly. During the November 2006 U.S. mid-term elections, for instance, the Democrats were the grateful recipients of political manna from heaven. In those races, a couple of exceedingly helpful, exquisitely timed sex scandals emerged, involving Mark Foley (Republican family values stalwart caught sending perverted text messages to congressional pages) and Pastor Ted Haggard (evangelical leader and anti-gay White House regular allegedly chasing methamphetamines and male prostitutes). Pastor Ted and former Florida legislator Foley provided swing voters with ample evidence that the Republican religious right were led by sweaty, debauched nutbars, not self-professed men of God. The GOP's unwillingness to quickly acknowledge their mistakes — and their appalling hypocrisy — helped to return the Senate and the House of Representatives to Democratic control for the first time in many years.

Now, it would be unfair to suggest only conservatives make big mistakes. Liberals do, too. Like me, for example.

In the lead-up to the October 2007 Ontario election, I had been doing my utmost to publicize the record of an anti-gay, anti-Native, anti-Quebec, anti-urbanite Ontario Conservative candidate named Randy Hillier. Lots of moderate conservatives were upset about Hillier's candidacy, and in late July one of them sent me a photo of Hillier onstage with party leader John Tory, federal Conservative Member of Parliament Scott Reid, and provincial Tory Lisa MacLeod. My Tory correspondent said Tory, Reid, and MacLeod looked very uncomfortable being onstage with the knuckle-dragging Hillier. He was right.

So I posted the photo on my website, www.warrenkinsella.com, with thought bubbles coming out of Tory's, Reid's, and MacLeod's heads. MacLeod's thought bubble suggested she'd rather be "baking cookies."

My wife, who is a lot smarter than me, thought it was a dumb, sexist joke. So I took the photo down — but too late.

An NDP politician who despises me (I had criticized her for her drug-smuggling past, among other things) issued a press release calling me sexist. The *Toronto Star*, whose ownership also despises me (I had criticized their willingness to take money for prostitution ads in one of their weekly papers), jumped on the story — which quickly moved to the national stage.

I made multiple unreserved apologies; I ate humble pie, big-time. By week's end, columnists and bloggers were saying the reaction to "cookiegate" was far out of proportion to the offence. (And more than one conservative acquaintance told me they suspected I had been "kicking the story" — drawing it out — to distract media attention away from a spending scandal involving an Ontario Liberal cabinet minister. I, um, have no comment on that.)

Bottom line? Mistake-making campaigners should, if the circumstances warrant, fess up, laugh at themselves, then move on. Periodically falling on one's sword is excellent politics.

The Orchestra Pit

Many years back, Roger Ailes started out as a prop boy on the *The Mike Douglas Show*. At its peak, it was one of the biggest TV shows in the world. By age twenty-eight, Ailes was executive producer. One day, Richard Nixon appeared on the show and was highly impressed with Ailes (who, as Joe McGinniss recalls in his seminal book *The Selling of the President*, bluntly told Nixon that "television isn't a gimmick"). Ailes went on to work for a string of Republican leaders, from Nixon to Reagan to Bush, racking up victory after victory. Ailes contributed one line to history that amply testifies to his political smarts. "It's my orchestra pit theory of politics," he said. "If you have two guys onstage, and one says, 'I have a solution to the Middle East problem' and the other guy falls in the orchestra pit, who do you think is going to be on the evening news?"

Statistics bear out Ailes's pithy observation. From 1960 to 1992, Thomas E. Patterson diligently tracked every story written in *Time* or *Newsweek* about major party candidates for his book *Out of Order*. In every U.S. election before 1980, good news dominated bad. After that, the situation reversed. In the 1960s, about 75 percent of political coverage was good news; in the 1990s, 40 percent. When given a choice, political reporters will always write negative stuff; it is their heroin. Candidates (and voters) who request that journalists publish or broadcast "good news for a change" are wasting their breath, and sound nauseatingly Pollyannaish as well. Give the nattering nabobs of negativity, as William Safire called them, the fix they want. It's the only way to get a reporter's attention, some days.

Spin Is B.S.

And not in the way that political reporters think, which is that so-called spin is false. As I opined a few pages ago, *spin* is merely a word that describes attempts to put a favourable gloss on something. It is akin to editorializing about one's own candidate or the opposition's candidate. Putting a favourable gloss on a falsity is, well, lying. And if you lie, you will get caught. Count on it. In my view, spin has become problematic because so many reporters are so suspicious of it — they sense that they are being manipulated by a backroom sleaze who has a bigger salary and a bigger car.

Unless you are invited to spin, don't. Even if you're invited to, proceed with caution. Reporters are in the facts business; give them the facts they need to do their job. That's the war room's number-one job. When they call, they already possess a thesis about the story they want to write; apart from the outbreak of World War Three, the only thing that prevents them from publishing or broadcasting that thesis is *fact*. Fancy talk simply won't work — or, as one politician once put it to me, "You can't shine shit."

Former Clinton advisor Dick Morris also dismisses spin, albeit from a slightly different perspective, calling it a "mutually reinforcing conceit." Says he, "Consultants and press secretaries overly pride themselves on their ability to manipulate press coverage, which they really can't. The media revels in the assumption that its slant and bias are so important that they are worthy of the skills of great manipulators, which they really aren't." There are simply too many daily newspapers and too many television stations for any single spin campaign to make much of a difference. As above: just the facts, ma'am. That's why God (or James Carville) created war rooms.

TV Is Pictures
Study after study show that the vast majority of voters get their political information from TV. (TV reporters, meanwhile, get their agenda and research from newspaper coverage, but not much else.) In political terms, the existential reality is this: if something did not happen on television, it did not happen at all. Step one: get your candidate on TV. Step two: on television, emotions count more than facts — or, as B.C. Liberal Premier Gordon Campbell once told me ruefully, "It's 10 percent what you say, 20 percent how you say it, and 70 percent how you look." Television news executives will try to deny this, but in the depths of their tiny black hearts, they know it is true.

Political news coverage on TV is all about melodrama. Former *NBC News* chief Reuven Frank, no less, confirmed as much in a memo which he circulated to his staff: "Every news story should ... display the attributes of fiction or drama. It should have structure and conflict, problem and denouement, rising action and falling action, a middle and end. These are not only the essentials of drama; they are the essentials of [TV news] narrative." Too much emotion in the "cool" medium that is television is inadvisable, as Marshall McLuhan lectured the world in 1960, after the cool John F. Kennedy beat the hot Richard M. Nixon in a televised presidential debate.

To evaluate the effectiveness of a political story or advertisement, I always watch it with the sound off. That way, I'm forced to consider the visual impact for what is a visual medium. Franklin Delano Roosevelt, for instance, understand the power of image — he allowed the media to take many pictures of him during his twelve years in the White House, but never wearing the braces that he was forced to wear after being struck with polio. So, too, Ronald Reagan's former advisor, Michael Deaver, who was obsessed with television images: "I have always believed that impressions are more important than specific acts or issues … I believe TV is a great boon to us in judging our leaders. It lets us see all the dimensions that, in the past, people could only see in person: the body language, the dilation of the eye, the way they perspire. We see them when they are tired, worried, under great crises. If television focuses on somebody every day, it shows all the dimensions."

Sound Bites Earn Earned Media

Those of us who love campaigns love earned media. As noted, it's cheaper than other forms of political advertising — and because the media is the source, it is regarded as more neutral, and therefore more credible, by potential voters. Writes political scientist William Kerbel, "Media coverage has become a campaign resource as important as money, for money will come only to candidates perceived to be viable — which is to say, perceived to be viable by the press." To capture earned media, therefore, you need to remember that folks in the news business love stuff that is dynamic. This means that many newshounds don't like to write about substantive issues; instead, they like to cover "process" stories — bad jokes about cookies instead of stories on program spending, for example. Most of the time, they think that politics is a game, so they churn out stories about how a particular campaign is a horse race, or a battle, and so on. (Heaven forbid that they should actually suggest that it is a clash of ideas.)

The brass ring in this horse race or battle or whatever it is is the sound bite. Campaigners and war roomers are perpetually dreaming up creative ways to get a sound bite (i.e. a pithy quote) on the news, because sound bites attract the interest of voters. Back in the late 1960s, the average U.S. network political sound bite was 42.3 seconds. By the end of the century, it had shrunk to 9.8 seconds.

This, to me, is not necessarily a bad thing; after all, if you can't say it in a few seconds, it probably can't be said. Dick Morris, who is smarter than the average bear, agrees: "A good campaign strategy may take months to formulate, but it should take no more than a few words to express." Good sound bites get earned media. Earned media gets money, credibility, and votes. Ipso facto, get a sound bite now.

The Media Is a Special Interest Group
So says the aforementioned Mr. Morris, anyhow. And he may be right.

One of the nastiest viruses that journalists are exposed to in journalism school is the idea that the public "has a right to know." Personally, I can't say if the public always has a right to know. (For example, I still cling to the belief that Bill Clinton's fling with a White House intern was between Clinton, his God, and his wife.) But I do know one thing: the public mostly does not give a rat's ass about what the media care about. To them, the media is just another special interest group. Therefore, reports about individual speeches by candidates, policy platforms, and scandals are usually irrelevant to voters. Plenty of studies show that voters tend to look for information that corroborates what they already believe or suspect; most often, they are not looking for something to change their minds.

In a five-hundred-channel universe, no single media outlet commands unswerving loyalty anymore: voters are very selective, and they see media reports as just one of a number of sources of information they use to make ballot decisions. To wit, voters care about issues, not blow jobs in the White House. Says William Kerbel, "Left to their own devices, citizens ... tend not to ask the sort of horserace, strategy or personality questions that obsess political reporters." But some reporters cannot help themselves. They are creatures possessed.

To sum up: the media is, arguably, a special interest group aligned with the enemy. They shouldn't be spoken to off the record. When you *do* speak to them, take every allegation seriously, even if it sounds crazy — and make sure to indulge their passion for sound-bite simplicity, war analogies, snappy visuals, and conflict. If you screw up, fess up and look for a sword to fall on. They'll love that, even if you won't.

And even when you're spinning them, don't admit that you are spinning them. They don't want to be spun, even though — sort of — they do.

Got all that?

Now, DON'T GET ME WRONG. I do not mean to suggest that the news media are all bad. Most of them, as noted, possess redeeming features. Quite a few of them are quite likeable. But a lot of political consultants and war room members don't feel as I do.

Some of this is due to sour grapes, of course. Politicos are frustrated by the fact that this rebellious, ill-mannered, ink-stained pack of jackals has, in a very real sense, more power and influence than they do. They are also irritated by their near-total inability to keep the media pack under control. But what politicos think, at the end of the day, is completely irrelevant. What matters is what the voters think, and, overwhelmingly, they hold journalists in as much contempt as they reserve for politicos and lawyers. (I've been all three — journalist, lawyer, and politico — so I know all about this contempt stuff, believe me.)

Regular folks think everyone in Ottawa and Washington is crazy, most days. My friend Randy McCauley, who was Jean Chrétien's press secretary and who worked with me in the 1993 Liberal war room, puts it succinctly: "Parliament Hill, or Capitol Hill, are a few square kilometres surrounded by reality."

Let me give you an example. In Washington, D.C., Route 495 is called the Beltway. On a map, the Beltway runs more or less in a circle around the U.S. capital and captures places where political hacks and flaks abound — Alexandria, Arlington, and so on. When something happens in Official Washington that excites reporters and politicos, it is said to be "inside the Beltway." In Canada, some of my friends and I have used a similar phrase. If a development has folks on Parliament Hill atwitter, but the ordinary voter doesn't give two hoots about it, it is a "north of the Queensway" story.

For thirty-six days in the fall of 2000, as noted, I was imprisoned in a small, grimy, and poorly ventilated space, helping out on the Liberal Party's national campaign. In all of that time, I can count on one hand the number of times a reporter called up to discuss bona fide policy issues. It did not particularly matter, it seemed, that more than 60 percent of Canadians who were polled during the election were saying that they considered health care to be their biggest concern. It did not matter that a sizable number also wanted to discuss taxation. No. What interested reporters were trivialities like what one leader was wearing that day, or what another leader listened to on his CD player, or what was going on inside the war room.

Sigh. If voters heard a lot about the political parties' war rooms over the course of the writ period, they can be forgiven for wondering why. Reporters were transfixed by that kind of stuff. Utterly and completely transfixed. I am not exaggerating when I say that every day a reporter or a producer of a program would dial up to request a tour of the Liberal Party's war room. We would always say no, because we naively believed elections should be about actual issues, and not about a bunch of young people and computers crammed into a smelly room, churning out press releases and whatnot. But they kept on calling. (One CTV crew even filmed the outside of the Liberal Party's headquarters, ostensibly hoping to spot something war-roomish through the mirrored windows.)

Occasionally, I would get irritated with a reporter making such a request and ask them whether "real Canadians" really gave a sweet damn about these so-called war rooms. Late in the campaign, an equally irritated CBC-TV producer said the subject was important. I asked him why, given what the polls said about what Canadian themselves considered important, things like the future of health care, and taxation, and social programs. His answer was simply to repeat that war rooms were an "important" news story.

That's a pile of crap. Everywhere the leaders went in the campaign, they tried to speak about the issues that count to Canadians. But the news coverage did not reflect that nearly enough. When no reporters were looking, I spoke to a few senior members of the Alliance, Tory, and

NDP parties to confirm that they all felt similarly. Far too many journalists, they told me, find writing about political process a lot easier than actually writing about policy. Reporters love talking about process, one cynical Conservative told me, because they are constant outsiders. Said he, "They love anything that lets them be players."

That's an overstatement, but it may explain why newspapers devote so much time to calculating which party, and which candidate, they plan to endorse near the end of a campaign. My advice? It doesn't really matter. Political folks spend way, way too much time worrying about opinion columnists. And I say this as a guy who writes weekly opinion columns for a national newspaper!

Opinion columns — like the unsigned editorials found every single day in any newspaper — don't change anyone's point of view. In fact, there is evidence to suggest that these editorials may actually persuade readers to embrace the *opposite* point of view. I kid you not. Claims made by newspaper opinion makers — that they are fostering public debate and boosting democracy — are facile and self-serving.

Every year, we collectively witness a raft of electoral contests, at every level. At any given time, on any given date, lots of ballots are being handed out, marked, and handed back. So have newspapers — specifically, newspaper editorial endorsements — affected the way in which voters made democratic choices in any of those places? Do they ever?

In January 2006, Stephen Harper's Conservatives were endorsed by every newspaper from the *Brandon Sun* to the *Winnipeg Sun*. Among major dailies, only the *Toronto Star* called for a Liberal government. But studies show that such editorials ultimately have virtually zero impact on voters. A 2004 Pew Center analysis, for example, measured media influence in that year's presidential campaign. Their surprising conclusion: "Newspaper endorsements are ... less influential than four years ago, and dissuade as many Americans as they persuade." An earlier review by the Annenberg Public Policy Center at the University of Pennsylvania had a similar result: the impact of endorsements, nationally or regionally, was "negligible."

Why? Allen H. Neuharth, the founder of *USA Today* — which adamantly refuses to make political recommendations — regards them with contempt. Editorial endorsements are an insult to readers, he says. When a newspaper publishes them, their political coverage "becomes suspect in the eyes of readers, rightly or wrongly," he adds.

Political partisans, of all stripes, quietly nod their heads at such assessments. Voters, too.

As much as newspapers like to claim that impenetrable walls separate news writing from editorial writing, increasingly few people believe it. Mostly, they see unelected, unaccountable corporate interests throwing their weight around during election campaigns. (Unless those interests align with their own, naturally, in which case all is forgiven.) Ask Bob Hepburn. In January, the *Toronto Star*'s genial editorial page editor acknowledged that some readers regarded the newspaper's enthusiasm for the Liberal Party to be "tantamount to interference in a federal election," as one wrote.

That's absurd. That's crazy. Having editorialized critically about politicians for four years, are newspapers supposed to go mute when a writ is dropped? No way. For his part, Hepburn, like many other newspaper editors, does not see his newspaper's endorsement as a means to influence a voter's choice. They merely hope that it "adds to the political discourse."

Okay, fine. But does it? Around the water coolers of the nation, it is impossible to measure the impact of one or two editorials. Prominent media analyst Jay Rosen, chair of the journalism department at New York University, dismisses the contention that such editorials promote democratic participation in any way. In fact, says Rosen, they often foster "misunderstanding and resentment."

In party war rooms, however, a fistful of editorial endorsements serve at least one useful purpose: they are helpful fodder when cobbling together end-of-campaign television advertising. That is, they have a reinforcing effect when voters see on a TV screen that others agree with their point of view. (See the next lesson-cum-chapter to see what I mean!)

At the end of the day, at the end of this particular chapter, where the media continue to have the greatest influence is in day-to-day news coverage, not on editorial pages. An ink-stained wretch can't really hurt or help a politician in an opinion piece. But take it from me: an angry ink-stained wretch can cause a lot of damage over on the news pages. A lot.

After all, they're the news media. It's their hockey rink — and, until further notice, they are the ones who get to determine who gets to play. And who gets to win.

Get Your Message Out
(For Money)!

I T BEGINS QUIETLY, WITH A LITTLE
girl. She appears to be standing in a field somewhere, with some trees and
branches visible behind her. The wind is blowing. It is warm enough for
the child to be wearing a sleeveless top and a pair of shorts. She has long,
straight hair, with bangs to just above her large eyes, which are preoccupied as we meet her. She can be no more than three or four years old.

She is a holding a flower — a daisy. In a child's singsong voice, the
little girl is counting the petals as she removes them from the daisy. "One,
two, three, four, five," she says, so softly she can barely be heard. She gets
her counting wrong, as young children sometimes do: "Seven, six, six,
eight, nine, nine ..."

And then she stops and looks up, startled and apparently frightened.
Abruptly, a man's voice, very loud, echoing as if amplified through a
loudspeaker, starts to count. As he does so, the camera moves closer and
closer to the little girl. "Ten, nine, eight, seven, six, five, four," he says, and
all that can be seen are the child's eyes, which are afraid. "Three, two, one
..." The shot moves into the dark centre of her eye.

Then there is an explosion — a huge, lingering explosion — and the child's iris is filled with a grainy image of an atomic bomb being detonated. As the mushroom cloud reaches upward, filling the sky, another voice is heard: the voice of Lyndon B. Johnson, president of the United States.

"These are the stakes," he says in the flat idiom of Texas. "To make a world in which all of God's children can live, or to go into the dark." Pause. "We must either love each other, or we must die."

The screen goes black, and a few words appear in white: "Vote for President Johnson on November 3." Then the last voice-over: "Vote for President Johnson on November 3. The stakes are too high for you to stay home."

MOST OF THOSE WHO HAVE SEEN the spot that came to be known as "Daisy" agree: it was, and remains, the most powerful piece of political advertising in history. Hell, I even named my company after it.

Some say "Daisy" marked the beginning of negative political advertising, but that is wrong on two counts. First, the genre of political communications it represents — that is, tough but accurate criticism of the public record of one's political opponent — isn't new. It reflects, in fact, some of the oldest campaigning there is. Second, it isn't accurate to dismiss "Daisy" as negative. The spot has a kind of poetry about it, and, visually, it is beautiful.

It is also wrong to suggest that "Daisy" belongs to the same category of advertising as the infamous and despised Jean Chrétien "face" ads, or some of the other more notorious examples of the politics of personal destruction. The Tories' 1993 spots — produced, in part, by John Tory, who now leads the Ontario Conservative Party — were a vicious, empty-headed attack on the Liberal leader's facial paralysis, and had precisely nothing to do with policy. "Daisy," on the other hand, did not mention once the name of President Johnson's opponent, but it was all *about* a policy: nuclear deterrence.

As a paid advertisement, it ran only once, on the evening of September 7, 1964. But "Daisy" profoundly altered modern electoral politics and the way in which political messages are communicated. Almost four decades later, it can still send shivers up the spines of seasoned political campaigners, the ones who claim to have seen it all. More than Ronald Reagan's 1984 "Morning in America" spot, more than George Bush's 1988 "Willie Horton" attack ad, "Daisy" was, and still is, the best.

On the night it ran, during *Monday Night at the Movies*, the effect was immediate. Within moments, recalled former Johnson press aide Bill Moyers, the White House switchboard lit up with hundreds of calls from those who wanted to protest the ad. Moyers even fielded a call from his boss, who also sounded irate. "Jesus Christ!" Johnson yelled at Moyers, who was part of the team that had produced "Daisy." "What in the world happened?"

"You got your point across, that's what happened," Moyers replied.

There was a lengthy silence. "Well, I guess we did."

They most certainly did. Other networks started to run the ad as part of their news coverage — for free. One Republican senator complained to the National Association of Broadcasters. The chairman of the Republican National Committee, Dean Burch, filed a formal objection with the Fair Campaign Practices Committee, stating that "Daisy" amounted to "a libel against the Republican nominee," Senator Barry Goldwater. More than thirteen hundred people called the Republicans to register their objections to "Daisy," including, allegedly, a Virginia mother who said the spot had reduced her four-year-old to tears before bedtime. "This horror-type commercial is designed to arouse basic emotions and has no place in this campaign," wrote Burch, who was only half-right. Yes, "Daisy" had been carefully designed to stir up basic emotions. But the message "Daisy" conveyed certainly *did* belong in the 1964 U.S. presidential race, because the stakes were very high that year.

Arizona's Barry Goldwater scared people. Even before he won the Republican Party's presidential nomination at the Cow Palace in San Francisco in July 1964, the hard-line conservative had alienated many Americans, and even members of his own party, with statements and allies better suited to the Wild West than a national election effort in a pluralistic democracy. In May 1963, while the U.S. war effort in Vietnam was escalating, Goldwater told an ABC news program that if one wished to expose arms supply routes to Viet Cong guerrillas, then "defoliation

of the forests by low-yield atomic weapons could be done." His ruminations caused an international uproar. In October 1963, Goldwater horri-
fied Americans by claiming that the nuclear bomb was "merely another
weapon." In 1964, he voted against the Civil Rights Act, thereby earning
the enthusiastic support of the Ku Klux Klan and the white supremacist
John Birch Society. He disavowed the support of neither.

At the Republican convention in San Francisco — which Norman
Mailer described, memorably, as "murderous in mood, [where] chimeras
of fascism hung like fogbanks"— Goldwater had not done much to re-
lieve himself of the extremist mantle. Near the conclusion of his acceptance speech, he made the infamous exhortation regularly repeated by
right-wing extremists: "I would remind you that extremism in the defence of liberty is no vice! And let me remind you also that moderation
in the pursuit of justice is no virtue!"

To the Democrats managing Lyndon Johnson's campaign, among
them Bill Moyers and Jack Valenti (who would later achieve distinction
as a powerful Hollywood lobbyist for the Motion Picture Association),
Goldwater had built himself a gallows. By attacking Goldwater, they were
merely granting the Arizona senator his desire for electoral euthanasia.
The advertising campaign they conceived was easily the toughest in U.S.
history. It was also, the Johnson team fervently believed, a valuable public service.

The parentage of "Daisy" is claimed by many. It seems clear, however, that the person most responsible for the spot was a New York City
adman named Tony Schwartz.

Though Schwartz was from New York, he was far removed from
Madison Avenue, home to the advertising agency establishment. In the
brownstone where he lived with his wife and two sons, he built a sound-
proof recording studio, filled with top-of-the-line cameras and editing
machines. He was a bit of a curiosity to the Madison Avenue types, many
of whom had long and enduring relationships with the Republican Party.
Schwartz had an interest in recording children at play, as well as in what
he called "the world of numbers." Long before "Daisy" would change a
presidential campaign, Schwartz said, he "wanted to do a record essay on
numbers without any narration, just the world of numbers. I saw a book
that IBM put out, called *The World of Numbers*, and I thought, I would

love to do a record to go with that … The most complex use of numbers was the countdown on the atom bomb or a rocket blast-off. The simplest use of numbers was a child counting from one to ten. I started fooling around with [that]."

By the summer of 1964, the advertising firm of Doyle Dane Bernbach (DDB) had been retained by the Democratic Party as their agency of record for the forthcoming presidential campaign. Moyers, Valenti, and the DDB admen had resolved to get tough with Goldwater from the start, reminding Americans about his extremism and fondness for the nuclear option. A DDB producer who had worked with Tony Schwartz asked him to come to the firm's Manhattan offices, without telling him why.

In an interview from his home — Schwartz rarely travels anywhere because he is agoraphobic — he tells me he remembers the genesis of "Daisy." Born in New York City in 1923, Schwartz is not as young as he used to be, but his memory is very sharp. In his soft New York accent, he tells his story: "A political ad is about things that are important to the people, at the time the election is taking place. The Daisy ad was an interesting thing, the way it came about. I went down to [DDB] and the producer held up Johnson's picture, and said, 'Would you work for him?' I said yes." He laughs. "They asked me to do the sound for six or seven spots for Johnson, and I said okay."

The Democrats and the DDB team wanted a spot to emphasize the fact that, as president, Goldwater would have his finger on the nuclear button. Schwartz told them he had just what they were looking for. "I told them I had it all done already. I had done a Polaroid spot for Doyle Dane Bernbach with my nephew, counting up to ten and getting all mixed up as kids will at his age — four or five," he recalls. He had also produced dozens of spots and radio essays for WNYC, the New York affiliate of National Public Radio. In one of them, he had an idea. "I added [to the spot featuring his nephew] a countdown from a rocket blast, and a bomb sound going off. And then I had an announcer say, 'In a world of nuclear weapons, we have to have a strong United Nations.' So I took that and played it for them. They flipped. Find a child, I told them, picking the petals off a daisy. And I'll produce it."

The little girl — four-year-old Bridget Olsen, whom DDB found through a city talent agency — was filmed with her flower while walking near the Henry Hudson Parkway north of the city. "The Democrats and DDB gave me five hours of Rose Garden speeches by Johnson," Schwartz says. "They had a script, and they had a little section they had marked off, which they liked. So I listened to all of the five hours of tape and found the section. I listened to it. It had no emotion, and I didn't like it at all. So I just went through the whole thing again and found this piece that I liked. 'These are the stakes ...' And I used that."

While not as many Americans saw "Daisy" as Schwartz or the Democrats would have hoped — most were watching NBC that Monday night — many later claimed to have seen it, or had it described to them. A surprising number insisted, to Schwartz or others, that Barry Goldwater had been named in the spot. Schwartz is vehement on this point: "We never mentioned Goldwater. The type on the end said, 'Vote for President Johnson' and so on. But Goldwater's name was *never* mentioned in it. Now, for years, this was called the beginning of negative political commercials. But it wasn't."

The unforgettable words that Johnson spoke, as it turns out, were not the president's, or Bill Moyers's, or Jack Valenti's. They belonged to the British poet W.H. Auden. "It turned out he wrote a lot of the Rose Garden speeches," Schwartz says, amused. Years later, members of the Auden family tracked down Schwartz and asked him how the New York City adman had persuaded the poet to write for a political commercial. He laughs at the memory, but Auden himself, apparently, had not been amused. A White House speech writer had appropriated the stanza from Auden's most famous poem, "September 1, 1939," written about the growing storms of war. When Auden finally saw "Daisy," he was livid. "I pray to God that I shall never be memorable like that again," he said, giving orders that the poem not reappear in any collections of his work.

Schwartz says he thinks he knows why "Daisy" worked: it confirmed the public's suspicion that Goldwater favoured the use of nuclear weapons, while Johnson did not. When the commercial came on, people asked themselves, "Whose finger do I want on the nuclear trigger? The man who wants to use them, or the man who doesn't?"

"Daisy," in this context, was not really a negative political spot at all. It was an advertisement about choices. It highlighted, in dramatic terms, the difference between Johnson and Goldwater on the nuclear question, and asked voters to make a choice. The way in which the choice was laid out — stark militarism versus a little girl with a flower — was, without a doubt, maddening to partisan Republicans. But, stripped down to its core facts, "Daisy" was not inaccurate. Goldwater *was* more willing to consider the deployment of nuclear weapons. He and his fellow GOP members may not have approved of the fact that Johnson had chosen to emphasize that point of difference. But it *was* a point of difference. And voters were entitled to be told about it.

Elections are about choices. And Tony Schwartz was, one might say, merely suggesting that one choice was infinitely better — infinitely safer — than the other.

IN HIS BOOK *The Responsive Chord*, Schwartz suggests that "Daisy" was effective — despite the controversy, despite the expressions of outrage — because it stirred up powerful, unarticulated emotions among those who saw the spot. "The best political commercials are similar to Rorschach patterns," wrote Schwartz. "They do not tell the viewer anything. They surface his feelings and provide a context for him to express those feelings."

Feelings were in ample supply after "Daisy" was broadcast, just that once, on September 7, 1964.

Barry Goldwater's mistake was to underestimate the power of the spot, which had become the talk of the nation. (He left a charge unanswered, you might say.) At first, he dismissed "Daisy" as "weird television advertising." Two weeks later, however, Republicans, including Goldwater himself, had woken up to the significant damage done to their campaign by Tony Schwartz, a little girl, and a flower. Desperate, they hauled Dwight D. Eisenhower out of retirement to prop up Goldwater's faltering presidential hopes. In a hurriedly produced sixty-second spot, Eisenhower and Goldwater were filmed chatting. Goldwater says, "Our opponents are referring to us as warmongers." Says Eisenhower, looking barely indignant, "Well, Barry, in my mind, this is actual tommyrot."

Actual tommyrot! Goldwater supporter Ronald Reagan also stepped forward to provide a filmed speech to assist Goldwater. Reagan's speech, called "A Time for Choosing," was masterful, and hinted at the promising political future that lay ahead for the California actor. It even attempted to throw back at the Democrats some of their own dark imagery. Said Reagan, "You and I have a rendezvous with destiny. We can preserve for our children this, the last best hope of man on Earth, or we can sentence them to take the first step into a thousand years of darkness."

It was not insignificant, perhaps, that the Democrats and the Republicans were making essentially the same allegation against each other — that the future was at peril in the presidential race. But it was the Democrats (or, more accurately, Tony Schwartz) who understood that, on television, the picture of a child was worth far more than any of Ronald Reagan's words. In politics, that basic proposition has not been challenged since: pictures equal emotion, which equals power. Words do not equal pictures.

When the results came in, early on November 4, 1964, Lyndon B. Johnson had won by a landslide. Barry Goldwater, meanwhile, barely won his home state, by less than 1 percent. Out of fifty states, the Republican nominee took only six. "Daisy" had won.

IF A CAMPAIGN CAN AFFORD IT — and a campaign should always *try* to afford it — paid media is worth it.

Unlike earned media, paid media permits a candidate or a campaign to say precisely what they wish to say, without being forced to go through a pesky news media filter. It permits you to say what you want to say, at exactly the right moment — and as many times you can afford. Most of all, paid media allows you to be creative and to punch through the data smog.

Data smog wasn't a problem, so much, back in the 1940s and 1950s. But an ability to effectively reach millions of potential voters *was* a problem. Thus, Thomas Rosser Reeves.

A book lover, a Virginian, and the son of a Methodist minister, Reeves does not seem the likeliest of candidates to have conjured up modern political advertising. In *Reality in Advertising*, published in 1961, he described himself as "a licensed pilot, a skilled yachtsman, a collector of

modern art, a Civil War buff, a musician and the writer of short stories."
He sported bow ties and horn-rimmed glasses, smoked cigarettes inces-
santly, wrote novels and poetry, and once acted as captain of the United
States chess team. In his early days, Reeves hoped to be a lawyer. The
Great Depression, however, forced him out of the University of Virginia,
and he became a reporter for the *Richmond Times-Dispatch*.

Of his many interests and avocations, it was for advertising that
Reeves became known — in particular, for advertising that used the new
medium of television to revolutionize political campaigns. Tony Schwartz
would create a genre, but it was Reeves who created the medium.

Until Reeves came along, political salesmanship was a primitive process. Candidates for national office were obliged to submit themselves to
gruelling, months-long campaigns — travelling great distances by train,
hollering themselves hoarse from makeshift platforms, grasping innumerable hands at innumerable rallies, and occasionally making use of
radio to broadcast lengthy speeches listened to by only a few. In 1948, the
year Harry S. Truman won the U.S. presidential race, Truman himself
estimated that he had "travelled 31,000 miles, made 356 speeches, shook
hands with half a million people, [and] talked to 15 or 20 million in person." Truman was unenthusiastic about other, more modern approaches
to communicating with voters. "My own experience is all personal contact," he declared. In the 1948 campaign, the Democrats had produced
just a single advertisement to be used in movie theatres or television. At
a post-victory press conference, when a reporter asked Truman whether
television had assisted his campaign, all the other journalists erupted in
laughter.

It would not be very long before people like Reeves would be doing
the laughing. The 1948 U.S. presidential campaign represented the final
hurrah of so-called retail politics: campaigning door to door, vote by
vote, with little or no attention paid to mass communication techniques.
In 1951, transcontinental cable led to the quick formation of national
networks in the United States, while in Canada, the CBC announced
plans for the debut of a national television service. By the following year,
more than 20 million television sets were to be found in homes in North
America, particularly in urban areas clustered along the Canada–U.S.
border. A lot of votes lived in those homes.

Much of the earliest television programming on privately owned networks — *I Love Lucy*, *The Milton Berle Show*, *The Ed Sullivan Show*, and so on — was sponsored, and ultimately controlled, by advertisers. Programs carried names like *Camel News Caravan* or *Texaco Star Theater*, and featured lengthy ads from only those companies. One Madison Avenue advertising executive, frustrated by the restrictions placed on the new medium, promoted the fact that advertising rates dropped dramatically in the broadcast minutes sandwiched between the sponsored programs. The executive — a young Reeves, who had abandoned Virginia for the big city — told his clients that they could use those minutes to reach as many households as Texaco or Camel, but at a fraction of the price. Developing shorter, memorable ads he and others called "spots," Reeves became rapidly known as an adman who could deliver cost-effective messages that produced results.

Reeves was indeed effective. Some of his advertising milestones remain well known many years after the fact. There was "Certs breath mints — with a magic drop of retsyn." And "How do you spell relief? R-O-L-A-I-D-S." And "Wonder Bread helps build strong bodies in eight ways." And, perhaps most memorably of all, "M&Ms melt in your mouth, not in your hands."

For a quarter of a century, Reeves worked at the Ted Bates Agency, where he was known as the Prince of Hard Sell. His view of advertising was unromantic. To Reeves, too many agencies were preoccupied with the development of advertising that won industry awards but did little else. He said, "Let's say you have a million dollars tied up in your little company and suddenly your advertising isn't working and sales are going down. And everything depends on it. Your future depends on it, your family's future depends on it, other people's families depend on it … Now, what do you want from me? Fine writing? Or do you want to see the goddamned sales curve stop moving down and start moving up?"

The advertising Reeves produced ultimately stressed simplicity, clarity, and repetition. (One of his spots for Fleischmann's, for example, mentioned the words "corn oil margarine" no less than seven times.) To Reeves, it did not matter whether a commercial was interesting or not. In his view, early television audiences were captivated by the new medium and were therefore very likely to see and hear an agency's spot. What mattered most, then, was not the artistry of an ad, but its effectiveness. Anything that detracted from a commercial's selling message, such as a clever visual or graphic, was a scene-stealer — what Reeves called a "video vampire." Originality and prettiness were simple distractions, he argued, that had been conjured up by egocentric advertising copywriters who placed creativity over selling the client's product. On one occasion, when challenged on his tough approach to advertising, Reeves replied, "No, sir. I'm not saying that charming, witty, and warm copy won't sell. I'm just saying that I've seen thousands of charming, witty campaigns that didn't sell."

Reeves called his no-nonsense advertising philosophy the Unique Selling Proposition (USP). In *Reality in Advertising*, Reeves writes, "Advertising is the art of getting a unique selling proposition into the heads of the most people at the lowest possible costs."

There were three components to the USP. The first was that the ad must make a proposition to the customer being targeted. The message needed to be more than words or a catchy phrase or a colourful graphic. To Reeves, it needed to say to the consumer, "Buy this product and you will get this specific benefit." The second was, as the name implies, uniqueness. The ad had to be able to make a claim about the product or service that the competition could not. The third was likely the toughest: the proposition needed to be strong. It needed to be one that could motivate the masses — in the television age, that meant millions of potential consumers — to purchase what was being sold.

In the early 1950s, using modern advertising techniques to market political candidates on television was not merely new, it was unprecedented. Earlier on, radio had been used in the campaigns of the likes of Franklin D. Roosevelt; being confined to a wheelchair, FDR used his mellifluous broadcaster's voice to great effect with his Depression-era fireside chats. But Harry Truman possessed a raspy twang, unsuited to radio. And, like Truman, many politicians in the U.S. and in other places were suspicious of television. In fact, most advertising agencies were still unsure how to make effective use of the new communications medium.

The Ted Bates Agency, where Reeves started working in 1940, was different. The Bates team had been involved with television advertising from the start, when few TV sets had meant few sales. But before long, the agency's knowledge of the fledgling medium started to pay dividends. Said Reeves, "We discovered that this was no tame kitten. We had a ferocious, man-eating tiger. We could take the same advertising campaign from print or radio and put it on TV, and, even when there were very few sets, sales would jump through the roof. It was like shooting fish in a barrel."

Reeves, a Republican, took his enthusiasm to Thomas E. Dewey, governor of New York and the Republican's challenger to Truman in the 1948 race. Reeves argued that the contest would be a close one. If the Republicans saturated key markets with effective Dewey spots, he argued, they would win. Dewey, who was referred to derisively as "the little man on the wedding cake" — a stiff and formal person — sniffed at Reeves's ideas, stating that they were undignified. He went on to be clobbered by Truman.

By 1952, when Truman's term was at an end, the Republicans were less quick to dismiss Reeves. Since 1948, television's growth had been explosive. Even Thomas Dewey, in his 1950 campaign for re-election as governor of New York, had changed his tune. Assisted by advertising executives at Batten, Barton, Durstine and Osborn, Dewey agreed to participate in an eighteen-hour marathon of talking, wherein voters from across the state would stand before television cameras and ask him questions. His ability to answer questions in detail and to speak extemporaneously, not to mention the fact that he was prepared to answer literally hundreds of questions for eighteen hours, won him re-election.

Reeves and his revolutionary ideas about television and politics started to seem less revolutionary. The first to come and pay obeisance was, fittingly enough, the Republican Party. Madison Avenue ad agencies had, from the outset, a pronounced Republican tilt, partly owing to the party's local and state-wide successes. Moreover, and more significantly, perhaps, many of Madison Avenue's corporate clients were run by businessmen who were committed followers of the GOP. So in the summer of 1952, when Reeves was summoned to the Racquet Club on Park Avenue by a group of Republican businessmen, he was unsurprised. Truman had earlier decided not to seek re-election, and the Republicans desperately wanted their candidate, General Dwight D. Eisenhower, to win.

The businessmen told Reeves that the Democratic candidate, Illinois governor Adlai Stevenson, had a great slogan: "You never had it so good." The Republican campaign of Eisenhower, meanwhile, offered a line that was less inspiring: "Time for a change." Could Reeves think of something better? "Ike doesn't need a slogan," Reeves told the businessmen. "He needs a strategy."

Reeves told the Republican businessmen that Eisenhower should make use of television spots. Recalled Reeves, "These [businessmen], they didn't know an advertising spot from Alpha Centauri, so I explained the whole theory." Reeves told the men that television was "so powerful that it's changing the whole media structure of the world," and that politics should not be immune from its effects. Nor could it be.

The businessmen were intrigued. Money would be no object, they told him. Go and develop a strategy for Eisenhower in the coming presidential election. Over a weekend, Reeves and an associate produced two memos for the Republicans. One of the memos, stamped "Confidential," remains a fascinating document and represents the first known attempt by a Western political party to address the powerful challenge represented by television. Titled "Program to Guarantee an Eisenhower Victory," the three-page, double-spaced memo uses language that, until that point, many of the Republican mavens and money men had never seen before. The enthusiasm it contains is almost childlike, but there can be little doubt that Reeves was ahead of his contemporaries. The memo reads:

> The betting odds may be even — some pollsters may say it's in the bag — but don't forget what happened in '48. Look at the number of electoral votes the Democrats now confidently claim — 293 (266 needed)— and look at the number the Democrats concede to the Republicans — a probable 78. Complacency and wishful thinking will not elect Ike. His top advisers know it is going to take plenty of work; lots of money; plus something new — something EXTRA AND SPECIAL. This program may well be it — so read carefully.

In the same breathless, enthusiastic tone, the memo goes on:

> Is *there a new way of campaigning* that can guarantee
> a victory for Eisenhower in November? The answer is:
> "Yes!" It is not a theory. It has been tried, tested and
> proven in local elections. Now for the first time this
> method is ready for national treatment, ready for Ike ...
> WHAT IS THIS "NEW WAY OF CAMPAIGNING?"
> This new way of campaigning, in essence is a new use
> of what advertising men know as "spots." A spot is a 15-
> second or one-minute announcement on radio — or a
> 20-second or one-minute announcement on television.
> Most people do not know the power of spots. How-
> ever, here are the cold facts. THE HUMBLE RADIO
> OR TV "SPOT" CAN DELIVER MORE LISTENERS
> FOR LESS MONEY THAN ANY OTHER FORM OF
> ADVERTISING. Let us repeat that. THE HUMBLE
> RADIO OR TV "SPOT" CAN DELIVER MORE LIS-
> TENERS FOR LESS MONEY THAN ANY OTHER
> FORM OF ADVERTISING.

The memo goes on to discuss the financial advantages offered by the use of spots placed strategically between sponsored shows featuring stars such as Jack Benny, Eddie Cantor, and Fred Allen, as well as Edgar Bergen and Charlie McCarthy. ("YOU GET THE AUDIENCE BUILT AT HUGE COSTS BY OTHER PEOPLE," Reeves gushed.)

The same summer, Reeves had spoken with public opinion pollster George Gallup about which issue was most important to Americans. Without hesitating, Gallup answered that there were three: corruption, taxes, and the ongoing Korean War. True to his USP credo, Reeves preferred just one issue, but Gallup insisted there were three. So Reeves concluded his memo with a section headlined:

> WHAT DO THE SPOTS SAY? Plenty! However, they
> all touch on just three problems — the "big three"
> which the largest number of people are worried about:

1. Corruption in government. 2. High prices and high taxes. 3. War! In these spots, Eisenhower identifies himself as one who fully understands the problems of Mr. and Mrs. America (which is 50 per cent of the battle in winning people's confidence). He sits down in personal interviews with people in all walks of life — cab drivers, schoolteachers, office and factory workers, housewives, etc. It is a way of having a big "TOWN MEETING" ... but letting 60,000,000 people hear all the questions and answers! This intimate, informal "spot" technique is ideally suited to [Ike's] warm personality.

While Eisenhower's campaign manager was skeptical, as was the national chairman of Citizens for Eisenhower-Nixon, Reeves's determination overcame all Republican resistance. Closeted away in a hotel room on Fifth Avenue for weeks on end, Reeves scrutinized Eisenhower speeches, spoke to Gallup, and typed out a total of twenty-two scripts. In mid-September 1952, Reeves and Eisenhower met for the first time at a film studio in Manhattan. At the start, Eisenhower resisted Reeves's approach. "To think an old soldier should come to this!" he remarked at one point. But he eventually succumbed to the adman's blandishments. The Republican nominee was persuaded to abandon his glasses and read Reeves's scripts off cue cards bearing giant-sized letters. In time, Eisenhower was racing through takes, while Reeves typed up seventeen more scripts in another room. (Eisenhower, warming to the task, apparently even wrote one himself, but no one seems to be able to recall the subject.) In all, forty were written and filmed, featuring Eisenhower briefly answering a question.

The questioners, mainly tourists, were rounded up and filmed over a couple of days outside New York's Radio City Music Hall. Reeves wanted Americans who were not actors — real people, wearing their own clothes, asking questions in their local accents. The tourists were filmed reading questions from cue cards. Later, the tourists' questions and Eisenhower's answers were spliced together, to magical effect. Each spot started with a slide that read "Eisenhower Answers America."

In one particularly brilliant spot, a dark-haired woman asks, "The

Democrats have made mistakes, but aren't their intentions good?" Replies Eisenhower, "Well, if the driver of your school bus runs into a truck, hits a lamppost, drives into a ditch, you don't say his intentions are good. You get a new driver." In another, which succinctly addressed Gallup's advice, a man in a plaid shirt says, "General, the Democrats are telling me I've never had it so good." Says Eisenhower, "Can that be true, when America is billions in debt, when prices have doubled, when taxes break our backs, and we are still fighting in Korea? It's tragic and it's time for a change." Another featured an elderly woman wearing a hat who says, "You know what things cost today. High prices are just driving me crazy." Replies Eisenhower, who at that point likely did not frequent too many grocery stores, "Yes, my Mamie gets after me about the high cost of living. It's another reason why I say, it's time for a change. Time to get back to an honest dollar and an honest dollar's work."

The spots, which cost $60,000 (the price of a few seconds' broadcast time in today's campaigns) were revolutionary and radical. When word leaked out about the ad campaign, however, the Democrats did what all political parties would later do when queried about an opponent's advertising: they went into attack mode. George Ball, executive director of Volunteers for Stevenson, attacked the Republicans' use of the Madison Avenue ad firm. Sniffed Ball, "[The Republicans are attempting] to sell an inadequate ticket to the American people in precisely the same way [advertisers] sell soap, ammoniated toothpaste, hair tonic or bubble gum."

In an advertising industry publication in early October, Ball said, "They have all the money, but no candidate ... Found with this dilemma, they have invented a new kind of campaign — conceived not by men who want us to face crucial issues of this crucial day, but by the high-powered hucksters of Madison Avenue." Stevenson himself picked up on the theme, stating that the GOP was showing "contempt" for the intelligence of the American people. In their criticisms, there was no doubt that the Democrats were partly right. Reeves, in fact, privately admitted as much: he *was* attempting to sell Eisenhower in the manner that toothpaste was sold, although doing so could hardly be labelled contemptuous of the voter. Condescension and contempt, after all, do not sell toothpaste; good messaging does. In the end, Democratic pieties did not matter much. Unfortunately for Ball and Stevenson (whose comments actually spurred a number of large contributions to the GOP to finance the ad campaign), and unfortunately for the Democrats (who fatally misunderstood, or underestimated, the power of television), Reeves's TV theories won the day.

His theories were durable, too. Even when the Republican ticket was later beset by trouble — when vice-presidential candidate Richard Nixon was accused of benefiting from a secret fund to supplement his income, with his wife, Pat, receiving a mink in the bargain — the adman's formula was employed to devastating effect. (The Democrats' charges were true, but also somewhat unfair: most political party leaders receive stipends and allowances from their partisan fundraisers.) In his "Checkers" speech, Nixon knocked the Democrats' allegations out of the proverbial ballpark. Looking straight into the television camera on September 23, 1952, Nixon said, "My fellow Americans, I come before you tonight as a candidate for the vice-presidency and a man whose honesty and integrity have been questioned." Nixon described what he and his wife owned, then said, "Pat doesn't have a mink coat. But she does have a respectable Republican cloth coat, and I always tell her she would look good in anything."

Nixon could have stopped right there, having perfectly vanquished his adversaries. But he went on: "One other thing I probably should tell you, because if I don't, they will be saying this about me, too. We did get something, a gift, after the nomination. A man down in Texas heard Pat on the radio mention the fact that our two youngsters would like to have a dog. Believe it or not, the day before we left on this campaign trip, we got a message from Union Station in Baltimore, saying they had a package for us. We went down to get it. You know what it was? It was a little cocker spaniel dog, in a crate that he had sent all the way from Texas — black and white, spotted, and our little girl Tricia, the six-year-old, named it Checkers. And you know, the kids, like all kids, loved the dog. And I just want to say right now, that regardless of what they say about it, we are going to keep it."

Dwight D. Eisenhower and Richard M. Nixon won the election with nearly 60 percent of the vote. Reeves, who died in January 1984, was characteristically modest about his own achievement, calling the spots "only an interesting footnote to history." Said Reeves, "It was such a

[Republican] landslide that it didn't make a goddamned bit of difference whether we ran the spots or not."

Others beg to differ. Lynda Kaid is director of the University of Oklahoma's Political Commercial Archive. The archive contains more than fifty-five thousand political commercials, in film, audio, and videotape, reaching back to 1936. Nearly two-thirds of the university's holdings are simply unavailable anywhere else. Kaid has probably seen more political commercials than anyone else on the planet, and she told me this about Reeves: "His work was enormously important — for its groundbreaking nature. Reeves realized that television spots could overcome selective exposure, thus ensuring that Democrats and Republicans would be exposed to Eisenhower's political messages." She added, "His intuitive sense about this was later borne out by some of the earliest empirical work on political television advertising. Reeves was also successful in using the spots to achieve a softening of Eisenhower's cold military image, helping to reshape his appeal into the warm fatherly figure Eisenhower is remembered to be."

WHEN THEY ARE PERIODICALLY POLLED on the issue of negative advertising, Canadians, like Americans, are of almost one voice: they insist that they do not like it. A November 1988 Canadian Gallup poll, for example, noted that 60 percent of Canadians expressed opposition to "political advertising which criticizes another party's policies and leaders." This finding, Gallup asserted, was consistent across economic, regional, educational, and linguistic divides. It does not appear, however, that Gallup probed a related, and more salient, question: namely, do critical campaign ads work? Even if Canadians profess to dislike them, do they not recall such ads more readily? Why has there been so much critical campaigning in recent decades, if voters say they aren't paying any attention and claim that they are unmoved by it?

In the only fairly recent study of the issue, three Canadian professors of political science and communications examined the issue at length; their findings are part of a volume that makes up the 1992 report of the Royal Commission on Electoral Reform and Party Financing. In their essay, titled "Negative Political Advertising: An Analysis of Research Findings in Light of Canadian Practice," professors Walter Romanow, Walter Soderlund, and Richard Price noted that there is indeed an increasing amount of negative advertising filling the airwaves. But why is there so much of it, the professors queried, if it is allegedly so harmful to a candidate's prospects?

The answer, they concluded, is undeniable: in Canada, as in the United States, "negative advertising works." There are two reasons for this. First, television is an emotional medium, and emotional messages work best with voters. "With too much information around," the professors wrote, "our senses are overloaded and advertisers have turned away from information-imparting ads to an approach that 'goes for the gut,' appealing to core values ... Negative ads are crafted in the best dramatic tradition: they contain characterization (implicit or explicit), plot and conflict." Second, they wrote, negative ads work because they are negative. "Simply put, negative information is more powerful in crystallizing decisions than positive information. In politics, it is said, 'mud sticks,' and negative ads are the way in which seeds of doubt about an opponent are introduced and negative perceptions are reinforced."

In Canada, as in the United States, negative campaign advertising is nothing new. "Historically," the professors noted, "negative or attack ads ... have played a significant part in the ad campaign tactics of the three major parties."

In his seminal 1993 work on the relationship between Canadian politicians and Canadian reporters, *Scrum Wars*, author Allan Levine emphatically agreed. Levine recalled that aggressive partisanship has always characterized Canada's public life. "In a world defined by whether one was a Grit or a Tory," he wrote, "it was usually good business for a newspaper to identify with one side or the other." Among other things, well-behaved newspapers — that is, ones that propped up the ruling party and brutally derided the opposition — were the recipients of lucrative advertising contracts and a loyal readership. In some cases, politicians such as Sir John A. Macdonald actually invested their own monies in the partisan journals. For the better part of a decade, for example, Macdonald worked with a group of followers — unsuccessfully, as things turned out — to establish a pro-Conservative newspaper to counter the debilitating effects of the Liberal *Free Press*. And in the 1860s, Canada's first prime minister actually contributed $5,000 of his own money to help launch the *Daily Telegraph* in Toronto; ironically, the paper ended up being one of the Conservatives' most ardent critics.

With political parties relying upon newspapers for partisan support, and in some cases owning them, there were not many compelling reasons in the late nineteenth century and early twentieth century to spend more money on expensive advertising campaigns attacking one's partisan opponents. As Canadian newspapers grew increasingly independent, however, this changed. It gradually became necessary for politicians and their advisors to develop their own communications vehicles, and not simply rely upon partisan broadsheets. The transition does not appear to have been difficult. The Liberals and the Conservatives threw themselves into vicious advertising campaigns with unrestrained enthusiasm.

The first use of wide-scale negative campaigning in Canada can be seen in the 1935 general election, with William Lyon Mackenzie King representing the governing Liberals and Richard Bedford (R.B.) Bennett leading the Conservatives. Both parties made some use of partisan newspapers, as they had done in the past, and both parties continued to make use of campaign posters featuring highly unflattering caricatures of King or Bennett. But the Tories, as things turned out, were the first to recognize the power of the new medium called radio.

The Conservative negative ad campaign had been the idea of Earl Lawson, a party organizer and Toronto member of Parliament. Relying upon a researcher named R.L. Wright at the Toronto agency of J.J. Gibbons Limited, Lawson first placed tantalizing display ads in different newspapers in September 1935. "Introducing Mister Sage," read the ads. "A shrewd observer who sees through the pretences, knows the facts, and understands the true issues of the present political campaign, discusses the election with his friends." There followed a listing of the radio stations that would be broadcasting Mr. Sage's ruminations, along with the relevant times. No mention was made that the ads had been placed by the Conservative Party.

The first ad was presented as a dialogue between two actors, the aforementioned Mr. Sage and one Bill. It pulled no punches. In fifteen short minutes, the radio ad alleged that King's Liberals were engaged in threats, blackmail, lies, and slush funds. For those who pine for a time when Canadian politics was more genteel and refined, the Mr. Sage broadcasts make the argument that no such time has ever really existed. In one blistering segment, Mr. Sage tells Bill, "In 1930 … I happened to be staying with my brother-in-law in Quebec. Mr. King's henchmen used to call up the farmers and their wives in the early hours of the morning and tell them their sons would be conscripted for war if they voted against King."

Later in the same broadcast, Mr. Sage notes that King had led his Liberal Party into "the Valley of Humiliation." The character named Bill is blunt: "Slush fund, wasn't it?" Mr. Sage responds, "Yes, Bill — over $700,000 — and that's the man who wants to be Prime Minister of Canada. Can you beat it?"

The second broadcast of Mr. Sage's musings took place a few days later, but ran for thirty minutes instead of fifteen. Mr. Sage lived in "a typical home, in a typical Canadian town," listeners were told, and was "our friend and neighbour" and simply a benign "political observer." In this segment, Mr. Sage essentially accused King of being a grasping, dim-witted, self-absorbed, vainglorious liar. In a chat with his wife — presumably Mrs. Sage — the "simple observer" states, "We've only got to take what that Mr. King said about Mr. Bennett … [King] said a lot of things, didn't he, but mostly harm … He doesn't care whether it helps or hinders the people of the country so long as it helps him to be Prime Minister. That's the pity of it: [King] is frightened of losing the leadership … It seems to me he's just like the movie star who is losing her appeal to her public and she's afraid that one of her smarter and better-looking rivals will put her nose out of joint. Mr. King's so fearful, that he does anything at all that he thinks will please the crowd."

Following a barrage of complaints to the Canadian Radio Broadcasting Commission, the earliest of our broadcasting regulators, the Conservatives were persuaded to identify a sponsor of the Mr. Sage attack ads. They claimed that it was only the Gibbons Agency's R.L. Wright, and not the Tories themselves. Outraged Grits continued to complain about the ad campaign, however, so the Tories relented: the sponsors were identified as "R.L. Wright and a Group of Conservatives." As would be the case with every subsequent target of a negative Canadian ad campaign, King did not resist unburdening himself about the Mr. Sage ads: they were "insidious," "libellous," and "scurrilous," he puffed.

Notwithstanding all the ad hominem nastiness, the Liberals possessed better chances in the 1935 general election: the Great Depression had dramatically eroded Tory support, and Bennett had become isolated from public opinion. The Grits, moreover, had a better slogan than the Tories: "King or Chaos." The Tories had the mundane "Stand by Canada" (and "Vote Bennett"). The Liberals were also better funded, and King had learned to make better use of the radio medium. (As he was later advised by the first Canadian *spinmeister*, Jack Pickersgill, what mattered most in broadcasting was sound, not content. Pickersgill was right.) By 1930, more than 75 percent of all homes in Canadian urban centres possessed radio sets. So when the Grit leader aired three FDR-style "talks," he was heard by many, and the broadcasts were well received. An August 1, 1935, *Ottawa Journal* editorial, for example, declared that King possessed "stately diction" and "an excellent speaking voice," and had acquitted himself "with distinction."

Voters, apparently, agreed. Slightly more than two months later, R.B. Bennett was drubbed by William Lyon Mackenzie King — 173 Liberal seats, compared to the Conservatives' 40. But Mr. Sage, while ineffective in attracting votes, was not forgotten by the newly elected Liberals. In his final campaign address in Ottawa, the *Citizen* reported on October 14, 1935, a fiery King declared that Mr. Sage–style campaign attack ads would be outlawed: "I will do all in my power to see to it that no man in future generations has to put up with that sort of thing through a medium over which a Prime Minister and his government has full control."

King may have won the election, but, as subsequent events and Canadians campaigns would demonstrably prove, his battle to purge the airwaves of negative political ads was a lost cause before it even got started. Following 1935, nasty campaign advertising became as all-Canadian as hockey and *Anne of Green Gables*.

JUST *MAKING* A POLITICAL SPOT, as noted, requires skill and money. But so too does the other part of the process, the part where a campaign buys time and decides when, where, and why to put the spot in a voter's living room.

The office of Tobe Berkovitz, tucked away in a bland, four-storey building fronting on Boston's Commonwealth Avenue, not far from the Massachusetts Turnpike and the Charles River, is a very crowded place. From the ceiling to the floor, the Boston University professor has jammed hundreds of videotapes of political spots, along with stacks of books about campaigns, consultants, and commercials. Here and there, Berkovitz has affixed buttons and banners from different campaigns — John F. Kennedy's, Jimmy Carter's, and many others.

Berkovitz stretches out, propping his running shoes on his crowded desk. With lots of dark hair, an unlined face, and a genial manner, Berkovitz does not look like a man who is just past fifty, or, for that matter, like someone who is considered one of the smarter political ad buyers in the United States.

He comes from Connecticut, and he got his start there in 1974, doing a fifteen-minute free-time film for Tony Discepelo, an independent candidate running for Congress. Berkovitz had been teaching television production and broadcast studies at the University of Connecticut when he got the call from the aspiring congressman's campaign staff. "We were essentially slaughtered," he says. "But the film I did for this guy — that was pretty good." When 1978 rolled around, he was living in Michigan and helping out Carl Levin, then the president of Detroit's city council. A long shot, Levin was seeking a seat in the U.S. Senate. His team hired Tobe Berkovitz to be its advertising coordinator.

Berkovitz knew enough about television to teach, and he knew how to read a poll. He also, as things turned out, knew how to read a television ratings book. "I just worked as [Levin's] in-house media buyer," he says. "And, lo and behold, Levin won. Knocked off a guy who had a couple decades of experience, a real senior senator." Berkovitz had placed Levin's spots on and around the TV programs most favoured by the voters Levin needed to reach. There is no point, Berkovitz says, in placing spots at times when nobody will see them, or at times that primarily attract voters who are already voting for your candidate. They need to be seen by the voters called "persuadables."

By 1980 Berkovitz had moved again, this time to Washington, D.C.

He worked on Capitol Hill for Democrats, and he toiled as a media buyer for a trio of Democrats seeking seats in the Senate. Two of them were Arizona's Morris Udall and Ohio's John Glenn. Notwithstanding that 1980 was the year that Ronald Reagan swept to the presidency and liberal Democrats were being toppled across the political landscape, Glenn and Udall were elected. Berkovitz, one of those credited with the Glenn and Udall wins, was on his way up.

In those days, he says, there were not many political consultants. No more than two dozen, he estimates, certainly not the hundreds of consultants and consultancy firms now found in every corner of the United States. "In the seventies, people said to me, 'Well, what are you doing?' and I'd tell them I was working as a media consultant. And no one would know what the hell I was talking about," he recalls. "It wasn't the era of the James Carvilles and all the superstar consultants. There was a small group of people who did this sort of work, but you were really talking about a dozen Democrats and a dozen Republicans and that was it."

In 1985, Berkovitz met one of those top-rung Democratic political consultants, Ken Swope. Swope is an award-winning writer and strategist who has led successful campaigns against clear-cutting in the western United States. He is a committed believer in political advertising, and he has suggested that good advertising, and a good ad buy, can turn around a twenty-point deficit in the polls in less than a week. Swope and Berkovitz struck an informal partnership and have been consulting on Democratic campaigns ever since. Says Berkovitz, "Most often, the media buyers are sort of backroom people, and the consultants are front-room people. Sometimes they will trot out their media buyer at a political meeting, but most often they won't. It's ironic, really, because [ad buy] is where most of your campaign's money is going. If you do it efficiently, then it's going to be good. But if you're not doing it efficiently, then you're going to end up wasting a fair amount of money." It is not just Berkovitz who feels this way. John Rowley is another Democratic Party ad buy expert, from Nashville. Speaking at that 2001 Washington gathering, he said, "Candidates and campaign managers will spend hours and hours debating whether we should say 'should' or 'must' in a script. And then, when it comes to the media buy, they just forget about it." On the importance of political ad buying, Rowley stated, "Television is a thermonuclear weapon. There's a lot of waste with a thermonuclear weapon, but it gets the job done."

In 1996, Tobe Berkovitz wrote a short guide called, simply, "Political Media Buying." The paper ended up in literally dozens of places on the Internet and is widely known in U.S. political circles. While it is only eleven pages in length, the guide has been tremendously influential in a number of U.S. campaigns. In his paper, Berkovitz defines political media buy this way: "The goal of media buying in an election campaign is to reach a defined target audience in the most efficient and economical way possible." To ensure that the media buy is done the right way, it is essential that the political campaign — its candidate and its consultants — are very clear about six elements.

The first order of business, Berkovitz says, is the development of a media plan that works. When buying ad time, consultants focus on what are called gross rating points (GRPs). GRPs, he writes, "are the sum total of ratings achieved for a media schedule." To figure out how much a campaign's media buy is going to cost — and in Canada and the United States, it is safe to assume that as much as 80 percent of a campaign's spending will go to ad buy — consultants multiply GRP by CPP (cost per point). It sounds confusing, but it is not. "The general rule of thumb is one hundred GRPs means the average TV viewer sees a commercial once. Therefore, five hundred GRPs should expose the average viewer five times to the commercial."

In the United States, if the media buy is "spot"— that is, in a regional media market — then five hundred GRPs is usually enough to influence what Berkovitz calls "the voting decision." In a national media buy — called a network placement — three hundred GRPs is considered about right. (In the closing days of a campaign, some consultants argue for GRPs of nearly two thousand.)

In the United States, a network buy during the newsmagazines *60 Minutes*, *Prime Time Live*, or *20/20* can cost as much as $200,000. That may sound pricey, Berkovitz concedes, but there are shows that are even more expensive. When *Murphy Brown* was on the air, he says, placement of a spot could cost up to $335,000, while one during *Friends* was $400,000. Says Berkovitz, "It's expensive. A million bucks — if I'm running in a rural part of Iowa — hell, with a million bucks, I'm going to do okay. But in New York, a million bucks? Great, that's a week [of buy]. Now what do we do?"

The second important element of a good media buy plan is timing. Since few candidates can afford to advertise from the start of the campaign through to election day, different patterns of advertising are commonly used. A continuity pattern airs spots at a single GRP level throughout the election. One of the dangers associated with such an approach, Berkovitz warns, is that a continuity pattern does not take into account the sorts of disasters that befall every campaign, such as candidates saying something embarrassing or issues unexpectedly attracting public interest. A pulsing pattern is what its name implies. A campaign team may, to use Berkovitz's term, "heavy up" a buy at the start and end of an election and do less in between. The idea, he says, is to ensure that "the weight and timing of the advertising is matched with the political objectives of the campaign." A flighting pattern, meanwhile, sees advertising going on and off the air. It allows a campaign to save precious funds and respond to issues only when a response is truly needed.

A third important consideration is the target audience: whom does the campaign wish to reach with its advertising? Without exception, the demographic that a campaign wishes to reach and influence is identified by the campaign's pollster, and it can vary significantly at different times during a campaign. For example, if a tax message (which is usually most popular with men) is not effective, then a campaign may wish to consider switching to an education or health message (which are typically more appealing to women). Women are just as susceptible to tough ads as men, Berkovitz explains, but an ad buyer needs to be sensitive to when and where an ad is placed. Says Berkovitz, "What are you running in the six o'clock newscast — lots of burn, slash and attack advertising. Maybe, earlier in the day, during the soaps, you want to be a little kinder and gentler — and a little more emotional and warmer."

Point number four is geography. Called variously the "Area of Dominant Influence" or the "Designated Market Area," these geographic regions are served primarily by clusters of broadcasters within the area. Broadcast planning and spending, Berkovitz says, are built around these regional clusters. Once polling is analyzed, weighting is done, meaning that an advertising budget is divided between the different geographic areas a campaign is trying to influence. Weighting forces a campaign consultant to determine which areas have priority, and to spend accordingly.

The media mix is number five on Berkovitz's list. In his view, and in the view of the vast majority of campaign professionals, television is the "prime medium for delivering the campaign's advertising message." Many more people watch television than read newspapers, and the people who watch it tend to come from diverse demographic categories. Notwithstanding the eye-popping costs mentioned above for placing a spot during television programs like *Friends*, Berkovitz argues that "on a cost-per-point basis, television is excellent for reaching overall audience."

Every broadcast day is divided into sections called dayparts. Advertising is then purchased for programs that fall within the dayparts. The early-morning daypart is principally filled with local news, network news, and information programs; these reach opinion leaders and high-interest voters. Next is the day daypart, which is filled with syndicated talk shows, game shows, and soap operas. This part of the broadcast schedule is watched mainly by women with little education between the ages of twenty-four and fifty-four. The early fringe of the late-afternoon daypart is made up of syndicated talk shows, sitcoms, and tabloid television. Again, the main audience is women who have no post-graduate education. The early-news daypart is important; it comprises local and network news, and reaches better educated viewers likely to vote. The access daypart is next, with syndicated sitcoms, game shows, and more tabloid TV. It has high ratings and is cost-effective for media buy; the types of viewers vary, but it is considered to be rich in potential voters. The prime daypart has high ratings as well as varied demographics and is what Berkovitz calls a "premium audience." Late news is the next daypart, and reaches highly educated people who can be counted upon to vote. The final daypart, late fringe, has a wide audience and is made up of late-night talk shows and syndicated sitcoms. (The importance of these shows shouldn't be underestimated either: in the 2000 presidential campaign, both George W. Bush and Al Gore did shows with the likes of Jay Leno and David Letterman, because an increasing number of voters are getting political information from these sources. In May 2001, Jean Chrétien was persuaded by one of my best friends, Liberal advisor Charlie Angelakos, to appear on CTV's *Mike Bullard Show*.)

Radio has a far smaller audience, but it must also be considered in the media mix. It has its advantages: it is far less costly than television, and it is better targeted to certain audiences. Middle-of-the-road stations attract the thirty-five-and-over audience that political candidates need to win. News and information radio stations are also efficient at attracting likely voters. Talk radio, which is usually right-wing ideologically, can boast a loyal audience that is highly motivated in elections. Contemporary hit radio and varied rock formats attract a younger audience that is less interested in public affairs and often does not vote. For political parties, the daypart segment with the largest radio audience is AM drive, reaching workers and commuters; following that, midday also has high ratings among people at work and at home.

Cable television, called "narrowcasting" by some, has become more important as an ad buy consideration in the past decade. John Rowley notes that "at any given time, half the people are not watching the big networks. Cable is a complementary medium, but it's not the primary place to deliver your message." Even the cable programming that attracted the largest audiences ever — CNN's coverage of the O.J. Simpson trial — never equalled the total for the average U.S. network newscast, Rowley notes.

The sixth and final element of a good media buy plan is commercial format. "The 30-second spot is the workhorse for campaign advertising," Berkovitz writes. "On television, 60-second spots are an effective way of communicating a deeper message to the voter, but cost twice the amount … this means that only half as many rating points can be purchased for 60s." Often, consultants are obliged to buy thirty seconds of air time to show two fifteen-second spots back to back. They are forced to do so because television stations and networks these days do not have many other advertisers developing fifteens.

Media buying has changed dramatically in the past two decades, Berkovitz says. "In the old days, they used to talk about counties and precincts and districts. But now you're talking media markets. Two years ago, we did a race for a governor in Rhode Island. I love doing Rhode Island, because you buy Providence and you get to carpet bomb the whole state. It's not cheap — we spent about a million bucks — but we were running commercials by the pound because it's a nice clean media market."

Canada has its share of political ad buy geniuses, too. The Liberal Party relies heavily upon the smarts of Toronto's Gordon Ashworth, while provincial and federal Tories have a former colleague of mine, Patrick Muttart.

On average, U.S.-based media buy consultants like Tobe Berkovitz will receive up to 15 percent of the costs of the advertising they place, which can be very significant. Along with placing spots, media buyers will review invoices received from broadcasters, to ensure that their candidate is getting what they paid for. They attend to the paperwork of the buy and monitor whether spots are actually broadcast when, where, and as often as desired. Simultaneously, ad buy consultants will track the placement and frequency of an opponent's spots, as well as those of any third-party organization seeking to harm their candidate.

Generally, ad buy experts will try to purchase air time far in advance of an election. In Canada, with election dates unknown to all but the prime minister (federally) or a premier (in most provinces), this is hard to do. In the United States, with fixed election dates, it is easier. But its predictability does not make it cheaper; in fact, the reverse is true. Broadcasters seldom, if ever, provide ad buy discounts to political campaigns. Says Berkovitz, "The stations are obviously trying to maximize what they can get out of you. They certainly all play at the edges and they don't cut you any slack. It's important to remember, though, that [in the United States] we are buying in the fourth quarter. That's the most expensive time of the broadcast year."

The decision to go negative with an ad buy should not, most agree, come at the start of an election campaign. Particularly in the case of challenger campaigns — that is, campaigns attempting to dislodge an incumbent, popular or not — it is important to first define one's candidate. Let the voter see the candidate at work, with family. Let them hear a little about the issues that motivated the candidate to run. It typically takes a few days for these issues to become defined in the public's collective consciousness and for the public to decide where they stand themselves. At that point, and only at that point, is it safe to start deploying toughly worded issue advertising.

The time of day a so-called attack ad runs requires a lot of thought, too. These types of spots generally have two effects: they either persuade a voter to vote against one's opponent, or they persuade the opponent's committed voter to essentially do the same thing by staying home. Detailed demographic data is therefore required to figure out when the target audience — the audience one wishes to stay home, for example — is most likely to see one's spot. Evaluating the data and making these decisions is tricky, most consultants agree, and can make or break a campaign.

Despite all of the apparent complexity of ad buying, and despite the political risks associated with it, Tobe Berkovitz is modest about what he does. Walking me to the door of his office, he shrugs. "You know what? I don't think media buying is that big a deal. It's really just tinkering at the edges. It's about when do we go on, how strong do we go on, that kind of thing. But I'm not sure that media buying wins or loses campaigns. It just contributes to it." He pauses. "But I guess you can say that you don't want to screw it up."

Get Creative!

HERE'S A BIT OF CAREER advice, free of charge. If you want to avoid risk — if you want to avoid getting embarrassed, or criticized, or maligned by your relatives and closest friends — don't get into politics. Most of all, don't ever set foot in a war room. Become a bureaucrat or something. You'll be happier. It's unlikely you'll ever produce a win for the candidate or the cause that you happen to believe in, mind you, but you'll be happier. (I guess.)

Let me provide a bit of background. One nice day in the spring of 1993, Senator Romeo LeBlanc gathered us around his chair for a little fireside chat. While I had been setting up the federal Liberal Party's war room earlier that year, Jean Chrétien — knowing me, and knowing the testosterone-charged lunatics I hung out with on Parliament Hill — had asked LeBlanc to keep an eye on us. He figured we needed some adult supervision, and he was right. So the good senator, who rarely swore and never lost his temper, gathered us around.

For us Grits, it was a good time. Brian Mulroney had announced his resignation to a grateful nation, our party was ahead in the polls, and we were already giddily shredding the public reputations of the contestants for the Progressive Conservative leadership. LeBlanc eyeballed us all for a moment. "Okay, guys," he said, softly. "Here's what I have explained to the leader. The kind of work we are engaged in — the kinds of things we are doing — are going to result in one of you losing a limb. It's inevitable. If you can't accept that, you're in the wrong fucking line of work."

I can't recall ever hearing Senator LeBlanc swear before, so his words had the desired effect. We were absolutely silent; he had our full attention. LeBlanc went on to explain, calmly and matter-of-factly, that some of us might be asked to resign the campaign if we got into too much trouble. And if we talked about the stuff we were doing with outsiders, we'd be fired. As he related all of this, he remained very calm. I, meanwhile, felt like I had just signed on to be an undercover cop or an assassin or a ninja or something. It was a bit weird.

But it was also the truth, and — as I would later learn, when I returned to the real world off Parliament Hill — it wasn't just true of politics, either. For businesses, for unions, for any goal-driven organization, it's always the same: *you can't achieve great things without taking great risks*. In the intervening years, I've yet to meet a corporate or labour leader who got where he or she is without trying, and failing (that's why this book talks about losing as well as winning campaigns, by the way). The fact is that God gave us all necks so we can stick them out.

Voters — and consumers, and citizens, and the news media, and just about any sentient being — are astute. They know when you are playing it safe. They know when you are being timid. When they sense you are being deliberately boring, they tune you out, sometimes permanently. Or, even worse, they will conclude that you are hiding something, that you have the much-feared "hidden agenda," and that you are accordingly dishonest. In politics, at least, it's a paradox: taking no risks is in itself risky.

So, in your campaign for votes or sales or support, it's okay to occasionally take a few risks. Be a bit louder, be a bit faster, be a bit funny, be a bit more aggressive. Most of all, be more creative. You won't always win, but one thing is for sure.

You'll never win if you don't *try*.

ON THE EVENING OF TUESDAY, November 14, 2000, with just under two weeks to go in the Canadian federal election campaign, the clouds parted, an angelic chorus sang and a gift descended from the heavens.

The gift took the form of a CBC television documentary by veteran journalist Paul Hunter. Titled *The Fundamental Day*, the documentary ran for only a few minutes, and it did not break any new ground (not, at least, for any of the bone-tired Liberal war room operatives who were watching it). But by the time he was done, Hunter had transformed the first Canadian national election campaign of the new millennium.

The Fundamental Day told the story of Stockwell Day, the telegenic former treasurer from Alberta, who, through a combination of luck, perseverance, and circumstance, had come to be the leader of Her Majesty's Loyal Opposition in the fall of 2000. Because he was functionally bilingual, and because he had an arguably good record as Alberta's minister of finance, Day was an early favourite to lead the Canadian Reform Alliance, the fledgling political protest party that grew out of the ashes of Reform. In a leadership vote held in a grimy Toronto hotel in early July 2000, Day had even soundly trounced the founder and leader of the Reform Party, Preston Manning.

Throughout the summer of 2000, the new leader of the Canadian Alliance received a lot of glowing press reviews, most often in the pages of the editorially conservative *National Post*, but also in the chain of newspapers owned by media baron Conrad Black. Black made no secret of his detestation of Liberal Party leader Jean Chrétien; in one *London Times* article in November 1999, in fact, Black had boasted that by the time he got through with Canada's prime minister, there would not be enough left "to squeeze through an eye dropper." So, in editorial after editorial, in news item after news item, Black's employees depicted Day in the most flattering light; conversely, they repeatedly characterized Chrétien as a criminal, a simpleton, or both. By the time fall rolled around, the Liberal Party's popularity had shrunk somewhat, while Day's Reform Alliance party was experiencing a modest growth in support.

Stockwell Day, however, had a past, and it wasn't one that would be terribly helpful to his political fortunes in a pluralistic, urban democracy. That was why Paul Hunter's documentary about Day's fundamentalist religious views was so important. For months, Liberals had been at-tempting to draw the media's attention to evidence of Day's views about gays, lesbians, abortion, and single moms (he didn't like any of them). For months, the media, particularly those many segments of it owned by Conrad Black, had declined to pay any attention at all.

The documentary started with a discussion of Day's involvement with a private Bible school in Bentley, Alberta, in the 1980s. The school, which was found by a December 1984 Alberta government inquiry to possess a curriculum that "violated principles of tolerance and under-standing [towards] Jews, blacks and Indians," employed Day as a pastor for more than five years. Hunter's story described how Day was indif-ferent towards the Conservative government's criticism of the Bentley Christian Centre. "God's law is clear," Day shrugged. "Standards of edu-cation are not set by government but by God, his Bible, the home and the school."

The CBC report went on to document Day's efforts to prevent a mu-seum in his riding from receiving a small grant for a study of gay and lesbian history; recognizing the historical contributions of gay and les-bians to Alberta's history was "a mistake," he declared. The documentary then described Day's attempts, as a cabinet minister, to prevent gays and lesbians from receiving legal protections against discrimination. A clip of Day recorded him stating, "I think people need the right to say no to, for instance, to sex education programs that would include homosexual material. We'll look at fences there. I think there should be fences around adoptions. We'll look at fences there."

After recalling some of Day's hardline views on abortion, Hunter's report turned to a final issue: creationism.

For many months, folks had been hearing rumours that Stockwell Day was an enthusiastic adherent of creationism. There had been no re-porting about any of this, however, and Day resisted saying much about his faith in public. Creationism itself, as a religious philosophy, contains many conflicting elements. Some creationists believe that the Earth is flat and is covered by some sort of dome or firmament. Others are geocen-trists who insist that, while not flat, the Earth is the centre of the solar system. Young Earth creationists, of which Day may be one, claim a lit-eral interpretation of the Bible as a basis for their beliefs, and believe that the planet is six to ten thousand years old, that all life was created in six days, and that death and decay came as a result of Adam and Eve's Fall. There are other creationist derivatives, including Old Earth creationism, cap creationism, day-age creationism, intelligent design creationism, and so on.

In Hunter's documentary, Day's particular variant of creationism is vividly described for the viewer by Red Deer College's Pliny Hayes. In 1997, Hayes recounted, Day had attended a discussion about evolution during the college's Christian Awareness Week. Curious, Hayes and some of his students wanted to see what Day had to say. Recalls Hayes, "He prefaced his comments with a smile and a question: 'Are any of my friends from the press present?' When no one responded, he then went on to say a number of things. One, that the Earth is six thousand years old. That Adam and Eve are real people. That humans co-existed with dinosaurs. That there's as much [evidence] for … creationism as there is for evolution. And that he's upset that creationism can't be taught in public schools."

I can't recall if, at the conclusion of Hunter's report, sitting on the bed in my hotel room, I was just smiling or laughing. I think it was both.

STOCKWELL DAY WAS A CREATIONIST. This, in and of itself, was politically irrelevant. Like every other Canadian, the leader of the conservative political party had a constitutional right to believe in whatever the hell he wants to. Like any aspiring politician, Day's religious views were immaterial to his fitness for public office. God bless him, you might say.

Now, if a politician rigorously maintains a distinction between his or her religion and his or her legislative agenda, no one could legitimately have cause for complaint. Courts, constitutions, and modern legislative decision-making in Canada and the United States have embraced the notion that a wall properly exists between Church and State. But what about politicians who consistently attempt to infect the public agenda with their religious views? What about them?

In a telling, and under-reported, speech before a group of educators in April 2000, while still a candidate for the Canadian Reform Alliance leadership, Stockwell Day made it clear that he was not one who believed a politician could, or perhaps even should, keep Church and State separate. "[It is not] possible to demand that the convictions I express on Sunday should have nothing to do with the way I live my life the other six days of the week," he said. Day was telling the truth. Throughout his political career, as a backbencher and as a powerful member of Alberta's cabinet, Day had consistently attempted to impose his personal morality, and his religious faith, on others. On gays and lesbians. On pro-choice women. On common-law partners. Stockwell Day did not ever hesitate to use the law to advance his religious convictions.

Now, with only a few days left in a high-stakes election campaign, a major Canadian media organization had confirmed that fact in a detailed and dramatic fashion. I believed that, whether they were creationists or not, Canadian voters had no desire to elect a prime minister who would attempt to stick his religion in their faces. Day, however, had already tried to do so in Alberta. How could (or should) Canadians be told that Day might do the same thing to the country?

James Carville, who knows a thing or two about doing battle with the sort of far-right political establishment that periodically offers up the likes of Stockwell Day, muses about this. Before Day's election as leader of Reform Alliance, I spoke to the Democrats' best political consultant. Told about Day's views on abortion, Carville suggested that Liberals resist the temptation to say nothing. If one's political opponent has dropped a sticky moral issue into the middle of an election campaign, one is entitled to discuss the issue, says Carville. "I think you have got to [be] pretty non-political … and, you know, kind of say: 'Sometimes in politics, people have to discuss unpleasant things, and you know we have some very real differences between us. And, unpleasant as it may be, the most unpleasant alternative would be for you not to know what they are.' You know?"

He paused. "[Day] states that he doesn't favour abortion, even in the case of rape and incest. So you should state that it is a long-held policy of our government that Canadian women are smart enough, and they should be able to make these choices themselves."

What about a case where criticizing a political opponent's views — his willingness to mix his religious views with his politics — is necessary?

Carville laughed. "The first rule is to make a joke about yourself," he said. "The second rule is that there is nothing wrong, since time immemorial, about going after someone in a nice funny way, you know? Nothing wrong with that at all."

So that's what I did. I thought about Paul Hunter's story, and I decided to take a risk. I decided to be a little creative, you might say. With the exception of one person — my friend Jean Carle, who was a long-time Chrétien assistant — I didn't tell anyone what I planned to do. No one. In the war room, we all joked about the documentary, but no one was quite sure how to make use of it without offending millions of religious folks. Just let the media the chase the story, most said. It's safer.

Given the fact that most of the Canadian news media was owned by an arch-conservative multi-millionaire who viscerally despised Jean Chrétien, I wasn't so sure that was a good idea. True to form, no other media organization seemed to be interested in pursuing Hunter's documentary about Day. Moreover, at that point in the campaign, we Liberals needed to scare more progressive voters away from the NDP and get them to support us; a Liberal majority, at that point, was not a sure thing. I was convinced we had to quickly make two points: one, Stockwell Day's religion played a significant role in his politics; and, two, he would jam his religious politics down Canadians' throats if he got half a chance. We couldn't give him a chance.

Early the next morning, I asked that every Liberal candidate be sent a videotaped copy of Paul Hunter's documentary by courier, along with a transcript. Some talking points were put together to highlight what the CBC had revealed. Apart from that, nothing else was done with the CBC documentary. Later that night, Carle and I had dinner at a pasta place on Elgin Street. I told him what I was going to do. In between fits of laughter, Carle half-heartedly tried to talk me out of it.

"Warren, you could get kicked off the campaign," Jean said. He laughed. He guffawed. He giggled.

"Sorry, buddy," I said. "If I'm gonna go down, I'm gonna go down in flames."

Throughout the election, I had been drafted by the Liberal Party to appear on various television and radio political panels. Because I was no longer an employee of the prime minister, or of anyone else in government, for that matter, I was able to say things that other Grits couldn't, or wouldn't. As a result, I had been likened to various canines: I was "an attack dog," said the *Globe and Mail*; I was a "Liberal pit bull," declared a columnist with the Sun Media chain. Meanwhile, Day's party had also called me a variety of names, with his caucus members grumbling about how nasty I was. One of their guys whom I actually liked, Member of Parliament John Reynolds, darkly pronounced on me in the *Toronto Star*, "He's the master of dirty tricks … I would put nothing past him." I collected all of the best insults and put them up on my website. My rule of thumb is that whenever your opponent starts calling you a statesman, it's time to worry. (But when they start going after your friends or family to get at you, it's time to get out the brass knuckles.)

Canada AM's political panel was regarded as one of the most watched in the country. I had appeared on the panel several times before and during the election, usually facing off with Stockwell Day's tough-talking chief of staff, Rod Love. Now I would do so again. The night before the *Canada AM* show, I quietly spoke with the director of the Liberal caucus research bureau. A young Liberal named Matthew Graham was asked to scour Ottawa and find what I was looking for. Late that night, Graham showed up at the door of my hotel room with the prize in a Wal-Mart bag. I wrote him a cheque, and he left, grinning.

Early the next morning, I met with some people in the war room, but I didn't tell them what I planned to do. They wouldn't understand. After that, I walked through the cold to the CTV offices, carrying a Labatt Blue gym bag. In the studio, I sat down beside the only other pundit present, the Alliance's Tim Powers, and placed the gym bag beside my chair. A technician clipped a tiny microphone to my lapel and looped an earpiece over my shoulder so that I could hear what was being said outside the Ottawa studio. Powers, a lobbyist and former Tory from Atlantic Canada, had joined the Alliance some months before the election. Despite the fact that we disagreed about most everything, Powers was bright and affable, and we had become friendly. (In the intervening years, we have become great pals, and I would walk through a wall for the guy.)

The host of the political segment was Valerie Pringle. In the Toronto studio with her were representatives of the NDP and the Progressive Conservatives; a Bloc Québécois talking head was being beamed in from Quebec City. Typically, when a network broadcasts one of these pundit segments, anywhere between five to eight minutes is given to the participants to duke it out. If that does not sound like a lot of time, it isn't. The minutes fly past like an express train. Normally, the host throws out a question about some issue in that day's headlines or about something that happened earlier that week. On the *Canada AM* panels, whenever the Conservative, NDP, or Bloc participant said something critical — most often about the Liberal government, but also about the Reform Alliance — I ignored them. There is no point, in these debates, wasting precious seconds on opponents who represent no real electoral threat.

In the case of Powers and I, however, the rule was "Leave no charge unanswered." He was my principal opposition, and vice versa. With an estimated 2 million Canadians looking on, we would go at each other hammer and tongs, exploiting whatever weakness the other side had, highlighting whatever achievement we needed to highlight. The best approach was to be tough, but not be a bully or a sulk. If humour could be used, that was good, too. Sometimes, if the conversation got too heated, the pundits would end up speaking loudly and at the same time. For the most part, however, Pringle and her co-host, Dan Matheson, kept us from doing that.

On the morning in question, the panel batted around the usual stuff: polls, policies, prognostications. Time was slipping by quickly. When it appeared that I might lose my opportunity, I interrupted Powers. "Yeah, yeah, yeah, whatever," I said. "Valerie, you say you want to talk about the past week. Let's do that. In the past day or so, we have learned that Stockwell Day apparently believes that the world is six thousand years old, Adam and Eve were real people, and — my personal favourite — humans walked the earth with dinosaurs."

Powers looked at me as I reached down to open my gym bag. I continued, "Valerie, I just want to remind Mr. Day that *The Flintstones* was not a documentary." I then quickly extracted a large, stuffed, purple Barney from my bag. I held Barney up to the camera while Powers collapsed in laughter, as did the guy pointing a camera at us. "And this is the only dinosaur that recently co-existed with humans."

Of all the things I have done in politics, few things have had the impact of those few seconds on *Canada AM*, waving around a Barney dinosaur and suggesting that *The Flintstones* "was not a documentary."

The Conrad Black–owned press was livid, naturally, and called it an outrage and defamation of organized religion; I got emails from evangelicals calling for my excommunication or promising me a lengthy stay in Hell. But in the next few days, the risk-taking seemed to be paying off. Respected columnist Paul Wells, in the *National Post* no less, wrote that "the transformation of Mr. Day, from Stock to Laughingstock, was complete." The stunt was later discussed in the pages of the *Economist*, the *New York Times*, and *Time* magazine, and got a tip of the hat in the June 2001 issue of the U.S. political magazine *Campaigns and Elections*, which declared that the Barney moment "drove home the point" that Stockwell Day was an extremist who couldn't be trusted. I've even heard that the Barney moment is a Trivial Pursuit question.

Powers and I left the studio together; he was still laughing. "We're fucked," Tim said. "We are well and truly fucked." We shook hands and parted ways. Back at Liberal headquarters, I was mainly greeted by an awkward silence. People weren't sure how to react, although a few of them were laughing and wanting to see Barney. One of them suggested we auction the doll off at a party fundraiser. Meanwhile, I heard that some of my detractors on the campaign — and on that campaign, I had plenty, most of whom worked on Chrétien's communications staff — were hissing that it was a terrible, awful, cataclysmic mistake, and that Kinsella should go.

I was back at my desk for a few minutes when John Rae, the campaign's manager, walked into my office. He stood near me for a minute, saying nothing. *Here it goes*, I thought. *I'm getting the chop.* But Rae merely gave a small smile. "Be careful," he said, and walked out. Whew.

A minute later, the phone rang. It was the Right Honourable Jean Chrétien, the prime minister of all of Canada. "Okay," he said, "tell me exactly what happened. *Exactly.*" I told him, and he laughed and laughed, and then he said, "Okay, now tell me one more time."

Was Barney a dirty trick? Plenty of people thought so. Conservative columnists screamed that I was a "smear doctor" and even a "hatemonger" and stuff like that. One race-baiting Ottawa-area radio host,

Lowell Green, devoted an entire program to the subject, calling me "a sewer rat" and "diabolical." He suggested that listeners pray for the redemption of my soul. The Sun chain's Earl MacRae, another knuckle-dragging mouth-breather, actually equated me with Joseph Goebbels. (Being no fan of Nazis, I would have punched MacRae out for that one, were he not so old.)

But Barney had the desired effect. It kept Paul Hunter's documentary in the news and in the opinion pages for a few more days; it kept Day on the defensive about his hidden agenda; and it unleashed, as one CTV reporter told me, "ten million water-cooler conversations about Stockwell Day's craziness, and whether he wanted to bash down the wall between Church and State." Which, of course, had been what I wanted to do all along.

The Barney stunt didn't defeat Stockwell Day — not even close. Jean Chrétien did that all by himself, admittedly aided and abetted by Stockwell Day. But the Barney moment provides a useful example about the necessity of occasionally trying something different, and the utility of taking chances. You know, taking risks. *Not*, I stress, playing a dirty trick.

Real dirty tricks have been a feature of election campaigns for a long, long time. Following the Watergate scandal in the United States in the early 1970s — when a perfectly awful synonym for dirty tricks, "rat-fucking," was publicized by one of the indicted players in that drama — so-called dirty tricks were deservedly unpopular. Spying, invasion of privacy, and so on became *verboten*, and for a time campaigns took notice. But it was inevitable that the pendulum would swing back, and it did. Towards the end of the 1970s, stunts, dirty tricks, and skulduggery were back with a vengeance. A dirty trick, by its very name, speaks to its essential illegitimacy.

Drawing a distinction between dirty tricks and stuff like the Barney stunt is easy. The best way to figure it out for yourself, naturally, is to talk to your mother. That's what I do. She and my wife are what I call my one-person focus groups. If your idea isn't something you'd brag about in front of your mom, it's safe to assume you are in dirty trick territory. If it's something that you and your mother would both find screamingly funny, and that she would repeat to her friends down in the bank lineup, it's no dirty trick. It's in the Barney zone.

You will not be surprised to hear that dirty tricks are as old as politics itself. As far back as 54 B.C., for example, letters written by Cicero to his colleague Atticus amply testify to the longevity of such electoral nastiness. The political system of Rome was then characterized by "*consules flagrant infamia,*" Cicero wrote, meaning "the consuls are ablaze with scandal." Cicero tells his friend that a closed-door session concerning the misconduct of several politicians was stirring up "*magnus timor candidatorum,*" or "great fear among the candidates." The problem apparently related to the revelation that a certain candidate had been bought, but did not stay bought. According to Cicero, one Gaius Memmius stood in the senate to read an agreement that he and a fellow candidate had made with certain Roman consuls to pay them a great deal of money for suborning witnesses, should they be elected. The agreement detailed sums to be paid and who was involved in the conspiracy. History goes on to record that Memmius was successful in his objective: he effectively destroyed the political careers of those he named, but, tellingly, did irreparable damage to his own career as well.

The types of dirty tricks available to political hacks are limited only by their imaginations, and, sometimes, by the law. Cell phones are monitored by companies that later sell tapes and transcripts to the media or political partisans. Private detectives are hired to poke through a candidate's garbage (a process called Dumpster diving) hoping to unearth some scandal. Telephone conversations are regularly recorded to trap or embarrass an opponent. Sometimes, campaigns are even infiltrated by moles from the other side. In the summer of 1984, I was a young Liberal, assigned to assist Senator Phillippe Gigantes in trying to elect some Grits under the very troubled leadership of John Turner. As the Liberal effort lurched from one disaster to another, the so-called strategists who supposedly ran the campaign were growing increasingly, and visibly, desperate. One memorable day, Gigantes met with one of these people (I will not name him because he left politics thereafter, and never came back). Following the meeting, Gigantes sat down with me, shaking his head. I asked him what was wrong.

The person with whom he'd just met "wants to pay for someone to act as a mole on the Tory press plane so that we can get some dirt, and find out what the reporters are writing," said Gigantes. "What an asshole."

"What did you say to him?"

Gigantes laughed. "I told him to save his money. I told him that, if there is any dirt to be had on a campaign plane, he can buy an account of it in the newspaper the very next day. And for just twenty-five cents!"

Dirty tricks do not work. They just don't: they turn off the very people the dirty trickster is allegedly seeking to influence. Other political consultants feel similarly. U.S. political commentator Larry Sabato argues in his bestselling book, *Dirty Little Secrets*, that "such tactics frequently go too far, becoming acts that either constitute or lead to significant impairment in the conduct of public affairs — [which is] our definition of corruption." The dividends paid by such tactics are far outweighed by the damage that inevitably results when one is found out. Polling data shows, not surprisingly, the voting public and the media look on such trickery as bad, bad, bad — and those who engage in such tricks are seen as worse than those they seek to expose. A February 1999 U.S. Gallup poll, for example, showed that fully three-quarters of those surveyed considered ethical political behaviour to be "very important."

In the 1962 Canadian federal election campaign, to cite another example, flamboyant Liberal cabinet minister Judy LaMarsh followed Conservative leader John Diefenbaker across Canada as part of a Truth Squad, providing what she called "constructive criticism" of the Dief and his policies. The Truth Squad effort dramatically backfired on LaMarsh and the Liberals, however, because Diefenbaker was able to persuade voters that LaMarsh was using gutter tactics to win popular support. LaMarsh was widely castigated for the effort — she was even forced to publicly concede that she was "accident prone" — and Diefenbaker was re-elected, albeit with a minority government.

In the unsuccessful 1996 provincial British Columbia Liberal campaign, in which I was intimately involved, we used one political stunt to great advantage. One sunny afternoon in May of that year, in a cluttered office space in Richmond, brewing executive James Villeneuve and I were speaking in a conference call with Gordon Campbell, leader of the provincial political party. Villeneuve, a superior political communicator who would later chair the successful 2000 campaign of Toronto mayor Mel Lastman, had flown out west to assist the B.C. Liberals in the race. We were preparing Campbell for his appearance on a radio drive-in show the next morning. The B.C. election race was well underway, and our stalwart group was struggling mightily to unseat the well-organized and well-funded New Democrats of Glen Clark. Our opponents were well ahead of us in the polls. At one point, I suggested that radio drive-in shows were not the ideal place to ruminate aloud about complex policy matters. Villeneuve recalled Bill Clinton's fabled saxophone recital on *The Arsenio Hall Show* in 1992. Laughingly, we asked the B.C. Liberal leader whether he played an instrument.

"Well, yes," he said. "I play guitar, sometimes. But I'm not very good."

Villeneuve and I pounced like the hungry jackals we so resemble. Could he think of a song or two to strum on the radio program? "Sure," said Campbell. He called back a few hours later. Not only had Campbell located a song to play, he had written one. It was a funny and catchy little ditty, sung in a respectable alto, and all about the three-dozen or so tax increases Glen Clark's NDP had foisted upon the weary voters of B.C. He called it "Taxman Glen."

The song was a huge hit; people loved to see a politician who did not take himself so seriously that he could not have fun. Everywhere Campbell went in the province, people requested that he sing "Taxman Glen." In a matter of days, the B.C. Liberals started to inch back up in the polls. And on election night, Campbell and his party actually acquired 41 percent of the popular vote, fully three points ahead of Clark's NDP, but, thanks to some good old-fashioned gerrymandering, the NDP eked out a few more seats.

Sending dead flowers to a losing campaign or ordering a lot of COD pizzas to be delivered to one's opponent are examples of the sort of stupid behaviour that some consultants and political veterans can succumb to. But pranks are best when they are funny, not malicious. Democratic campaign operative Joe Trippi recalls one wonderful example of this in Sabato's *Dirty Little Secrets*.

Trippi, a smart Democrat who was the first guy to truly figure out how to make use of the Internet as a political tool, had been part of the team overseeing the 1984 presidential campaign of Walter F. Mondale. Recalled Trippi in the book, "I was running Pennsylvania for Mondale in the 1984 primary against Gary Hart. We had this huge Mondale for

President dinner, with four or five thousand people there. Then, after dessert, I see out of the corner of my eye that all the waiters are bringing out plates of fortune cookies, and it hits me about ten minutes later that I never ordered any cookies. To my shock and horror, Mondale gets up to give his speech, grabs a cookie, opens it, and reads, as they all did, 'Hart Wins Pennsylvania.' Mondale got this horrid, pale look on his face …"

SUGGESTING THAT A CAMPAIGN or a war room "get creative" is, I admit, a bit odd, with a vaguely West Coast feel to it. Let's all hop in the hot tub, throw on some Fleetwood Mac, fire up a fatty, and "get creative!" Peace, man!

That's not what I mean. (Besides, Fleetwood Mac sucks, and so do hot tubs.) And it's not something I can neatly summarize in a ten-point list, either. "Creative" doesn't describe a type of thinking, necessarily. In a war room context, it describes a type of person.

Being creative, in a campaign for something or someone you care about, isn't for everyone. Let me give you a literary reference point, one we have all been familiar with (or should have been) since the age of sixteen: T.S. Eliot's "The Love Song of J. Alfred Prufrock." Remember Eliot's withering dismissal of those folks who always opt for the safe and the bland? The "Do I dare? Do I dare?" and the growing old, wearing white flannel trousers rolled, a pair of ragged claws on the floors of silent seas? Remember all of that? I love that poem. Whenever I'm in a political capital like Ottawa or Washington, I recall "Prufrock" and how perfectly it describes the armies of drab, colourless people I imagine toiling behind the grey walls, in airless cubicles. Sending emails about nothing to nobody.

Campaigns and war rooms have their Prufrocks, too. They tend to be nice, inoffensive people who always opt for the course of least resistance. They equate lots of meetings with progress, and too many syllables with meaning. You forget their names ten minutes after you meet them.

Being creative — taking risks, rolling the dice, pushing the envelope, getting outside the box, call it whatever cliché you want — isn't for the Prufrocks who work among us. It's for risk-takers. Over the years, I've observed certain characteristics common to these risk-taking types.

A non-Prufrock person is, to the J. Alfred Prufrocks of this world, a crazy bastard. To the Prufrocks, naturally, risk-takers seem both erratic and idiosyncratic. But the non-Prufrocks aren't crazy at all, and they're quite strategic. They know nothing will ever get better if they remain cowering in the foxhole. So they pull the pin on the grenade, scramble over the side, and start running like hell towards the other guys — the other guys being the ones pointing guns in their direction. The risk-takers and the creative types aren't sociopaths, however; and they aren't superheroes. They know if they make a mistake they can get hurt, and (even worse) they know that the people around them can get hurt, too.

The best risk-takers, therefore, are a bit like the best athletes: they make it all look easy. They always seem like they are improvising, but they're not. Every move, every step, has been choreographed in advance and practised a thousand times. They work according to a *plan*. If something goes dramatically wrong —just as Senator LeBlanc warned us when we were starting up the 1993 Liberal Party war room — then there are unpleasant consequences, among them being dropped from the team. Risk-takers, as others have observed before me, need to be creatively intentional, and not just wildly improvisational. Improvisation sounds like a lot of fun, but it's really just a fancy word for doing stuff without a strategic plan. And, as per Lesson One, getting a plan and sticking to it is a prerequisite to winning.

During the 2000 federal election campaign, it is true that we had no *specific* plan to use a purple dinosaur to draw attention to Stockwell Day's willingness to govern Canada according to his religious views. But, long before the campaign got underway, we all agreed that the general campaign theme was about choices — one choice being moderate, and the other choice being extreme. Everything we did, including Barney, needed to remind Canadians that one of the choices was extreme. And that they needed to consider the consequences of that for themselves, and their country. Barney, therefore, *reflected* the plan, even though he wasn't exactly *part* of the plan. Barney did the trick. (And I was indeed ready to be fired if it went awry.)

Another characteristic common to risk-takers is their ability to express, in understandable terms, simple solutions for complex problems. Whenever facing a stressful situation, Prufrocks have a tendency to convene lots of meetings and write lots of memos and use lots of fancy-sounding, multisyllabic words. Instead of trying to eliminate needless complexity, Prufrocks embrace it. It helps them to avoid solving the problem.

Risk-takers tend to be good communicators, and they're also impatient. Wartime generals are great communicators, for example, because they have to be: whenever you are asking people to literally risk their lives for a cause, the very least you owe them is clarity, and not a pile of bureaucratic bafflegab. Now, General George S. Patton was seen by wartime Prufrocks as certifiably insane. But he won plenty of battles in Africa, Sicily, France, and Germany, and his U.S. Third Army would have followed him to hell and back, and did. (To wit, more than twenty thousand of his men volunteered to act as his pallbearers after his untimely death in December 1945.) Patton got into lots of trouble for his profane and blunt way of communicating, but he knew how to speechify in a way that ensured he'd be understood by his soldiers. He knew the value of communicating. And, like all great risk-takers, he was ahead of his time on important issues, too.

The command of the first African-American tank unit, the 761st "Black Panther" Tank Battalion, was assigned to Patton in the fall of 1944. As they were about to enter a key battle, Patton addressed them, in a wonderfully blunt and honest bit of speech-making: "Men, you're the first Negro tankers to ever fight in the American Army. I have nothing but the best in my Army. I don't care what colour you are as long as you go up there and kill those Kraut sons of bitches. Everyone has their eyes on you, and is expecting great things from you. Most of all your race is looking forward to you. Don't let them down and, damn you, don't let me down."

They didn't. The 761st did the job Patton required of them, and were victorious in many other subsequent missions, too. Three decades after being deactivated in 1946, Patton's Black Panthers received a Presidential Unit Citation for their Second World War service.

A third and final identifying trait of creative, non-Prufrock risk-takers is that they always strive to have the best possible sense of what people think. They always seek to be in sync with what people will accept and what they won't. And they don't arrive at this profound understanding through qualitative and quantitative public opinion research, either. To achieve this higher state of knowledge, they trust their gut over their noggin, ten times out of ten. In a war room, I usually tend to distrust the guy or gal who endlessly quote what the pollsters think. I want to hear what their *mothers* think!

Here is the advice I received from a wiser and older Liberal friend, as we were getting ready for another Chrétien campaign. Said he, "I know you, Kinsella. You are a CBC Radio and *Globe and Mail* Liberal. You're a Bay Street Liberal. You need to become a Main Street Liberal, and listen to AM Radio, and read a subway give-away paper. Main Street is where the votes are, Kinsella."

Well, that wasn't exactly what he said, since I don't take detailed notes when I'm having a beer with friends, and neither do you. But you get the drift, and my friend was of course correct. Here, then, is another gratuitous literary reference, *gratis*. Listening carefully to Main Street is what J.D. Salinger did when he was getting ready to write the greatest book about teenagers ever written, *The Catcher in the Rye*. To capture the colloquial idiom of adolescence, to give his book the authenticity it still has, Salinger allegedly lurked in the places where teenagers lurked, listening to the way they talked, learning what it was that preoccupied them. He took notes. It gave his book an astonishing genuineness that has made it one of the best-loved books ever written in the English language.

Like Salinger, the risk-takers know that if given the choice, Joe and Jane Frontporch will always choose a plan that is more hope than fear. They will always succumb, first and foremost, to the appeal to the heart, and not just the cold play for the intellect. They will always choose to listen to the person who talks *to* them, and not just *at* them. They will embrace the leader who is willing to take risk and isn't just playing it safe — as *they* do, every single day, juggling mortgage payments and utility bills, trying to catch up their sleep, worrying about keeping their jobs, and saving up every damned penny to give their kids a better life than the one that they had.

As in campaigns, as in life: real creativity is attained through risk-taking. And risk-taking generally only happens with certain kinds of people — people who work hard, people who know how to communicate, and people who know in their guts how to capture hearts and minds.

Most of all, they are people who know that you never, ever accomplish great things without taking great risks.

Ever!

Get Tough!

I DESPISE AND LOATHE Big Tobacco. I hate the people who run Big Tobacco. It's time to get tough with Big Tobacco. But how?

A little while ago, I was invited to speak to a global conference of people who work against Big Tobacco. I didn't know any of the hundreds of people at the conference, and they didn't know me. But I told them I was willing to bet that for them, as for me, the subject matter of the gathering was personal. Intensely personal.

All of them, I suspected, had lost someone to the terrible scourge that is tobacco — one of the great avoidable plagues of our time. They had lost someone in their family, or a friend, or someone they had known in their lives. So in that sense, what I wanted to talk to them about was not merely something to be debated and focus-grouped and spun out in a strategic communications plan.

It was more than that. It was more than what the media call, in their bland, antiseptic way of describing the great dramas in a human being's life, "an issue." It was *more* than that word. It was, and is, personal.

My personal experience with this terrible tobacco virus, I told them, was bookended by two memories.

One memory, at the age of seven or so, involved me sending away for Cancer Society anti-tobacco posters to put up on my bedroom walls. It also involved the younger me praying to God every night, really praying, that my parents would not smoke — my mother, cigarettes sometimes, my father cigars and pipes. If the prayers didn't work — which they didn't, not for a long time — I would find their tobacco and quietly throw it in the garbage.

They'd know who did it, eventually, but they never got mad at me for it. Because they knew that, even though I was seven years old, I was right. My father, who was a doctor and who gave up cigarettes when I was born, knew that most of all. That is one memory that I told the conference delegates about. That was one personal experience.

The other personal experience came one year, five months, ten days, eight hours, and a few minutes before I stepped onstage to speak to the conference delegates.

It involved me sitting on a chair on the third floor of the Kingston General Hospital — where, three decades earlier, my father had worked as a physician, saving and bettering lives — and watching, from what seemed like a distance of a million miles, my father relate to my mother and me that the cough that had not gone away was more than a cough. It was cancer, it was in his lungs, and in three weeks it would kill him.

That is what I remembered, and that is what I told the delegates. And as my parents held each other and I sat there stupidly, unable to comprehend, I remembered my father's words very clearly. He said, "We are going to join a class-action suit against the tobacco companies." That's what he said. We are going to go after the tobacco companies.

We never got a chance to do that. The cancer was without mercy, as it often is, and it moved through him as if it had been fired from the barrel of a gun. We buried him a few weeks later, on my parents' fiftieth wedding anniversary. I can tell you that, at that point — and despite having practised the speech a few times at home — I got a little upset.

After a pause, I told the delegates that that was my second personal experience with the issue that brought us together that night. The image of my father holding his high school sweetheart and telling us it was time to go after these people who know — who *know* — that they peddle death for a living, like terrorists do. Although from my perspective, terrorists at least tend to be a bit more forthcoming about their culpability.

That is how I wanted to start with the conference delegates. Talking about my own personal experiences, in the knowledge that they, too, undoubtedly had a personal experience that was just as painful and that made them just as angry as I was about these killers in $5,000 tailored Armani suits.

It wouldn't be entirely true to say I was there that night just because of my dad. The truth is that the anti-tobacco folks had me going way, way back when I was seven years old. Back when I was taping those anti-tobacco posters onto my bedroom wall.

But it *was* true to say that I was there with a renewed focus — as someone who was alleged to know something about running campaigns, and as someone who wanted to use what I had learned to assist in one of the greatest campaigns of all: the campaign to rid ourselves of the dirty pestilence that killed my father, and perhaps killed someone close to you, too. This plague that has killed too many people, in too many places, for too long.

I told the delegates that I am known in Canada as a political activist, someone who runs campaigns for candidates and political parties and different causes. They listened. I work for people I believe in and whom I like, and I am pretty busy at that. Along the way, I told them, I have learned a few things about how to conduct all sorts of campaigns.

In every campaign I have helped to run, I have found it worthwhile to take a bit of time — *before* the campaign and *after* the campaign — to evaluate the effectiveness of our strategies and tactics. When we do that, we always learn something new, and we always learn that we could have done something better. So I offered a suggestion about the strategies and tactics we could perhaps use in our campaign against tobacco and those who sell it.

The tendency a lot of us have, when facing off against a group as well funded and as evil as Big Tobacco, is to be sucked into a war of statistics and to try and win the day with columns and graphs and charts and numbers.

It's easy to see why those of us who despise Big Tobacco do that, sometimes. In our case, in our cause, it is because the statistics are so clearly on our side of the debate. Our facts and statistics are irrefutable, I told the delegates. They certainly support our contention that tobacco will kill you, if you let it.

But here is one thing I have learned on the political campaign trail (and that I related earlier on in Lesson Two). It is one of the first things I inevitably tell my fellow campaign workers on day one of the campaign. In the new reality — this twenty-four-hour-a-day, seven-day-a-week, five-hundred-channel universe — statistics will not work. What works best is a story, a short, simple story that puts a human face on what you hope to say.

Besides, I told them, if we come up with a scientist, Big Tobacco will buy a scientist. If we come up with a medical report, they will buy a doctor's soul and produce false medical reports. If we come up with charts of tobacco mortality rates, they will come up with more charts, filled with lies.

They've got a lot of money, after all — they had enough money to re-cruit former Conservative prime minister Brian Mulroney's chief of staff as their head lobbyist. And, when the political winds were changing, they made sure a former Liberal prime minister, Paul Martin, was on one of their board executives for years. They have lots of money, and too many people willing to work for them.

But if we come up with a hard-hitting story — a short, simple, com-pelling story, told with emotion and conviction, over and over — they cannot equal that. *They will lose.*

Their fake science and fake medicine and fake charts cannot ever equal what happened to my father, or someone's mother, or your brother or sister, or someone who was loved and whom we lost. If that is the battlefield — real stories, filled with real people living real lives — the tobacco merchants will never win the war. *We will beat them.*

That is one piece of advice I gave to the delegates: always put a hu-man face on the story you want to tell, and never lose the passion you feel in wanting to beat them. Here is the second bit of advice: pulling your punches will not work. Taking the high road all the time will not work. Looking for the reasonable middle ground will not work.

Like I said, and like the anti-smoking delegates already knew, this is a war, a real war with real casualties. As in any war, and as in any political campaign, I have always found — as James Carville memorably said — that it is pretty hard for an opponent like Big Tobacco to punch me if they already have my fist in their face. And I mean *hitting hard.* Making it hurt.

In political campaigns, that's sometimes called "going negative." I don't think it's that, I told the delegates. I don't think it's ever, ever negative to tell the truth.

At about that point in my speech — and as I looked out at their faces — I kind of knew what the delegates might be thinking. Going negative doesn't work. Or it's a sign of a desperate campaign. Or the media don't like it. Or when people get polled about it, they say they don't like it.

And that is certainly true. If you commission a quantitative poll or set up a qualitative focus group, and you ask people, "Do you approve of negative political advertising?", they will always say no. It's kind of like asking them if they approve of death, or if they like paying taxes. They will always say no, if that's the question.

But that's not that the question! What's worse, I told the delegates, that's letting language do our thinking for us. The question is not whether people *approve* of negative communications in campaign, or whether they *think* it works. The question is whether they have ever seen tough, critical, but factual messaging that *worked on them.* Do they approve of that?

They may say they don't pay attention to it, but they do. They may say they are not influenced by it, but they are. Getting tough — war-room tough — in campaigns works. Always has, always will. In fact, what voters and consumers say and what voters and consumers are influenced by are completely different things.

That's why, when I am running a war room, I am always prepared to tell the critical facts about an opponent. If they have done or said something on the public record that is hypocritical, offensive, or stupid, then it is right and proper for me to go at them, factually and forcefully. It's my job, in fact. (Yours, too.)

So, I told the delegates, when you are formulating your next campaign against Big Tobacco, don't hesitate to hit them, and hit them hard. Kick the crap out of them. You may get a couple of Nervous Nellies on your board, or among your donors, who profess to be unhappy because of your tough, factual messaging. But don't listen to them, and don't pull your punches. Don't look for a reasonable middle ground with human garbage who do, in fact, profit from peddling cigarettes to kids.

This war in which we are all engaged, I told the delegates — against a lying, venal, disgusting, soulless opponent that is better funded and better equipped to run broad-based campaigns — is, like I said at the outset, intensely personal. All of us anti-tobacco fighters have deeply held convictions and beliefs. It isn't academic to us.

But here is my personal view: we owe it to each other — and to our fathers and mothers and brothers and sisters, now gone — to be better and faster and smarter and stronger than our adversary. We owe it to them to build campaigns, I told the delegates, that will defeat our enemy, once and for all.

Now, as you read this book, and as you consider the detestation I feel for Big Tobacco, you may say to yourself, "That's Kinsella's passion. That's not my passion."

Fair enough. But if this book is successful at anything, I want it to be successful at persuading folks to join campaigns to make their personal passions real. The cause doesn't have to be fighting Big Tobacco. Fighting the seal hunt, fighting racism and anti-Semitism, fighting for aboriginal rights, fighting for the boreal forest, fighting for diverse and tolerant public education: those are some of the other campaigns in which I have been involved, recently and over the years. In every case, I've advocated getting tough with our opponents, because first, the new media environment doesn't reward subtlety; second, your opponent, knowing that, will almost certainly get tough with you; and third, the stakes are too high to do otherwise. As one of my punk rock pals once said, talk minus action equals zero. True enough.

So get passionate. Get involved. Get tough.

Now, when my dad was getting sicker, and when I was shuttling back and forth between Kingston and Toronto, I wasn't paying much attention to the 2004 federal election. It just wasn't all that important.

But you do a lot of waiting when a loved one gets sick — in hallways, at home, and at hospital bedsides. During those times, I wondered what the Liberal Party's leadership could have done differently in the 2004 federal election campaign, given that, in the view of most everyone, the campaign had been managed very poorly. Given that it blew a near-certain majority and ended up with a slim minority government. Given that it paved the way, in just a few months time, for a healthy Conservative minority government.

In the interest of full disclosure, I should confess that I am no fan of Paul Martin, or the senior people he had around him. I disliked them, and they disliked me.

It had gone on for years, but after a while, you get tired of fighting all the time; sometimes, you forget why you were fighting in the first place. So, on the cold Toronto night in December 2003 that Paul Martin took the Liberal leadership, I put on one of his buttons, walked up to his campaign manager, David Herle, and offered my hand. As a few others looked on, Herle mumbled something, turned around, and walked away. He didn't shake my hand. A little bit before that, in October 2003, I had made a similar attempt to make peace and sent an email to another top Martin aide, Brian Guest (a guy who is now a senior — and controversial — advisor to Stéphane Dion). Here's what it said:

> Brian, it's been pretty obvious for some time that your team didn't need a lot of outside help in the lead-up to the next election — particularly my help. As I've told whomever asked, the Martin team seemed to be doing rather well all on their own, and I was fully confident they would win the next election handily. They didn't need my help, etc.
>
> Today's news about a possible Canadian Alliance-Tory merger hasn't changed that prognosis, yet, but it can't be denied that (if successful) a single conservative party, coupled with a resurgent NDP, will change the landscape dramatically. A single conservative option, with a new leader, presents a threat.
>
> There's no point in rehashing here a lot of grievances, on my side of the divide or yours. Suffice to say that, at

the end of the day, I am a Liberal. So … I am offering my help. I am fully confident said offer of help will be declined by others. But at least I will be able to tell myself that I offered it.

… I look forward to discussing [this] one day. Best wishes in the weeks ahead.

That email received no response from Guest or anyone else, which was fine. At least, as I wrote, I had made an attempt to help out. As it was, I was busy enough with provincial Liberal political stuff, and it was time for a new team and some new faces. I, and others, moved on. At the time of Chrétien's resignation, the Liberal Party was supported by more than 50 percent of Canadians, and Martin looked to be sailing towards another Parliamentary majority. (Although, after the Canadian Alliance and the Conservatives successfully concluded their merger, I publicly predicted that a minority was likely, which attracted media attention. That didn't endear me to the Martin folks, and understandably so.) It got quiet for a while.

Then, early in 2004, all kinds of shit started to happen. Hell broke loose. For us Chrétien folks, it was flat-out crazy. It was insane.

Here's a only a partial list. The Martin guys tried to push out Sheila Copps, a party stalwart and a former deputy prime minister. They dumped Stéphane Dion from cabinet and attempted to orchestrate a nomination challenge in his riding. They started to fire anyone who had been associated with Jean Chrétien, contrary to the law and contrary to the basic principles of fairness. They recruited a separatist, Jean Lapierre, to be their Quebec lieutenant, and called Jean Chrétien's popular separatist-fighting *Clarity Act* "useless." They started to recruit so-called sovereignists to run for them in Quebec and issued a press release to brag about their desire to sign up "nationalist" candidates, at which point I decided not to vote Liberal for the first time in my life.

But it got worse, a lot worse. In mid-February, senior staffers in Martin's office told reporters that Chrétien's government had actively concealed "criminal" activity — that's a quote, folks — in the sponsorship program. They declared that they would hold a judicial inquiry into the program, and said this, before it even got underway: "This public inquiry is going to pin it all on them." This, despite the fact that Chrétien was the guy who had called in the auditor general, and then the RCMP, to probe wrongdoing in the ill-fated program. This, despite the fact that Chrétien had offered to stick around and take the heat on the sponsorship mess. This, despite the fact that when he left office — and while the RCMP was conducting criminal investigations into the affair — the Liberal Party of Canada was topping the polls in voter support. None of that mattered, apparently. The inquiry, with its rigged terms of reference, would "pin it all on them."

Then the geniuses around Paul Martin made things worse — for themselves. They sent Martin across the country, in every region, to say he was "mad as hell" about the Quebec sponsorship mess, and to point the finger of blame at everyone but himself — him, the guy who (as finance minister) knew where dollars were being spent. Him, the guy who (as the most senior Quebec political minister) knew everything that was happening on the ground in that province. Mad as hell: that's what he said, and the media started to make mock him for it, calling it the "Mad as Hell Tour." The Liberal Party lost nearly fifteen points in voter support in a week, and it never got them back. It was a political cataclysm unlike anything any of us had ever seen before. Fifteen points in a week! Suddenly, to a lot of people, my prediction of a minority didn't seem so crazy anymore.

With the Martinites declaring their intention to pin the blame on us Chrétien folks, my position hardened. I decided I was going to persuade as many disaffected Liberals as possible to vote against Martin. So I energetically took to criticizing the Martin junta in the media and on my website, www.warrenkinsella.com, knowing that it would attract media attention. Which it did. I trace my conversion from a Liberal supporter to a Liberal critic to the day that the Martin thugs called me, and lots of other good people, "criminals." That tends to get your attention, particularly when it's coming from the highest political office in the land. So I started to get tough, very tough, with the party I had been associated with for my whole life. The way I looked at it, I didn't have much choice.

Paul Martin, however, had a choice. He didn't need to commit regicide. He didn't need to set off a massive civil war in his party to satisfy his own ambition. He didn't need to turn a majority government into a minority government. It was all unnecessary and avoidable. I gave a speech about what Martin could have done that spring and talked about the four big rules I believed Martin and his cabal had broken. I called them "Kinsella's Four New Rules of Media Management." Here's what I said.

Number one was the Crisis Management Rule. Even if you are in the middle of a big, hairy crisis, don't call it one. If you are panicked, don't say you are. If you are "mad as hell," don't travel to every major media market in the country to say that, thereby encouraging everyone within earshot to be mad too. (At you, Paul, mostly.)

The second rule I called the Public Servants Rule, and it was based on a true story. When I was in government, I would make every new political staffer follow me outside my office door. I would introduce them to all of the secretaries, the mail delivery people, and the receptionists. "This is the public service," I would say. "These people have more power than you, because they were here before you, and they will be here long after you are gone. They do good work. Be nice to them." In the spring of 2004, that also meant not going on national television — as Paul Martin had done — to accuse public servants of crimes, destroying their lives in the process. It's not fair. They cannot defend themselves in the manner, say, politicians can. Public servants don't say much, I opined, but they always, always have the last word. Paul Martin learned that lesson the hard way.

The third rule I called, indelicately, the Don't Do Stupid Things Rule. It was a dumb name for a rule, but that was because it was really two rules in one. The first part is called "Keeping Your Stories Straight." That means, for instance, it's probably not a good idea to say one thing in a press conference attended by lots of reporters (i.e., that you, Paul Martin, didn't believe Jean Chrétien knew about criminal wrongdoing), and then let your staff run around saying the exact opposite thing to a lot of the selfsame reporters (i.e. that Jean Chrétien covered up criminality). It's confusing, and life is too confusing as it is. The second part is called "If You Take a Swing at a Professional Political Brawler from a Small Town in Rural Quebec, Like Jean Chrétien, Make Damn Sure You Knock Him Out But Good." Otherwise, he's liable to get up and beat the shit out of you. Which, eventually, Chrétien did.

The final rule was the Party Leader Rule. Unless you are from Mars,

I suggested, your political party has only one leader. That's how we do things down here on Earth. Therefore, it's a good idea to protect your leader at all costs (those of you who know me know this is the rule I take really, really seriously). Don't put your leader front and centre on some stinking mess, as the oxymoronic Martin brain trust had done. Hand the messes to solid, dull, factual, unflappable guys to answer all of the questions, until people get bored and start playing bridge again. After all, that's why God invented solid, dull, factual, unflappable spokespeople. To watch your back.

As the Liberals slid ever deeper in the polls, I started to receive panicky emails from people asking me to come back to the party, stop being so tough on poor old Paul Martin, blah blah blah. At the time, I was too preoccupied with my dad and didn't really care what happened to the Liberal Party. Eventually I publicly laid out the two things that needed to happen before I could ever consider returning. I wanted Paul Martin to say that his senior staff were wrong to call Jean Chrétien and the people around him criminals. And I wanted to be assured that all federal Liberal Quebec candidates, to use Stéphane Dion's phrasing at the time, had "resolutely and unambiguously ceased to be separatist and reconciled themselves with the Canadian ideal."

None of that happened, of course. I continued to defend my friend Chrétien, and I continued to predict that Paul Martin was going down to a minority. Which he did, decisively and deservedly, on June 28, 2004.

Could Martin have done better? Sure. As in campaigns, so too in life: you can always do better. When my dad was getting sick, I would sit beside his bed, and we would talk about politics. He loved politics. Together, we formulated a list of things Martin could have done, all of them necessitating getting tough — but not with Jean Chrétien, whose name wasn't even going to be on the ballot. They necessitated getting tougher with Conservative leader Stephen Harper, whose party's name *was* on the ballot.

I won't replay everything that was on the list, but three things bear repeating. Early in 2004, before things got out of hand, Paul Martin made his predecessor his political target — not the guy who was actively campaigning to be his *successor*. Big mistake. Martin needed to echo Harry S. Truman and assert that the buck stopped at his desk. He should have paid back every cent donated by the so-called Liberal-friendly ad firms in the sponsorship affair. He should have promoted the fact that he was doing it. And, at the start of the controversy (not during the election), Martin should have made the following statement: "I didn't know this was happening, but as finance minister, I should have. I take full responsibility for this. The buck stops here. I am sorry, and here are ten things I plan to pass into law to make sure it doesn't happen again." He didn't do that, either.

Getting tough? Paul Martin should have gotten tough with Stephen Harper. On December 12, 2000, for example, Harper authored a statement to the effect that Canada was a second-tier socialistic country with second-rate status. You could have built a whole campaign around those words; personally, I would have made that the most infamous statement ever made! On every Grit TV commercial, on every billboard, the tag line would be "First Rate" or "Number One" or something like that. Every photo of Paul Martin, flashing the number one. Every speech: "Canada's number one, Stephen. We're not second-rate. Shame on you, etc." Remind people of what they already know: that Canada is the greatest country in the world. He didn't do that.

Finally, Paul Martin needed to remember how he won the Liberal leadership in the first place. You shouldn't ever run from your record, particularly if it helped to get you elected with the three majority governments, in 1993, 1997, and 2000. Embrace it. It was a winning record, after all. He didn't do that, either.

Bye-bye, Paul. You're not missed.

I SENSE YOU REMAIN UNCONVINCED. I sense you think getting tough is unwise.

To win you over, let me pass along a few observations. First, just because someone tells you something is negative campaigning doesn't mean that it is. Negative ads and negative campaigns have been defined in so many different ways that no one is quite sure what "negative" means anymore. What too many people seem to accept, however, is that negative politics is bad for democracy. It isn't.

One of the better studies in this area is by the Annenberg Campaign

Mapping Project (ACMP). ACMP divided campaign discourse into three types: advocacy, which are arguments in favour of a politician's position; contrast, which are arguments contrasting two or more political choices; and attack, which are arguments critical of an opponent or the opponent's position on something. Only the last type can be fairly seen as negative, but all three are often lumped together as just that. It is worth remembering that the Annenberg study found that attack ads actually contain a far greater percentage of "policy words" and more issue content than contrast or advocacy ads. And a 1998 national U.S. poll, also by Annenberg, concluded that voters regard contrast ads as "responsible" and "useful."

So what's negative about any of that? Nothing. Reporters (who are more negative in a day than you will be in a lifetime) like to call tough campaign messages negative because they prefer to report on conflict not agreement. Political opponents like to call the other side's ads negative because they know voters believe they don't like negative ads, and they hope to win support by condemning the opposition's use of them. Don't believe the hype. Most of the time, when you hear a politician is being negative, it's not true. They're merely being political.

Second, so-called negative campaigning isn't becoming more widespread. It just isn't.

Every campaign I have worked on, one wag once remarked, has always been called the most negative campaign yet. It's true, too: after every campaign, editorialists and political scientists churn out pious thumb-sucker opinion pieces about how awful and nasty and unpleasant the latest election was.

But the academics who know this area best, such as the University of Pennsylvania's Katherine Hall Jamieson, have produced plenty of studies to show that so-called negativity in political campaigns has become *less* frequent over the years, not *more*. Because the press love to focus on the inflammatory stuff during elections, you will see and read more about it. But that doesn't mean it is *happening* more frequently. According to Jamieson, attack campaigning has actually remained steady since 1960. Claims that the widespread use of negative advertising is to blame for shrinking numbers of people casting ballots are also suspect. Contrast ads, which Jamieson tracked in the 1996 Clinton-Dole presidential race, actually "increased both turnout and vote share." So there.

Third, don't be suspicious when you hear that political campaigns are researching the public record of the other side — be grateful. Politicians and aspiring politicians have records, and by that I don't mean criminal records (although some of them have those, too). I mean public records that tell voters something about how they can be expected to conduct themselves in office: things like their stands on different policies, or if they have a fondness for junkets and expense accounts, or their willingness to put partisanship ahead of principle, or whether they are dummies or not.

Not things like extramarital affairs or divorces or past use of marijuana, nothing like that. Just the things that matter — the things that are found on the public record. Whenever the media learn that opposition research teams are taking a look at these things that matter, they will call it a dirty tricks. But letting voters know about a politician's public record isn't a dirty tricks — it's a public service. If the media aren't inclined to do it, then it is incumbent upon political parties to step up to the plate.

There are clear limits to what is acceptable in oppo, and the public knows what they are. A 1998 survey by the Sorensen Institute for Political Leadership at the University of Virginia found that its respondents considered it to be "very or somewhat fair" to criticize one's opponent for "talking one way and voting another" (80.7 percent), "his or her voting record" (75.8 percent), "his or her business practices" (71 percent), and "taking money from special interest groups" (70.7 percent).

Political consultants are also well aware of the limits to political discourse. In January 1994, for example, the American Association of Political Consultants passed a code of ethics bylaw calling upon members not to make appeals based upon racism, gender, and so on; to refrain from false and misleading attacks on an opponent and the opponent's family; and to document carefully each and every criticism they voice about an opponent. Opposition research, when it restricts itself to the public record of a candidate, is always right and proper. If you still doubt that, cast your mind back to 1972: do you think a crook like Richard Nixon would have been re-elected had the Democrats been doing some smart oppo on the activities of his aptly named Committee to Re-Elect the President (CREEP)? Not on your life.

But can a war room go too far? Can a campaign get too tough? Can it backfire?

Yes, yes, and yes. Let me provide you with an example.

In 1993, on day thirty-eight of the forty-eight-day national election campaign, the Liberal war room snapped to attention. Late on a Thursday evening, while a few of us were still around campaign headquarters, CBC-TV reported that the Conservatives had prepared two attack ads on Jean Chrétien, which were to start airing the next night, a Friday. When the story aired, you could almost hear jaws dropping.

According to David McLaughlin, who acted as Kim Campbell's senior political and policy advisor during the 1993 federal election, the Tories' earlier attempts at campaign ads had been "decidedly curious [and] ineffective." No shit, Sherlock. They showed a seated Campbell speaking into the camera about some of her policy positions. Each ad concluded with the tag line "It's Time." What this meant, or what it was intended to achieve, was unclear to most everyone, including Conservatives. It's time for *what*? In *Poisoned Chalice*, his 1994 dissection of the failed Conservative campaign, McLaughlin noted, "[The tag line] said nothing to voters, thereby confirming the essential vacuousness of the campaign. In that sense it too was reinforcing, confirming the worst impressions voters were concluding about the Tories."

The new ads were different — very different. Using photographs that had been taken at Liberal campaign events just a few days before, the advertisements featured Jean Chrétien's face in close-up. In each, Chrétien's facial paralysis — acquired when he was young — was prominent. While the photographs flew past, unidentified voices could be heard criticizing the Liberal leader. "Does this look like a prime minister?" the ad asked, before the closer: "Think twice." One of the anonymous voices, belonging to a woman, said, "I personally would be very embarrassed if he were to become the prime minister of Canada." It was clear that the woman was referring to Chrétien's facial paralysis.

As the CBC news item on the new Tory ads was broadcast, two dozen Liberal campaign bosses crammed into Saturation Plaza to watch. When the ads were finished, there was silence in the room. No one knew quite what to say. Someone swore, as I recall. It was probably me (I swear too much).

It was possible, certainly, that the Progressive Conservatives had just committed ritual political suicide on a historic scale. There was also a possibility, however, that their ads, like most political campaign ads, had been rigorously tested in focus groups and had been found to be effective at some strategic level. Much later, in fact, we all heard that the principal instigators of the spots — the Conservatives' pollster Allan Gregg and future Ontario Conservative leader John Tory — had played them for focus groups without encountering any criticism.

Could such an approach work? The campaign's boss, John Rae, decided we should not respond right away. It was the right decision, but sleep, if it happened at all, was pretty brief for the members of the Liberal war room that night. Very early the next day, many of us were huddled around a table in the Liberal campaign's cluttered main conference room. We scanned the papers. Without exception, the Conservatives were being excoriated in the media for their decision to produce and broadcast the "face" ads. Editorial commentary, from coast to coast, was uniformly negative. In the avalanche of press criticism that followed, veteran *Globe and Mail* writer Kirk Makin spoke for many of the pundits:

> With the supposed *crème de la crème* of advertising people and pollsters at their disposal, the Tories have managed to step in every cow flap in the field ... The notorious Conservative ad showing Jean Chrétien's face frozen in contorted positions has won hands-down as the most bone-headed act of the election campaign. In 30 seconds of symbolism, the Conservatives seemed to confirm what disaffected voters have been telling anyone who will listen for weeks: politicians have no scruples. Politicians will do anything to get elected.

So-called attack ads had become relatively commonplace in the United States since 1988, when the Republicans' George Bush destroyed the Democrats' Michael Dukakis with a series of brutal spots. In Canada, however, those kinds of ads were seen far less frequently. Around the conference table at Liberal campaign headquarters, everyone knew that the Conservative ads had introduced a dramatically new dimension to the 1993 federal election campaign.

As was the case the previous night, we didn't know how, exactly, to react, or whether we should react at all. Once the newspapers, clippings, and broadcast summaries had been digested, there ensued a quiet debate about tactics. All of us were ardent Chrétien loyalists, and we were all pissed off by the nature of the attack on our guy. One group wanted to hit back, hard, and unleash some of the material that had been saved for what Roméo LeBlanc had called "a rainy day" — documents detailing several new Tory mini-scandals, most of them involving patronage appointments. Another group, no less angry, wanted to wait and see what happened; it was particularly important, they noted, that nothing be done until Jean Chrétien could comment on the ads. He would be doing so later, during a campaign stop in New Brunswick or Nova Scotia.

Whatever approach was taken — hit 'em hard and right away, or wait and see — all of us were a bit nervous. The Canadian media were climbing rhetorical heights to condemn attack advertising in general, and the Tory ads in particular. That was to be expected. But we also knew that attack ads were not used because politicians enjoyed being figuratively crucified by the news media; they were used because, often, they *worked*.

Gregg and Tory's campaign spots mocking Jean Chrétien were desperate and despicable and destructive. On that point, every adult Canadian agreed. Before any decision could be made on what to do about them, however, we Liberals needed to know whether the ads could harm the party's upward momentum. There was a possibility that the two thirty-second spots were the political equivalent of a Hail Mary pass. Or it was possible (probable, even) that the Tories possessed polling data showing that, in the eyes of one segment of the electorate that had been drifting away from them, the spots were effective.

Roméo LeBlanc observed us without comment, occasionally cupping his hand behind one ear to compensate for some hearing loss. When the debate appeared to have run its course, LeBlanc held up two fingers. "Two things," he said, arching his eyebrows. "First, we cannot be seen to be manipulating all of this. Canadians are very mad at the Tories, and we cannot risk them getting mad at us, too. They do not want to see us taking political advantage of this situation. Secondly, we need to remind them — without it looking like we are reminding them — that these Tory ads are un-Canadian. We need to take them to a place, a room, where they look around and say, 'I don't like where I am.' Do you understand what I am saying?"

"I think I do," I said. I waved a stack of pink message slips. "These are just a few of the messages our volunteers at the reception desk out front have been getting. People are plenty pissed off. And the ones who are calling in aren't just Liberals — a lot of them are Tories. Most of them are Tories, in fact. It's like they are calling us to confess, so we can give them absolution."

"Um, I have a bit of a confession to make," said one war room guy. "We called Tory headquarters already, and said we were concerned citizens — which we are. And the woman who answered sounded really, really frazzled. She said they've been getting calls all night. And she indicated that a lot of them are from Conservatives."

"There you go," I said. "There you go. We don't need to respond with outrage and indignation, or anything like that. We just need to make sure that our friends in the media get these." I waved the pink message slips around.

The Liberal war room discussed ways to ensure that the names and numbers of angry Canadians were disseminated to the news media. In that way, the story would mostly take care of itself. The strategy, in effect, was to let the Tories' error kill the Tories; there was no need to "pile on," as someone said. Some of us would contact media in Ottawa, some would notify reporters travelling with the Liberal leader, and some would find the press contingent travelling with Kim Campbell, so that she could be peppered with questions when she emerged from her hotel room. LeBlanc approved the plan.

The Liberal war members made their way back to Saturation Plaza, but I stopped to scan the Canadian Press (CP) newswire machine, clattering away in a corner. There was story after story about the Chrétien "face" ads, as they were starting to become known. While tearing off sheets containing CP stories about the Conservative-ad backlash, one of the receptionists approached me. A man was holding on one of the lines, she told me, and he said he wanted to speak with someone in charge. "He says he is a senior Conservative."

"I'm not in charge of anything," I said. "But then again, I doubt he's very senior."

"I'm not sure. He says his name is Sinclair Stevens."

I dashed back to my desk, located a notepad and a pen, and signalled for quiet. Sinclair Stevens was first elected to the House of Commons back in 1972, and was re-elected in every contest that followed until, as minister of industry in the government of Brian Mulroney, he became enmeshed in a nasty conflict-of-interest scandal. He resigned from cabinet in 1986, and did not run in the 1988 election that saw Mulroney returned to power with another big majority. Stevens, a lawyer, had a reputation for being tough and partisan. The notion that he would be calling a Liberal Party office for anything was bizarre.

I went through the preliminaries with the caller, trying to determine whether it was a prank call. The voice on the other end of the line certainly sounded like Sinclair Stevens. After being assured — falsely — that he was speaking to someone in a position of authority in the Liberal campaign, Stevens said that he was outraged about the CBC report about the Conservative ads.

"We have received many calls about the ads, Mr. Stevens," I told him. "Many of the calls are from Tories, too."

"Well, I think they are terrible, and I want Jean to know that there are some of us who weren't consulted about them, and we condemn them," he said. He went on like that for another couple of minutes, saying that he wanted the Liberal leader to know that he disagreed with what had been done.

"Do you think you could put that in writing, Mr. Stevens?" I asked him, going for broke. "Mr. Chrétien is on the road, as you know, but I could personally ensure that a letter from you gets to him very quickly."

There was a long pause. In Saturation Plaza, there was no sound. Finally, Stevens said, "Yes. Yes, I think I could do that. What is your fax number?"

At 3:12 p.m. that afternoon, the Honourable Sinclair Stevens's letter arrived at the war room, from his home in King County, Ontario. I read it aloud to the Task Force members in the war room, some of whom were punching the air in victory. Stevens wrote:

Dear Jean,

As a life-long Conservative, I am embarrassed at the tone of certain PC TV ads being currently run which attempt to depict you in an unfavourable light. This is beyond the bounds of decency and in my opinion should have no place in our democratic system. Certainly, as a 26-year member of our Queen's Privy Council, of which you also know I am a member, you deserve better. I have written to the Prime Minister, Kim Campbell, and requested that she immediately apologize to you and cause the offensive ads to be withdrawn forthwith. During my years in the House of Commons, when we were often on opposite sides of an issue, I found you to be an aggressive combatant but always fair. That is why I find it so reprehensible that certain current campaigners would discard years of tradition in their attempt to make an unfair point. It is a reflection not only on the Progressive Conservative Party, but also on the institution of the Parliament of Canada itself. Such ineptitude and contempt for traditional decent behaviour is shocking. I only hope you will get a decent apology.

> Sincerely yours, Sinclair Stevens.

The war room erupted in cheers as I made my way to the fax machine. Cover pages had already been made up.

An hour after Sinclair Stevens's letter to Jean Chrétien appeared on a fax machine at the Liberal Party's campaign headquarters, the Conservatives conceded that they had made a terrible, terrible mistake.

Speaking at an impromptu press conference in the lobby of the Hilton in Quebec City, where she had just met with a newspaper editorial board, Kim Campbell declared that the ads would be immediately stopped. "I would apologize to Mr. Chrétien and anyone who found them offensive," she said. The words seemed grudging, and anything but heartfelt. Campbell turned away from a stand-up microphone to return to her hotel suite, reporters shouting questions at her back. Upstairs, she broke down in tears.

According to David McLaughlin, her apology came after a "hellish" Friday morning. There had been calls to Campbell from assorted cabinet ministers, demanding that the ads be pulled. One of them, Public Security Minister Doug Lewis, issued a press release to that effect. Tory candidates across the country swamped the PC campaign staff with angry phone calls. Lawn signs were actually being returned by long-time Conservative supporters.

Initially, at least, the Conservative campaign's stalwarts elected to ride out the storm. A sheet called "Lines on the ads" was issued to candidates. "Our ads focus on the very questions we have been asking Mr. Chrétien for the last three months," the document stated. "We are simply raising questions about leadership — questions that Canadians themselves are asking. The photographs are not the issue — they are no different than the cover of the most recent *Maclean's* magazine, and were taken in one day last week. Our new radio ads ask the same questions in the same manner." Real Canadians had been used in the spots, the "Lines" document noted, not actors.

In the space of a few hours, the "face" ad controversy mushroomed. A disabled member of the Alberta legislature had filed a complaint about the ads to the Canadian Human Rights Commission on the grounds that they "exploited a disability." A spokesman for the federal broadcasting regulator, the Canadian Radio-television and Telecommunications Commission, confirmed that the advertisements were being investigated. Our Task Force, meanwhile, had obtained a copy of an internal memorandum of the Telecaster Committee of Canada, a watchdog that scrutinizes all television commercials to ensure that they contain no "portrayals likely to be offensive to the majority of viewers." According to the memo, issued to networks and stations across Canada, the commercials "may be offensive to some viewers as they may be interpreted as a personal attack on Jean Chrétien. These spots may be seen as ridiculing Mr. Chrétien's facial paralysis and we have received complaints from viewers and member stations. You may therefore wish to view these commercials prior to airing." That memo, too, was circulated to the news media by the Liberal war room.

Because he knows a thing or two about politics, Jean Chrétien also knew it was important to approach the issue of the Progressive

Conservative's two thirty-second spots with great care. So, when he appeared at a campaign stop in New Brunswick, Chrétien said, "It's true that I have a physical defect. When I was a kid, people were laughing at me. But I accepted that, because God gave me other qualities and I'm grateful." The crowd erupted in cheers and applause; the Tories' humiliation, at that point, was complete.

Some years later, Allan Gregg sits in his cluttered office on Avenue Road in Toronto, a block or so north of the Four Seasons Hotel and the Royal Ontario Museum, his feet on his desk, remembering.

"The weak link for Chrétien was economic knowledge and representing Canada abroad," he says, words spinning out of him at a pace that reflects the exceedingly smart person that he is. "Those are always tough for an Opposition leader. So we sent a photographer out to a Liberal rally and got a bunch of pictures. And I remember talking to Tom Scott, and saying these are the ones we've chosen. We chose them because they weren't particularly flattering, but they also weren't particularly awful. There were worse ones we could use, and there were better ones we could use. We thought those ones were really typical."

When the two thirty-second spots were put together, Gregg and Scott showed them to a focus group. "Lo and behold!" says Gregg, laughing. "The response was really good. Really good." He pauses. "The story, which you can believe or not believe …" He trails off, shaking his head, scratching at his beard.

It is apparent that Allan Gregg does not have many fond memories about his work on the 1993 Progressive Conservative federal election campaign, and no one can blame him for that. After all, he had experienced many more wins than losses until that point in his political career: more than fifty campaigns, most of them victories. An Edmonton native, with a bachelor's and a master's degree from the University of Alberta, Gregg was drawn into Tory politics while pursuing a Ph.D. at Carleton University in Ottawa in the 1970s. He had long hair, he swore a lot, and he dressed like a member of a rock band, but he won a job at the Research Bureau of the Opposition leader on Parliament Hill.

Within three years of his arrival on Parliament Hill, Gregg was number three in the Tories' campaign hierarchy. His understanding of the intricacies of public opinion polling techniques, along with how to make use of polling data to craft effective campaign communications and strategy and tactics, made him unique in Canadian politics. The Liberals had their own pollster, Marty Goldfarb, and their own media manipulators, such as Roméo LeBlanc, but no one else had a pollster and a media manipulator embodied in a single person. Gregg helped Conservatives win elections, federally and provincially, time after time.

He went on to found multi-million-dollar companies like Decima Research and Public Affairs International, but the events of the fall of 1993 stuck with him like an unwanted house guest. Years later, Conservatives continue to blame the Chrétien "face" ads for a large part of the 1993 election rout, where they saw their 169-seat parliamentary majority reduced to 2 seats. Many of those same Conservatives also still blame Gregg — and Tom Scott, and senior campaign strategists John Tory and Tom Trbovich — for what happened.

There is a pause, so I ask Gregg The Question, still unresolved after so many years. In her bestselling book, *Time and Chance*, Kim Campbell called the spots "completely unintelligent" and "disgusting," and suggested that Gregg and his colleagues were "obtuse" to have developed them in the first place. She emphatically denied that she had seen them in advance, let alone approved them. So, I ask, why did Gregg and Tom Scott and John Tory and the others actually conspire to put the ads on the air without Kim Campbell seeing them, or any of her senior campaign staff, or anyone else?

He looks as if he is about to spit. "I talked to Kim Campbell *that* morning, *that* morning that they went on the air," he says, his finger stabbing the air for emphasis. "The whole campaign group saw them. Everyone. What was never anticipated by any of us was that the allegation would be made that we were making fun of Chrétien's face. When you think about it, when you actually stop and think about it, and you assume for a second that I and John Tory and Tom Trbovich and Tom Scott are stupid, and that we're all bad people. And we're sitting around a table and we're twenty-one points behind the Grits, and we go, 'You know what? You know what will really work? Let's make fun of the guy's face!' Fuck!" He laughs, long and hard. "We would never do that in a million *years*! We just never anticipated the reaction we got. It never came up in any of the focus groups — at all. But once the allegation was made, holy shit *la merde*!"

IN 1991, A STUDY conducted by the Royal Commission on Electoral Reform and Party Financing concluded that tough stuff would almost certainly become an ongoing feature of future Canadian elections. The study noted:

> Throughout our interviews with party strategists and advertising agency executives, we were struck by the number of respondents who remarked, unprompted by our questions, that the "old rules" about what was permissible in campaigns, particularly in campaign advertising, had been shattered. While not dismissing obvious sins of past campaigns, a number of those whom we interviewed felt that they had been dealt low blows in the last campaign, and at least some looked forward to settling the score. According to one respondent, "We never believed anybody could stoop that low. We were wrong. We'll shoot first next time!"

The Tories "face" spots were, along with being offensive to many people, probably unoriginal. In September 1968, in the United States, the Democratic Party's advertising team produced a spot called "Heartbeats" to support the effort to elect Hubert H. Humphrey and Edmund Muskie and defeat the Richard M. Nixon/Spiro Agnew Republican ticket. In the ad, a camera pulls back to reveal a single, simple question: "Agnew for Vice-President?" In the background, an unidentified person is heard — according to the spot's storyboard — laughing "uncontrollably." The tag line to the ad read, "This would be funny if it weren't so serious." Twenty-five years later, Nixon speech writer William Safire called the spot "the most distasteful, unfair and audience-insulting commercial" he had seen in years.

Unlike the Americans, Canadians have been relatively silent on the subject. American academics, columnists, and television analysts endlessly poke through the entrails of political spots, in some cases even running regular "Ad Watch" features in newspapers, to determine the reliability of claims made in campaign commercials, but Canadians usually do not.

One exception came six years after the 1993 election, when a group of Ontario and Quebec professors dispassionately dissected the television advertising campaigns of the Liberals, Conservatives, New Democrats, and Reformers in that campaign.

In their slim study, the professors, mainly from the universities of Laval and Windsor, examined all of the advertising broadcast during the 1993 campaign. According to the rules promulgated in the Canada Elections Act, partisan ads were permitted only for the final four weeks of the campaign period, with no advertising allowed on the day before voting and on election day itself.

The Tories were the most enthusiastic advertisers: their spots account for thirty-five of the fifty-seven English-language ads run by the four major parties contesting the 1993 election. The PC commercials ran 230 times, which meant that the Tories took up nearly 50 percent of the political advertising broadcast time. The Liberals came next, with eleven different ads, almost all of which ended with Jean Chrétien saying, "I have the people, I have the plan. We will make a difference." The Grit contributions were televised 123 times, giving the party 26 percent of the overall total.

The New Democrats ran nine ads on eighty-one occasions, many of them very negative; four of the spots, called "Voices," were shot in black and white and showed various Canadians literally yelling about health care, patronage, free trade, and unemployment. Despite their third-party status, the NDP telecast percentage was not far behind that of the Liberals, at 17 percent. The nascent Reform Party, meanwhile, broadcast two ads on democratic reform and fiscal responsibility, ending with the tag line "Reform — now you have a choice."

The French-language campaigns of the Tories and the Grits were more evenly matched, with the former producing eleven spots and the latter sixteen; overall, the Liberals were on air in Quebec most often, with 40 percent of the total political telecast time, compared to the Conservatives' 35 percent.

Most of the parties' English-language ads ran on the CBC, with 72 percent of spots airing on the public broadcaster, while a puny 28 percent could be found on its private sector rival, CTV. The vast majority of the ads produced by all of the parties were the same length — nearly two-thirds of them were thirty seconds. The remainder clocked in at a minute or two.

The arguments for pulling the infamous Jean Chrétien "face" ads were straightforward enough. One, the negatives evidently far outweighed the positives; after all, even Conservative candidates were taking to the air to condemn them. Two, Chrétien had, in Allan Gregg's own words, "brilliantly" counter-punched with his comments in New Brunswick, and thereby deflated any benefits the spots could offer. Three, and most compellingly of all, pulling the ads was simply the right thing to do. The political discourse had, in the view of a lot of people, been demeaned by a pair of poorly executed television commercials. In politics, criticizing an opponent's public policy record is fine. Criticizing their physical appearance is not.

In the end, and contrary to the Parliament Hill mythology that developed in the years that followed, neither the Liberal Party nor its war room single-handedly stirred up public outrage against the ill-fated Conservative attack ads. The Tories did that all by themselves.

And what did the academics think about the Chrétien "face" spots? Two of them, Laval University communications professor André Gosselin and University of Windsor political science professor Walter Soderlund, interviewed a number of partisans to assess the damage caused by the ads. Long-time Conservative Bill Neville claimed they cost his party more than fifty seats. A New Democrat strategist, Michael Balagus, estimated that the spots defeated Tory candidates in more than two dozen ridings.

"Whatever the likely number," note Gosselin and Soderlund, "the decision to run these two ads has to rank as the single greatest blunder in the history of advertising in Canadian elections."

No arguments here!

IN THE 2000 FEDERAL ELECTION CAMPAIGN — and in many campaigns since — others and I stayed up until all hours, working on punctuation.

That's right, punctuation. Where a period or a comma should go, where an ellipsis can be placed. I recall one day where a dozen of us sat in a cramped room at Liberal headquarters and debated where the dot-dot-

dots needed to go in a quote we were attributing to Canadian Alliance Leader Stockwell Day in a terrific television commercial that had been put together by Don Millar. We didn't get in trouble, as things turned out, for the placement of the ellipsis. We got in trouble with the *Globe and Mail* for when, exactly, the newspaper's name flashed on the TV screen as a source. I kid you not.

When getting tough with an opponent — in paid media (with advertisements) or in earned media (with a pithy quote) — there are three rules you must always observe. One, the critical statement of fact you are making about your opponent has to be scrupulously accurate. No ifs, ands, or buts. Check it a dozen times, then check it again. Two, the allegation you are making must be an even-handed take on the facts — that is, it can't be so wildly out of context that it offends people's sense of fairness. It should heap ridicule on an opponent, not invite it against you. Three, the critical statement must be on the public record — what is sometimes called "quotes and votes." Nothing about a person's personal life. (And particularly, nothing that attacks the way that they look.)

If you don't obey these rules, you will end up doing a lot of damage to your cause, your candidate, and yourself. Ask Allan Gregg or John Tory, or the other geniuses behind the "face" ads. They'll tell you.

Pick your fights, goes the saying, and the saying is right. You shouldn't take a swing at everything that moves. Instead, pick a fight you can win. Pick a fight when you are ready. Most of all, pick a fight only for a cause you believe in. *Don't waste your passion.*

For me, it is — among other things — the fight against Big Tobacco. For you, it might be something else. Find out. Then get passionate, get involved, and get tough!

Get the Facts and Numbers!

It being September 6, and the first Saturday in the 2003 Ontario provincial election campaign, nobody was really expecting it to be all that busy. It's Saturday morning, right? What could happen on a Saturday morning?

Plenty, as things turned out. Mid-morning, my BlackBerry and cell-phone started to buzz like crazy. Our leader, Dalton McGuinty, had been doing a leisurely meet-and-greet thing at Toronto's St. Lawrence Market with some candidates and supporters. Everything had been swell until a young guy — an exceedingly well-groomed young guy — started hollering at McGuinty.

The young guy yelled that teachers' unions had ruined his education, that he disliked McGuinty's policies, and blah blah blah. Sounded like a Tory, so one of our guys — long-time Liberal Michael Colle — hollered back that the young guy was "a Tory plant," which was eminently plausible. He then swore at the young guy, which was understandable, but not always a good idea when reporters are nearby.

The young guy started to taunt Colle, as our advance team hustled to get McGuinty out of there. "Are you going to hit me?" he said to Colle, who looked like he had certainly entertained the thought.

A couple of reporters started asking the young "student" who he was. He declined at first, and then nervously mumbled that he was nineteen years old and his name was John Leahy. He said he was at the St. Lawrence Market to "pick up apples." Uh-huh. Sure. Call me crazy, but nobody with a haircut *that* neat is hanging out in the market early on a Saturday, looking for apples.

One of our advance guys caught the guy's name and flipped it on his BlackBerry to my pal Charlie Angelakos, a Chrétien-era legend who was running our tour operation. Charlie jogged into my cubbyhole in the war room and gave me John Leahy's name.

Google didn't immediately provide what I wanted. I tried variations on his name, and on the spelling. Pay dirt! Our "student" was the director of recruitment for the Progressive Conservative Youth Association. I printed out a copy of his official résumé before someone could remove it. Then, with my tape recorder whirring away, I called Conservative headquarters. "Hi," I said. "Is John Leahy there?"

Said the nice receptionist lady, "Oh, no, dear, he's out at an event right now. Would you like his voice mail?"

"No, thanks, ma'am," I said. "I've got what I need."

We quickly notified the leader's tour team, so they could tell the reporters travelling with them — some of whom were still in the process of leaving St. Lawrence Market. We put together talking points making fun of the Tories, calling them dishonourable and nervous about McGuinty's momentum and stuff like that. And then we faxed and emailed Leahy's résumé to every reporter covering the election.

From the moment the neatly barbered Tory hack had started yelling at Dalton McGuinty to the dissemination of his resume and the talking points, about forty-five minutes had gone by. I was irritated about that, frankly. Typically, we aimed for a thirty-minute response time — from the happening of an event to the issuance of a press release, or a backgrounder, or a call to a reporter, or something on our website. But for a Saturday, not bad.

Within hours, all of the radio and TV stations were reading the Broadcast News copy, over and over: "Tempers flared on the campaign trail when Liberal member Mike Colle angrily confronted a student during a morning meet-and-greet at a Toronto market with party leader Dalton McGuinty. When a student in crowd began shouting that teacher unions had ruined his education, Colle became incensed, accusing the teen of being placed in the crowd by the Conservatives. The Liberals produced a resumé saying the young man, John Leahy, was a recruitment director for the PC Youth Association of Ontario. Leahy rejected suggestions he'd been planted by the Tories, saying he was at the market to pick up apples."

End result: the Conservatives looked stupid, dishonest, and desperate. We looked — reporters later told us — fast and organized. As one remarked to me: "This opposition research stuff actually works, doesn't it?"

It does, it does: on campaign 2003, for instance, we didn't encounter too many hecklers after that Saturday. In any campaign, facts and numbers are pretty important. You need the facts to tell compelling stories about both you and your opponent. And then you need the numbers — otherwise known as public opinion research — to see if your facts are persuading folks to vote the right way (that is, for you, or, at the very least, against your opponent).

That's what this chapter is about: getting the facts and the numbers you need to win.

NOTWITHSTANDING THE MANY MYTHOLOGIES that have developed around James Carville's War Room, and just about every other war room, opposition research is neither new nor glamorous. It is, instead, frequently boring work that has been done in political campaigns since the beginning of time.

Sometimes it wins campaigns, and sometimes it doesn't. But it's *always* worth doing.

Two hundred years ago, for example, oppo researchers with the Federalist Party campaign discovered that Thomas Jefferson, the author of the Declaration of Independence, had several mistresses, all of them slaves. The researchers even determined that Jefferson had fathered children with one of the slaves, Sally Hemings (DNA testing of Jefferson and Hemings's descendants in 2000, almost exactly two hundred years after the fact, determined that the story was almost certainly true). When the Federalists made their charges public, Jefferson never responded. Anti-Jefferson newspapers warned voters against him, and not very subtly, either: "Murder, robbery, rape, adultery, and incest will be openly taught and practiced, the air will be rent with the cries of the distressed, the soil will be soaked with blood, and the nation black with crimes." Jefferson was elected anyway, and served as president for nearly a decade.

The Thomas Jefferson story is a useful one to remember, right off the top: while oppo is vital to any modern political campaign, and while it can be effective — as with our apple-buying, clean-cut Tory heckler — it shouldn't be the central focus of the campaign. That is, criticizing an opponent isn't all you need to do to win.

Oppo is just one part of a large and complex campaign organization, drawing together press relations, polling, field organization, debate preparation, advertising, and the candidate's own retail politicking. At best, an oppo team's damaging revelation will throw an opponent off his or her campaign message for a day or so, like our St. Lawrence Market discovery did. But rarely will it wipe out a strong contender's chances. Thomas Jefferson proved that.

Until 1992 or so, few campaigns could afford the sort of oppo team that people like James Carville and George Stephanopoulos perfected. In local campaigns, particularly, candidates could not find the money or the technology needed to do proper opposition research. Some hired private investigators, but these were expensive, and, if voters found out, they could be politically costly, too.

By the early 1990s in the United States, however, oppo started to come into its own. Larry Sabato, one of the most acute observers of the unloved, misunderstood species that calls itself a political consultant, estimates that there was a 200 percent growth in opposition research firms in the U.S. in this period. Such paid, full-time professional political consultants, as opposed to the ad hoc, decidedly amateurish political consultants that had preceded them, had become a big, multi-million-dollar business.

One reason for the huge growth in the number of professional political consultants was the injection of large sums of cash into the system by aspiring politicians and advocacy groups. Both the politicians and the special interest lobbies needed people who could run effective campaigns in a complex and competitive media environment. A second reason, in the United States at least, was a continual election cycle, encompassing myriad never-ending congressional, senatorial, primary, and presidential races. There is, as things turned out, always a market for campaign specialists. A third reason was the technological advances that enabled the media, and politicians, to do things that had been previously only dreamed of. In the case of politicos, for example, computers permitted even the most modest campaign to develop crucial databases containing information about supporters, as well as information about the activities and statements of opponents.

Despite its successes, and despite the fact that oppo is now a component of virtually every large election campaign effort in the United States, Canada, and Europe, it is not always popular with the people who ultimately benefit from it. Politicians will often express hesitation, or even hostility, about the need to undertake opposition research (I always insist on doing on it my side's candidate as well as the other side's). James Carville, for one, doesn't agree with the naysayers. "Look," he told me, "the best way to do this game is to get all your information, and then get all your information out. The voters deserve more information, you know? We're not in this business to be mean or negative. We're in it to draw distinctions, and to draw distinctions that favour our side. So we just go out and try and be very honest about these distinctions, these differences."

Along with being (hopefully) both accurate and factual in highlighting what Carville calls political distinctions, it is also vital that the oppo work be done as quickly as possible. That twenty-four-hour, seven-days-a-week news cycle leaves you with no other choice. These days, he and others note, "opposition research" and "quick response" are usually mentioned in the same context. One isn't very effective without the other.

Carville recalls that the team he headquartered and built from scratch in Little Rock knew that the information they passed on to reporters had to be both reliable and quick. Says Carville, "Well, it was one of those ideas that just kind of grew out of necessity, you know? We have these sort of compressed news cycles now. A long time ago, I would have eighteen war room guys, and one of them would be pecking away on an Underwood typewriter, and the rest of them would come and look over his shoulder. And that was about 80 percent of what was going on." He laughs. "But now, if you have a political event, the media guys — these guys on CNN and MSNBC and all the talk shows and the columnists — are going to be dying to find out what's going on before it does. So you just got to be on top of everything that is going on, and you got to be on top of everything fucking fast. I mean, that is the whole name of the game now."

Fellow Clinton confidante Betsey Wright agrees with Carville about the need for speed (although the pair often clashed about strategy during that first Clinton presidential campaign). "We had to be in the same news story [in Houston], to try and minimize any damage [the GOP] would try to do. They were just wild with made-up stories," she says. "There were Republican people walking all over Arkansas, handing out tens of thousands of dollars to people to make up stories and lie, and we were doing our best to keep up with that. You have to be in the same news story. Otherwise, it gets engraved in the public's minds without your response, and the next day they and the media move onto something else."

How do oppo types do oppo? Most of the time, by poring over stacks of mundane reports and newspaper clippings. This kind of work is done by studious, methodical political staffers who pay attention to detail. Once something is found — something that is embarrassing, or outrageous, or just plain wrong — it is checked, then rechecked, then saved in a database or a filing cabinet. At the appropriate moment, the quick response team will kick into gear. The quick response types, unlike their opposition research counterparts, are communicators. (Some of them, like me, are bigmouths, too.) Their stock-in-trade is aggressively marketing what the oppo researchers dig up — to reporters, or voters, or whoever is paying attention. Quick response people throw whatever they can at whatever wall is available, and see what sticks. Their favoured tools are repetition, pithiness, and volume.

Most of the time, opposition research focuses upon a politician's public life — the votes he or she made in the legislature, the curriculum vitae he or she bragged about, the travel costs he or she passed along to the taxpayer. Few folks would argue that an opponent's public record should be exempt from scrutiny. It is one of the main ways, and sometimes the only way, voters can make informed choices on election day. A louder debate, naturally, rages about the ethicality of probing a politician's personal life. Is it fair to publicize long-ago bounced cheques, or drug use, or draft dodging? Is it right?

As a rule, and as I've said before, I don't like it. But, as in most matters political, not everyone agrees with me. There are situations, I concede, where it is fair to probe someone's personal life. In the 1992 presidential race, for example, George Bush's campaign warriors were fighting a battle on two fronts. On the one flank were the likes of James Carville and Betsey Wright, emphasizing the negatives in Bush's record and responding quickly to attacks on Bill Clinton's. On the other flank were the crazed, far-right Republican forces of Patrick Buchanan, who was challenging Bush for the GOP nomination. Buchanan — a knuckle-dragging mouth breather who applauded Hitler and called Capitol Hill "occupied" Israeli territory — was a former speech writer to Richard Nixon and Ronald Reagan. With his goofy "America First" themes, he struck a responsive chord with delegates interested in protectionist and/ or xenophobic bullshit.

Bush's sharp opposition researchers did not have to look very far, or very long, to produce evidence, taken from Buchanan's private life, to demonstrate that their opponent was a rank hypocrite. Buchanan, they learned, drove a Mercedes-Benz sedan, a European car. Bush's oppo team quickly developed a spot depicting the noisy Republican challenger as an utter hypocrite. No one, apart from Buchanan's puny band of kooky followers, suggested that digging into an opponent's personal life, in this instance, was inappropriate. It was, in fact, the right thing to do. And it worked: after Buchanan showed some early strength in the primaries, Bush went on to decisively beat him.

In developing an oppo file on a political adversary, particularly one who has a long record of public service, there are many and diverse public sources of information. The first place to look for material, generally, is a candidate's voting record: most jurisdictions now place the information on-line. It is also considered to be the safest area to probe. Public opinion research consistently shows that how a politician casts a vote —

in a legislature, in a committee, or anywhere else — is of greatest interest to voters.

At this level, opposition researchers are always interested in votes that a politician missed. While voters generally will put up with a small amount of incumbent absenteeism — say, missing one in four votes — politicians who miss a lot of votes are potentially exposing themselves to a lot of trouble. Speeches made to support, or oppose, a proposed law should also be scrutinized for contradictions, fibs, or embarrassments. Sponsorship of a bill or a legislative change is always worth examining, too.

One of George Bush's most effective political operatives was the late Lee Atwater, and one of Atwater's oldest disciples is Rod Shealy, a rumpled and bearded southern Republican. His tough approach to politics, particularly in direct mail campaigns at the constituency level, has earned him rebukes on the front page of the *New York Times* and even on *Court TV*. But the Republican tactician is unrepentant. "I don't do negative campaigns," he says. "I say that anything that is on the public record, that's not negative." Atwater taught Shealy that the timing and the credibility of the charge are critical when getting tough with an opponent. "It has to be fair game," says Shealy. "And anything that is on the public record, that is about a public official discharging their public duties, is obviously fair game."

To opposition researchers, one of the best sources of material are reversals made on previously held positions — the cherished "flip-flops."

In the 1993 Canadian federal election campaign, the Liberal war room put together a list of Conservative government reversals, particularly those of their newly minted leader, Kim Campbell. (I'll use Campbell as a bit of a case study, here, because she provided such a rich vein of oppo material for us nasty Liberal war room types.) In a confidential talking points document I wrote in September 1993 for use by Liberal candidates, we accused Campbell of whiplash-inducing flip-flops on Medicare user fees, research and development programs, deficit reduction, and a program to assist impoverished groups in their court challenges. But the focus of the document was another reversal: Campbell's decision to cancel an order for seven of fifty multi-million-dollar EH-101 helicopters. For most of the spring, Campbell had repeatedly insisted in the House of Commons that the government was right to spend $5.8 billion on the high-tech machines. But with the economy way down, and unemployment and the deficit way up, the Liberals decided to turn the purchase into an election issue. I wrote in the talking points:

> With today's cancellation of part of the copter purchase — one of the largest expenditures of its type in Canadian history — Campbell portrayed herself as indecisive and desperate and without a coherent plan for governing. For months, Liberals have called upon Campbell and her Tory government to cancel the EH-101 program, and spend money where it is needed — on job creation, on infrastructure, on cash-strapped social programs like Medicare … Kim Campbell's election-eve, death-bed semi-repentance on the EH-101s speaks volumes about her desperation, indecisiveness and lack of credibility. It speaks volumes about the decision-making ability of a politician who can say for months how crucial something is, then suddenly decide — when voting day is nearing — that a change of heart will gain an extra few seats.

In the document, I harped upon Campbell's decision-making abilities because secret Liberal Party polling had revealed that the public was uncertain about whether she could be trusted to make the right decisions, and to stick with them. To drive home the point, we dispatched a young Liberal to don a chicken suit and chase Campbell at an Ottawa speech, mocking her for her refusal to publicly debate the wisdom of the helicopter purchase. The Grit chicken was mentioned in most news stories written about the EH-101 "flip-flop."

For opposition researchers, another rich vein of public record material is what is sometimes called "resumé inflation." In any campaign, big or small, a smart oppo operative will closely examine an adversary's resumé to find contradictions, exaggerations, or plain old lies. In 1982, for example, long before she would become a household name in Canada, Campbell was a law student and was seeking an elected position with the

Vancouver school board. A *Vancouver Sun* reporter asked Campbell, and all of the other candidates in the race, to provide a short biography and position statement. In part, Campbell's read: "A graduate of the University of B.C. and the London School of Economics, a political scientist, a teacher and third-year law student, Kim is running for her second term on the school board."

While she was certainly a UBC grad, Campbell had not graduated from the London School of Economics. She had received funding from the Canadian government to attend the prestigious British institution, but she never completed her thesis, one of the conditions of her receiving financial support in the first place. Using Access to Information legislation, our team of oppo workers and other Liberals obtained all of the letters authored by Campbell and the government bureaucrats hounding her about her unfinished thesis. We also made certain that the letters found their way into the hands of reporters, resulting in two damaging stories: one, Kim Campbell apparently fibbed about graduating from the London School of Economics. Two, she didn't pay back the money taxpayers provided her to *attend* the London School of Economics. Oops!

Along with voting records and curricula vitae, oppo teams love expense account embarrassments — details about how much an opponent spent on a taxpayer-funded trip, or for staffing a political office, or for office renovations, or for a meal at a ritzy restaurant. Abuse of so-called franking privileges — mailing out tons of political propaganda at taxpayer expense — is also important. Another favourite is voting for one's own pay raise, which all politicians regularly do, or inflating one's pension. In the big scheme of things, of course, with governments and legislatures disbursing billions on all manner of goods and services, such stuff shouldn't matter much. But with voters, as one wag once put it, political graves are often dug with small shovels. It's the little things that'll kill you. (And, like Michael Marzolini told us, a lot of voters don't know how many million are in a billion. But they sure as hell know what it means when a politico spends hundreds of taxpayer bucks on a boozy dinner with his mistress — it means the end of said politico's career.)

Following Kim Campbell's victory in June 1993 at the Progressive Conservative leadership convention, the Liberal war room flooded Access to Information bureaucrats with demands for Campbell's expense accounts and travel spending. The Conservative government dragged its feet in releasing any documents, naturally. That wasn't a surprise. So we pulled out an atlas and calculated how many kilometres Campbell had travelled since her installation as prime minister, and multiplied that figure by the per-kilometre cost the Canadian auditor general had established for the use of government Challenger jets. To dispute our math, Campbell's minions would've been forced to release the real numbers. They never did.

There are other sources of public documents that candidates sometimes neglect to closely examine: court records of bankruptcies and lawsuits (someone sent us nasty affidavit material about one of Campbell's divorces, but we refused to make any use of it); property records (to see who holds mortgages or liens against the property of candidates, which, in Campbell's case, was nothing inappropriate or out of the ordinary); and lists of political donors. Who is donating dough is very important in any opposition research effort, and has always been a source of political embarrassment and scandal and whatnot.

From 1992 onwards (before Kim Campbell was appointed minister of national defence by Brian Mulroney in January 1993, and before she had won the Progressive Conservative leadership in June 1993), the Liberal Party's war room carefully scrutinized the names of companies and individuals that had donated money to Campbell during her campaign to represent Vancouver Centre in the 1993 election. One of the oppo staffers assigned to the task, my buddy Marc Laframboise, noted that one of the companies that had donated to Campbell shared the same name as a company that received a lucrative national defence contract after Campbell became minister of national defence. If the two companies were the same, or somehow related, it could have meant a huge political scandal. After many days of investigation, Laframboise determined that the two companies were owned and run by different people. The shared name was merely a coincidence. So we dropped the matter, a little disappointed, but relieved that we had checked. Checking one's facts is always a good idea.

The Conservatives, who maintained their own oppo/quick response team during the 1993 Canadian federal election, learned this lesson the hard way.

In September 1993, stories had been swirling about what Jean Chrétien planned to put in his campaign platform, and when he planned to release it. It was dubbed the Red Book by those of us in the campaign (mainly because its covers would be Liberal red), and a vigorous debate had taken place about whether to release it at the start of the campaign (thereby risking that its contents, and news value, would be lost by the end of the race), release it at the end of the campaign (thereby risking that it would arrive too late to positively influence voters), or break it up into pieces and release it at different points in the seven-week campaign (thereby diluting the impact that a single dramatic release might have). The decision, appropriately, was made by Jean Chrétien — to release all of the Red Book close to the start of the election, on September 15.

A lot of hype and speculation preceded the launch of the Red Book, and the Tories were clearly spooked by it. Lacking any kind of a coherent campaign document of their own, Campbell's campaign made the right decision — to pull out the stops and attack the Liberal platform with every weapon in their arsenal. The Tory oppo team, PC Caucus Services, got to work.

On the afternoon of September 14, the day before we were scheduled to reveal the Red Book in an Ottawa hotel, the Tories struck. They chose the late afternoon because, they knew, it was not too late to get something into the next day's papers and that evening's broadcasts, but it was probably too late for a reporter to properly check out whatever the Conservative war room was offering up. As it turned out, what they were offering up was pretty impressive: a thick blue binder, 102 pages long, couriered to reporters all over Parliament Hill. We were able to intercept a copy by pleading with a friendly journalist.

The blue binder contained a number of out-of-context snippets of speeches by Liberal members of Parliament, policy statements, and some press clippings. Campbell's former key election aide, David McLaughlin, describes it best in *Poisoned Chalice*: "Conservative headquarters decided that the most effective focus of attack on the Liberal platform was its putative costs. On the day before the platform was released, PC Caucus Services (the party's research arm) made public its calculations of Liberal promises to date, which they claimed totalled some $22 billion. This pre-emptive strike was designed to knock the Grits off-balance and drive the media questioning of their platform the next day."

But the Tories, as McLaughlin himself admits in his book, made a fatal error. They injected way too much spin into their oppo.

For example, the blue binder stated that the Liberals planned to spend "0.7 per cent of Gross National Product for international aid, as soon as possible." That was equivalent to $17.8 billion, by far the largest chunk of the Tories' $22 billion spending figure.

We quickly brought together some of our best campaign people. It was essential, everyone knew, that we rebut the international aid claim. A couple of guys noted that the "0.7 per cent of GNP" figure was in fact merely a goal, and not a firm commitment. What's more, we were told, the Liberals weren't the only ones who had pledged this. Both Brian Mulroney, the former Conservative prime minister, and Jean Charest, the minister of the environment and Campbell's principal opponent in the Conservative leadership race, had told the June 1992 Rio de Janeiro Summit that the 0.7 percent target was one the Tories supported, too. A quick scan of our four-thousand-quote database demonstrated that no less than Kim Campbell, in May 1993, had also backed the Rio target. Ha!

Clutching the quotes from the likes of Campbell, Charest, and Mulroney, I jumped in front of the nearest computer terminal and started typing. A couple of war roomers hovered above me, contributing lines. The heading: "Liberal Response to the $22 Billion Tory 'Big Lie' Document."

"If Kim Campbell and her Conservatives spent as much time trying to repair the damage they have done to the Canadian economy as on their 102-page 'Big Lie' document, we would all be in a lot better shape," it began. "The Conservatives are running scared[,] that is why they have prepared a document that responds to a Liberal platform that hasn't even been released yet! ... The Canadian people won't be fooled by the politics of desperation."

As things turned out, neither was the Parliamentary Press Gallery. The Tory attack had failed. McLaughlin admitted as much, when he later wrote that our group had "undermined" the Tory war room: "It took [us] weeks to overcome the credibility problem with the media that ensued." After scanning our document and the Conservative binder, the *Globe and Mail*'s bureau chief (and now its editor), Edward Greenspon, said, "Man, did [they] ever fuck up."

We knew we had scored a bit of a coup when, shortly after we distributed our talking points hither and yon, CBC Newsworld's Don Newman held them up, live and on camera. "These are from the Liberals, responding to this," he said, then holding up the blue binder. "We got the Liberal response to the Tory document before we had even received the Tory document. Canadian politics, it seems, has embraced the high-tech, quick-response techniques of American politics."

We cheered and clapped each other on the back, partly because we had beaten the Tories, but partly because Don Newman was right. The rules of the game had changed: oppo was here to stay.

Told this story many years later, James Carville gives another one of his famous laughs. "You know," he says, "you may have been a lot more sensitive about your politics in Canada way back when. But, in Canada and everywhere else, the media age has kind of changed things, you know? You used to have a little less aggressiveness in your politics, and a hell of a lot less than in American politics. But that's all different now, ain't it?"

IT AIN'T "DEWEY DEFEATS TRUMAN," admittedly, but you have to concede — quite a few of the media prognostications and predictions about the Liberal Party's year 2006 leadership race were dramatically, hilariously inaccurate. Let me refresh your memory.

"Dewey Defeats Truman," history buffs will recall, was the headline on the front page of the November 3, 1948, edition of the *Chicago Daily Tribune*. Mixing equal parts partisanship and incompetence, the newspaper's staff wrongly proclaimed Republican presidential candidate Thomas E. Dewey's victory over incumbent Democrat Harry S. Truman. Oops.

The *Tribune*, like most of the nation's newspapers and columnists that year, had been relying heavily — way too heavily, as things turned out — on the nascent public opinion polls of the Gallup organization, which had shown Dewey in the lead. "This is for the [history] books," said a grinning Truman, when handed a copy of the *Tribune*. It sure was.

Which brings us, about six decades later, to the leadership race of the Liberal Party of Canada, and what assorted Canadian polling and media organizations had told us all to expect in the lead-up to the Grits' so-called Super Weekend of delegate selection — wherein, like a U.S. presidential primary, a whole bunch of partisans were voting for delegate spots at the leadership convention, to be held in Montreal that December. Prominent among those whose forecasting went awry: the *Globe and Mail*, *Toronto Star*, the *Sun*, Strategic Counsel, Gandalf Group, Ekos Research, and a CanWest columnist (not me!).

On the Monday morning after the Super Weekend — with most of the 469 accredited ridings, Liberal organizations, and campus clubs reporting — Michael Ignatieff was way out ahead of the pack, with nearly 30 percent of the total delegate vote. The former Harvard University professor was rumoured to be disproportionately favoured by the so-called *ex officio* vote, too — that is, former MPs, senators, and candidates — likely pushing his total closer to 35 percent or so of the total. That's what those of us in the highly scientific political consultancy business call A Great Big Honking Lead!

Former Ontario NDP premier Bob Rae, another candidate for the leadership? Less than 20 percent support — and with a distant third-place finish in Ontario, too. Former Ontario education minister Gerard Kennedy? Just under 17 percent of the vote — but, astonishingly, with only 1 percent of the Quebec delegates. Count 'em — that's eighteen delegates, out of more than a thousand up for grabs in *la belle province*. Among the second tier, only Liberal constitution wars scrapper — and the leadership's ultimate winner — Stéphane Dion was happy.

Having been relegated to also-ran status for months, Dion captured 17 percent of the delegates, and was — like Ignatieff, who would come second on the final ballot — in respectable shape in every region of the country. Others, like hockey great Ken Dryden? Following Super Weekend, they all saw their Liberal leadership hopes had come to a shuddering halt. Dryden got less than 5 percent support. Ouch.

However, if you relied upon a mid-September poll of something called the Gandalf Group — as did the Parliamentary tabloid called the *Hill Times*, for which I write — you could be forgiven for being gobsmacked. There, the newspaper and Gandalf reported that Dryden was supported by approximately 20 percent of Liberals (and Canadians) nationally, with

Michael Ignatieff running a distant third. Um, wrong, by a factor of 400 percent, nineteen times out of twenty.

Next up for a trip to the woodshed was the *Globe*, with another mid-September poll, this one by Allan Gregg's Strategic Counsel (he's the guy, along with John Tory, who cooked up the anti-Chrétien "face" ads, by the way). In a front-page story accompanied by a large headline (to wit, "Ignatieff clings to slight lead"), Gregg said, "If you had money to put on it, you'd bet Rae right now." Uh-huh. Sure. And then you'd *lose* your money, Allan.

By a unanimous decision of our panel of judges (me, myself, and I), the *Chicago Daily Tribune* Foul-up Finalist was the *Toronto Star*, for the paper's September 25 page-one headline fumble: "Rae now poised to become Liberal leader." In Linda Diebel's accompanying news story, Ekos Research asserted that Bob Rae had "emerged as the leading candidate in the Liberal leadership race." Ekos president Frank Graves said Liberal respondents in his poll underwent a "very careful screening process." Apparently not careful enough!

There was a smattering of other wince-inducing boners following that historic weekend, such as the *Toronto Sun*'s Peter Worthington ("conventional wisdom" was that Rae had the "momentum," wrote the veteran conservative columnist), or the *Vancouver Sun*'s Barbara Yaffe (Ignatieff was "a long shot … he should get himself a good set of worry beads, pronto").

So who is to blame for this kind of stuff? The media organizations (with some justification) blame the pollsters. The pollsters (again, with some grounds) pin it on the folks responding to their polls, who are increasingly unenthusiastic about confessing their innermost thoughts to complete strangers on the telephone. The loser, naturally, is the reader. The reader deserves better. And if polling mistakes keep getting made, then the media needs to re-examine its enthusiasm for polls.

Ask Harry S. Truman. He knows.

DESPITE ALL THAT, there's no doubt that politicians, hacks, and war roomers love — and I mean deeply and truly *love* — good polling and good pollsters. Because you need both to win, in my experience.

For nearly two hundred years, politicians and their campaign teams have flat-out adored solid public opinion research. The first known published political poll showed up in the *Harrisburg Pennsylvanian* newspaper in 1824. In the survey, popular support was measured — "without discrimination of parties," the newspaper declared — and Andrew Jackson was found to be the most likely winner in his presidential race against John Quincy Adams. Jackson eventually did win, but the results were ultimately decided in a narrow vote in the House of Representatives. Following 1824, such polls were not uncommon in the United States, and were sometimes even commissioned by newspapers. (Hotels commissioned polls, too: guests registering for the night were asked to indicate their presidential choice.)

These embryonic political polls all suffered from one big shortcoming: the pollsters made no attempt to ensure that their results reflected an accurate sample of the voters they had contacted. Put simply, the sample used by the pollsters did not properly reflect the total voter population; the raw polling data had not been weighted to ensure that the final result did not over-represent the opinions of a particular demographic category or geographic region. The most notorious case of bad sampling came in 1936, when the much-read *Literary Digest* declared in a section titled "America Speaks" that Kansas governor Alfred Landon would defeat Franklin Delano Roosevelt in that year's presidential race by a factor of two to one. (He didn't.)

To arrive at the wrong result, the *Digest* had mailed out an incredible 10 million ballots and received 1 million replies. The publication's well-publicized error could be traced back to the fact that its mailing list was made up not of registered voters but of phone directories and automobile registrations. In the midst of the Great Depression, it had occurred to no one at the *Digest* that the vast majority of those Americans found on such lists would be well-to-do Republicans, and not a more representative sample of voters. The *Digest* folded the next year.

A better approach to polling and sampling came shortly before the *Literary Digest* would destroy its reputation. In 1932, one Mrs. Ola Babcock Miller achieved the distinction of being the first political candidate to employ a scientific, and properly sampled, public opinion poll. Miller, a former newspaper publisher in Iowa, where no Democrat had been elected to high state office since the Civil War, was placed on the party's ticket, but given little hope of success. Miller had a secret weapon, however: her son-in-law, George Gallup, who had just finished his Ph.D. in psychology. Using what he taught himself about proper poll sampling techniques, Gallup determined that his mother-in-law would win. She did, becoming Iowa's secretary of state.

The work of Gallup and the likes of Elmo Roper, Louis Harris, and others helped to ensure that public opinion research would become a vital part of the modern political process, or a part, at least, of every well-funded North American political campaign that was to follow in the latter two-thirds of the twentieth century. As any seasoned politico should know, the so-called horse race figures that emerge from public opinion polling (e.g., "Who will you vote for on election day?") are interesting but not crucial. What a campaign needs to win, and what good polling hopefully provides, is information on which a political team can base its decisions. These typically focus upon three areas: the candidate, the public, and specific topics or issues. For example, a political poll early in a campaign will ask voters whether they have heard about a candidate and the candidate's opponent. If the answer is yes in both instances, the poll will then try to find out whether the impressions of those candidates are positive or negative, and why.

At the next level, respondents will be probed on more than their impressions about the field of candidates. They will be asked for their views about particular issues as well. Statements will typically be made about a certain issue — for example, "Nuclear proliferation is a dangerous trend" — and then potential voters will be asked to indicate whether they strongly agree, agree, disagree, or strongly disagree. Another important series of questions concerns the voters themselves — their age, gender, occupation, income level, place of residence, political affiliation, and so on. This helps to determine if a certain issue is important to a certain group of voters, and whether the candidate has a reasonable prospect of attracting those voters by speaking up about that issue.

More than perhaps anyone else in Canada, my friend Michael Marzolini knows polling. For twelve years he was chief pollster — and one of the top strategists — to my former boss, Prime Minister Jean Chrétien.

He helped us to win, and win big, in 1993, 1997, and 2000. Over the past couple of decades, Marzolini has helped more than four hundred political candidates across North America and Europe. Almost 90 percent of them were winners.

Before he started the public opinion and marketing research firm Pollara — and, full disclosure, I use Mike as a pollster a lot of the time, and encourage my clients to do likewise — he was a consultant with a bunch of market and behavioural research organizations in Canada and the U.S. Prior to that, he provided demographic analysis to Prime Minister Pierre Trudeau, and — get this! — he was an apprentice pollster in Ronald Reagan's first successful campaign for president. (Everyone is entitled to one youthful mistake.)

How do I know he's good? Well, as pollster for *CTV News* in 1988, Marzolini called the federal election of that year bang-on, with a 0.0 percent margin of error. He is the only pollster in the history of the world to call a national election perfectly, as far as I'm aware. It's actually kind of creepy, when you think about it.

Sitting in my office, looking as dapper as always — I've never seen him not wearing a tailored suit, and he rarely sees me wearing a tie — he agrees that there are basically four steps to developing a good political poll. The first step is determining the appropriate sample, which means avoiding the *Literary Digest* faux pas. How does one identify a very small fraction of a much larger group in such a way that the fraction accurately reflects the composition of the whole? For the most part, random sampling is the answer. If a poll is, as is most often the case, being conducted on the telephone, some kind of random digit dialing computer program will be used. The size of the actual sample is largely determined by how large a margin of error is acceptable, because the smaller the sample, the larger the margin for error in the projected results. How much the campaign can afford to spend also helps to determine the sample size; the bigger the sample, the bigger the cost.

The second step is preparing a questionnaire. In a push poll, for example, the scrupulously neutral approach usually employed in the development of a good questionnaire is abandoned. While a series of loaded questions may produce results that make a candidate feel good, they don't usually offer up results that truly reflect public opinion. That is why a campaign must retain a pollster with experience in developing a series of questions that do not dictate a certain result. Says Marzolini, "Public opinion has to be measured very, very carefully. Objectivity is the name of the game. You can't allow yourself to be biased in any way, or swayed by partisan considerations. What we try to do is look at the state of public opinion today, and what it can be tomorrow." To prepare the right kind of questionnaire, he says, can therefore take two or three days.

The third step is collecting the data — that is, reaching out to the folks you've targeted. This part of the process almost always involves the telephone. In my view, newspaper, magazine, direct mail, and Internet surveys tend to elicit results from only the most committed voters, and are therefore suspect. While there are some weaknesses associated with the telephone — for example, it is often difficult for a pollster to connect with a respondent, and the ubiquity of answering machines, call display, unlisted numbers, and whatnot makes it very difficult to actually reach people these days — it remains the best available technology for collecting public opinion data.

Marzolini concurs. "It helps to establish a rapport," he says. Marzolini maintains a call centre in Bathurst, New Brunswick. "Most of our people have been with us from eight to ten years. They're very capable people, hard workers, and very warm and friendly. It's the Atlantic Canada way. Just recently, we did a forty-minute interview with someone who wasn't interested in the subject matter, and who had never done a poll before. They asked to speak to the supervisor, so they could say that our person made the whole process easier, and made the subject more interesting, too."

The fourth and final step is probably the most complex of all: interpreting the numbers. Says Marzolini, "In a political campaign, we're trying not so much to *measure* public opinion [as] we are ultimately trying to *manage* it. We want to learn how to change behaviour, or how to make a policy be seen much more positively." It's not enough to simply provide the "who is winning" numbers, he says. You need to probe attitudes and ascertain peoples' past views in order to extrapolate future views.

There are a number of different types of polls. The first has no official name, but some folks call it a pre-decision poll — Marzolini calls his recon polls. For those who can afford it (and many cannot, as a good one may run to more than $20,000), it's a device that helps aspiring politicians to determine whether or not to throw their hat into the proverbial ring. It tests name recognition and an opponent's areas of vulnerability, and it also provides a summary of issues important to the voters and which way the voters are leaning in their voting intentions. "It'll be a smaller sample in a recon poll," says Marzolini. "Six to eight questions, all designed to answer the 'should I run' question. It's a simple look-around, examining the obstacles, and then you follow it up with a good battle plan."

Another important type of poll is the baseline — the poll that a campaign must do if it is to do any polling at all. The baseline is a "line in the sand," for lack of a better description. As Marzolini says, "A baseline is your major study. Leader, policy, party — all of those things are measured. It's your broader examination of the political situation. It can be expensive, because it's a lengthy interview. But you have to do it — it's the major strategic stuff."

A third type of survey, called tracking polls, allow campaigns to measure daily fluctuations in public opinion and to decide whether a decision made earlier was a good one. "In a campaign, you do them nightly," says Marzolini. "Some people call polls 'snapshots.' Well, a tracking poll is like a movie — it is a moving picture."

A fourth type, focus groups, is not really a poll at all. Focus groups bring together small groups of people, usually no more than twenty, to discuss a predetermined set of questions, led by a moderator and observed by a cameraperson behind one-way glass. Focus groups take several hours to do properly, and, unlike polls, are not quantitative but qualitative. That means they are used to probe deeper on opinions of the public, but don't necessarily get a statistically accurate sampling.

The ill-fated Paul Martin regime loved focus groups. It focus-grouped everything that moved, and a few things that didn't. And it sure didn't seem to help them in the end, did it? "Focus groups aren't a good way of saving money," Marzolini says. "They're been abused by governments in the past, too. It was one of the big problems of the Martin administration. They made major decisions based on the views of eight to ten people — even though the margin of error can be about 44 percent!"

Wrapping up, Marzolini cautions against doing what the Martin crew — and other politicians — have done in the past: namely, governing by poll alone. "Public opinion research should *never* dictate policy. It should *never* replace leadership. We elect people, with different skills — and sometimes no skills — to debate and deliberate ands decide. You can't replace any of that with polling. Polling is useful in a democracy — but it shouldn't *replace* democracy."

FOR MANY YEARS, debates have raged amongst pollsters, politicos, and media types about whether polls are actual communication vehicles; that is, does the reporting of a poll result have some kind of impact on voting decisions? It would seem most governments believe it does.

In many Western democracies, for example, the reporting of polls is often restricted during electoral writ periods, presumably because some fear that the results will stampede voters in one direction or another. And during most election campaigns, parties regularly leak polls to the media in order to give the impression of momentum or to counter a suspicion that a campaign is in trouble.

Pollsters, meanwhile, generally maintain the public position that there is no evidence to show that publicity about surveys has an additional effect on public opinion. Privately, however, they will admit the reverse. They know that voters read polls, and that polls influence voters' thinking, particularly near the end of a campaign.

Jean Chrétien, for one, believes that the simple reporting of poll numbers by the media can be an effective communication tool. And he should know: he had more than thirty years of experience in national politics and is the most popular prime minister in the history of polling. In his autobiography, *Straight from the Heart*, Chrétien rejects notions that polls are benign. He writes, "While it is still debatable whether [polls] reflect instability or cause it, no one can doubt that they have changed the electoral process. Every time they fluctuate, great careers and important policies go up and down with them. The media distribute them as news items, yet their effect is incredible."

Even though he's a conservative, Haley Barbour agrees. At the relevant moment, the former chairman of the Republican National Committee and former lawyer from Yazoo City, Mississippi, is at the 2000

Republican National Convention in Philadelphia. Standing in a noisy corridor at the Loews Philadelphia Hotel, shifting from one foot to the other, pausing to shake hands with those walking by, Barbour is the man who in 1994 single-handedly rebuilt the GOP in Congress. And he is also the man who ensured that the party narrowly recaptured the White House with George W. Bush in the fall of 2000 by being better organized on the ground in places like Florida.

Barbour grins or shares a quick joke with some of the conservative partisans who pause to exchange a few words with the man who, possibly more than any other alive, knows how to get their fellow Republicans elected. He is of average height, and of slightly more than average weight. He has thick, greying hair and a Mississippi accent that is as smooth and sweet as syrup. He is funny — quipping that Bill Clinton could sell "Fords to Chevrolet dealers." He is partisan, too — noting that Clinton is also the "factually challenged" president. Haley Barbour is a diehard, never-give-up Republican. He always has been.

Between handshakes and small talk, Barbour returns his attention to his Canadian acquaintance and is unfailingly polite in answering questions, even though the questions concern negative campaigning and how to make use of some of the new technology to "go neg" in a manner that is effective. Barbour is clearly familiar with all of the methodologies mentioned by his inquisitor — the Internet as a communications tool, push polling, frugging (fundraising under the guise of research) — but he is wary. As long as he is on the record, he will only say that tough, no-holds-barred campaigning does indeed work, and that technology helps to ensure that it works. But the chief practitioners of negativity, he says with a straight face, are the Democrats of Al Gore, and not the Republicans of George W. Bush. "There's no doubt," Barbour says. "Negative campaigns and negative ads work. But they don't always work. There is a risk involved. And Gore, particularly, is subject to that risk because he has such high negatives going in."

All around Barbour there is an awful lot going on. The convention that will see the election of George Bush and Dick Cheney to the position of GOP standard-bearers is a cyclone of activity and sights and sounds. An estimated forty-five thousand people are in attendance at the convention, with just under five thousand of those being actual delegates and alternates. Outnumbering them are ten thousand or so volunteers and fifteen thousand accredited media people, as well as thousands of observers and retailers. Over at the convention centre, the Republicans have put on something called PoliticalFest. Those who are so inclined can get their picture taken stepping out of the door of an Air Force One set, or sitting behind the desk of a fake Oval Office, complete with vases filled with flowers and important-looking papers placed here and there. Beneath red, white, and blue banners, Ronald Reagan's shiny black armoured limousine has been put on display, along with one of Pat Nixon's gowns. There is a pair of Teddy Roosevelt's shoes, and a seat liberated from Ford's Theatre, where John Wilkes Booth assassinated Abraham Lincoln. In the streets between the hotel, the convention centre, and the Comcast-Spectacor's First Union Center, where the actual voting and speechifying are taking place, there are a lot of protestors, but they are generally behaving themselves. The delegates are overwhelmingly white and clean-cut.

Haley Barbour, born in 1948 in the sweaty Mississippi Delta, surveys what he sees, but does not let on whether he thinks it is good or not. He believes George W. Bush will win, but he is cautious. He believes Republicans will retake Congress, but he is cautious about that, too. He is well known for this refusal to engage in an overabundance of GOP jingoism. On the contrary: when the party makes mistakes — and it has made plenty in the past decade or so — Barbour will not hesitate to be critical. Around the time Bill Clinton clobbered Bob Dole in the 1992 presidential race, and around the same time he became chairman of the Republican National Committee, Barbour warned Republicans of the dangers associated with policies that many Americans considered to be extremist. Like Dole, Barbour is a "big tent" Republican — a Republican who tries to broaden the GOP base beyond wealthy, white, heterosexual males. "We need our heads examined if we let abortion be the threshold issue of Republicanism," he says. In his maiden speech as GOP chair, he bluntly assessed what he saw at his party's 1992 convention in Houston: "We came across as shrill, strident, and hard-edged."

In person, Barbour is funny and charming. He listens carefully to every question that is posed to him, nodding slowly. When he is asked about push polling, however, the nodding stops. "You know," he drawls, his eyes diplomatically searching the ceiling of the Loews Hotel, "when I first came along, push polling actually meant something. It was when you took a poll and you'd have pushy questions in it. The purpose of the push poll wasn't to see what someone's position was on an issue. It was to try and poison the environment. And, um …" He trails off.

As a Republican bigwig, there is good reason for Haley Barbour to be hesitant about push polling. In early 2000, with the outcome of the nomination for the Republican presidential candidate still far from certain, Barbour's party was seriously bruised by the issue. In February of that year, John McCain accused George W. Bush of push polling in South Carolina; that is, getting his supporters to dial up Republicans and ask them a series of loaded questions calculated to destroy McCain's reputation.

The Bush campaign did not deny that it was asking voters what it called "tough questions" about John McCain. But it strenuously denied that the questions were part of a push poll. To buttress the point, the Bush people released the script of the survey about John McCain. The release did not assist Bush's cause. One question asked respondents how they felt about McCain's plan to "increase taxes on charitable contributions to churches, colleges and charities by $20 billion." Another queried whether Americans approved of McCain's "legislation that proposed the largest tax increase in United States history." The survey went on to question whether McCain deserved support, since his "campaign finance proposals would give labour unions and the media a bigger influence on the outcome of elections."

The American Association for Public Opinion Research (AAPOR) defines a push poll as something very much like what George W. Bush's campaign authorized in South Carolina. Says AAPOR in its code of ethics:

> A push poll is a telemarketing technique in which telephone calls are used to canvass potential voters, feeding them false or misleading "information" about a candidate under the pretense of taking a poll to see how this "information" affects voter preferences. In fact, the intent is not to measure public opinion, but to manipulate it — to

"push" voters away from one candidate and toward the opposing candidate. Such polls defame selected candidates by spreading false or misleading information about them. The intent is to disseminate campaign propaganda under the guise of a legitimate public opinion poll.

The issue, in the South Carolina controversy, was about whether the critical information passed along was in any way misleading or inaccurate. At its depths, the South Carolina contretemps saw McCain claiming that a fourteen-year-old boy had been reduced to tears by one of the Bush push pollsters, who had called the war hero "a cheat, a liar and a fraud." Perhaps even Haley Barbour, in a candid moment, would have been forced to acknowledge that the "facts" underpinning the Bush campaign poll were not entirely above reproach.

For example, McCain's relevant legislative record as a senator was as follows: he had attempted to oblige tobacco companies to pay some $500 billion of smoking-related medical costs. He had worked to remove loopholes and deductions from the United States tax code. He had made an effort to ban unregulated contributions to political parties, including his own. In the hands of the Bush campaign's spinners, and its alleged push pollsters, those legislative measures became "the largest tax increase in United States history," an increase "on taxes on charitable contributions to churches," and a way to "give labour unions and the media a bigger influence on the outcome of elections." Were the Bush campaign's characterizations of McCain unfair or inaccurate? The best judge, in this case, is the best political columnist in the United States, William Saletan of the on-line magazine *Slate*, who dismissed the Bush poll as a sham. Wrote Saletan, "[The Bush poll's] purpose is not just to measure public opinion but to alter it, by figuring out how to deliver a message full of negative, distorted information that will push voters away from McCain ... Is push-polling worse than 'real' polling? Yes, because it's more dishonest."

A push poll is really not a poll at all. It is a political communication technique, or, sometimes, a telemarketing technique, disguised as a poll. That's it. Unlike legitimate public opinion surveys, push polls are not developed to collect information; they are, instead, designed to disseminate information (or rumours, or even lies) unhelpful to an opponent. Because push pollsters must reach a large number of voters to be effective — usually thousands, as opposed to hundreds contacted for a standard survey of public opinion — push polls are very brief. Although he did not say so in his interview in Philadelphia, Haley Barbour and his fellow Republicans might have known that George W. Bush's alleged South Carolina push poll was, at a minimum, twenty minutes in length. Even with a campaign as well financed as Bush's, spending that much time with thousands of potential voters is neither cost-effective nor smart. If the South Carolina effort was in fact a push poll, it was a poorly designed one. Suspicious voters can spot push polls by more than their abbreviated length; if a polling firm does not clearly identify itself at the outset, the chances are good that a push poll is about to follow.

Almost all political polling, to be fair, contains information that is critical of an opponent. The information considered negative is presented to potential voters, or to potential consumers of a product, to determine what kinds of messages or facts will affect a voting or buying decision. Russell D. Renka, a Missouri political scientist and expert on polling techniques, emphasizes this point: "Be warned — it is perfectly legitimate for good polls to address the most touchy or delicate subject. In fact, those are often the things most worthwhile to know and understand." Most often, exploring touchy subjects with polling is the means by which a campaign will decide how (or if) it should launch an attack on some aspect of an opponent's record.

In 1994, Haley Barbour lived up to his reputation as a smart political operator and developed one of the first systems to "inoculate" against push polling. Barbour recalled that in 1982, 1986, and later years, the Democrats and their allies in the labour movement had, in his view, made use of push polling, with great effectiveness, to frighten senior citizens about what Republican candidates would do to Social Security. By 1990, the Republican National Committee had developed an early warning system in certain states to alert GOP operatives about Democrat efforts to fearmonger on the issue. By 1994, Larry Sabato reports in *Dirty Little Secrets*, Barbour concluded, "What the hell, we know they're going to do it, they've shown their hand, so let's go on out there and take remedial action before they go after us." At a cost of $800,000, Barbour developed his inoculation plan. More than twenty-five thousand seniors would be called in fifty key swing districts in the Midwest of the United States and would hear the following message: "Republicans are for the Balanced Budget Amendment, and you are going to get called and told that Republicans will cut Social Security to balance the budget. But Republicans won't touch Social Security. So when you get called, I hope you will tell whoever calls that you know it's not true." The inoculation worked, and the Republicans captured Congress.

Push polls are not the only unethical weapons in a campaign's arsenal. While few politicos wish to discuss the practice, polling agencies exist, on both sides of the border, that will produce results that reflect not the political reality but what their client wants. Following the 1984 federal Liberal leadership campaign, for example, many supporters of candidate Jean Chrétien believed their man was sandbagged by polling done by a West Coast Liberal firm that had "torqued" the results — manipulated the numbers to make Chrétien look bad and John Turner look good. The danger inherent in such practices is obvious; notwithstanding the attempt to fool Grit delegates and the media, John Turner went down to one of the worst election results in the history of the Liberal Party in September 1984. False polling numbers may be persuasive to delegates at political conventions, but they are far less meaningful to voters.

Another unhelpful polling industry trend — and one that is more recent — is on-line polling. Everyone seems to be doing it, but that doesn't make it acceptable to guys like me.

Now, I have heard from pollsters who tell me that exclusively on-line polls are cheaper to do. They are less intrusive for the folks being called. They provide pollsters with a willing pool of pre-selected folks who have indicated they are willing to answer questions. They're not bogus pop-up polls, like you find on pro-conservative aggregator sites like Bourque Newswatch or the Drudge Report. Yada-yada-yada.

But on-line polls shut out the 30-plus percent of Canadians who aren't on-line. Among those on-line (and as the blogosphere demonstrates daily), important demographic groups are significantly underrepresented: older people, rural residents, those with lower incomes, and women. And, despite what some of what even the respected pollsters claim, pollsters aren't being terribly scientific in their recruitment efforts.

Hell, some of the firms — and one Canadian firm in particular — are letting people register to "vote" on-line more than once!

Most importantly, on-line polls destroy, utterly, what made polling so valuable in the first place: random sampling. And that's why so many pollsters were getting results so dramatically wrong in the 2004 and 2006 Canadian federal election campaigns, I suspect.

Despite the occasional lapses, which include push polling and number manipulation, the vast majority of public opinion polling in North America, political or otherwise, is conducted ethically. Guys like Michael Marzolini are the rule, not the exception.

And, despite what some media folks and aggrieved politicians will tell you, oppo is ethical, too. It's legitimate, it's fair, and — as long it's about someone's public record, and not their private life — it's the right thing to do.

Get the Handle Scandal Manual!

S PONSORSHIPS WORK.

Yep, you read that one right. Read it again.

Sponsorships work. Sponsorships are worthwhile. Sponsorships are effective. And they're *cost*-effective, too. And don't just take the word of this die-hard Chrétien-era Liberal, either. Flip through the pages of your favourite newspaper. Watch a local TV station broadcast. Listen to the radio in the car. You'll read or see or hear plenty of proof. The media know that sponsorship — that is, providing funds or support in exchange for brand name recognition, at local sport meets or charity fundraising events or cultural festivals — is a terrific way to promote their product and services, to boost awareness of their corporate brand, and to give back to the community where the media organization does business.

That's why the media generally spends more on sponsorships than any other organization — including government — by a long shot. Some years, the media pays for 70 percent of sponsorships in Canada and the United States. Other big sponsorship spenders, historically, include brewers, distillers, and even evil tobacco companies. Those private interests aren't in business to lose money. They want to turn a profit. And sponsorships help them to do that. That's a fact.

Governments do sponsorships, too, as everyone in Canada above the age of twelve now knows. From little sponsorships (like the side-of-the-highway sign that tells you what levels of government contributed to the costs of construction) to big sponsorships (like tourism promotion campaigns, which benefit millions of citizens), governments do sponsorships all the time. And they should keep doing them, too. Because they work. While we're in tell-it-like-it-is mode, here's another fact: I worked at the federal department Public Works and Government Services Canada under former Prime Minister Jean Chrétien. Proudly.

I was there as a minister's executive assistant, and I knew a lot about advertising and polling. (And, yes, I knew the controversial bureaucrat named Chuck Guité, too. I — along with all of his bosses in the public service, who promoted him over two decades — thought he did a good job.)

Back during the 1993 federal election campaign, whilst I toiled in the war room, the Liberal Party made promises about cleaning up and cutting advertising and polling. On the day the new government was sworn in, Chrétien reaffirmed those commitments outside Rideau Hall. A few days later, on December 20, 1993, the new prime minister sent a letter to his cabinet telling them to "minimize expenditures" for polling and advertising until new guidelines were in place.

In another letter the prime minister sent, on May 9, 1994, he told his cabinet that "contracting procedures … must follow a competitive process, similar to procurement of other services purchased by the government."

Those two letters became our mandate in 1994 and 1995: one, cutting spending on polling and advertising; and, two, creating a competitive process for those services, for the first time in Canadian history. With the assistance of a lot of dedicated, professional public servants, we did both. By the end of June 1995, we had radically cut spending on both ads and polls. In the last full fiscal year of the soulless, perfidious Brian Mulroney administration, advertising spending was $117 million. In our first full fiscal year, we reduced spending on advertising to $30 million —

that's an $87-million reduction, folks. In the last fiscal year of the corrupt, nasty, horrible Conservative regime, public opinion research was costing at least $14 million — "with many projects not accounted for," as the public servants dryly noted. In our first full year, we slashed polling spending to $4 million — a $10-million drop. Not bad.

And sponsorship? We didn't spend anything on sponsorships, because the program didn't yet exist. It wouldn't come into being until 1997, until well after Quebec's referendum, the auditor general later noted.

But was it the right thing to do? Should the sponsorship program have been created in the first place? Yes. In the November 1995 referendum, Canada came within a 1.16 percent margin of breaking apart the greatest nation in the world, forever. (It was in all the papers.) One reason for the separatists' near-win was that the separatists had long used pro-sovereignty sponsorship programs. For years, at cultural and sporting events across the province, the Quebec "brand" was aggressively promoted — while the Canadian equivalent was nowhere to be seen. This permitted the separatists to repeatedly argue that their tax dollars were going to Ottawa, but nothing was coming back.

Because Mulroney and his heartless regime did not want to provoke separatists, the Canadian concept had not been promoted in Quebec for a decade. Hell, when we got into office, Canada Post told us they had a policy to not fly the Maple Leaf at Quebec post offices anymore! (I'm not making this up, much as I wish that I were.)

But — fair's fair — we Liberals were to blame, too. We Liberals (including my friend Chrétien, and the historical footnote named Paul Martin) had been doing a lousy job of promoting Canada in Quebec. The referendum result made that obvious. Therefore, Liberals had to make big changes. *The Clarity Act* was one of those changes. So was boosting Quebec cabinet representation (which resulted in the recruitment of another guy I'm fond of, Stéphane Dion). And so, too, the sponsorship program — flying the Maple Leaf at federal buildings again, and fighting for the Canada logo to be displayed where federal tax dollars had sponsored an event.

The sponsorship program was the right thing to do. Was it properly managed? No! Obviously not. That's why Jean Chrétien — when he learned about the problems in the sponsorship program — personally called in the auditor general, and then the RCMP. It wasn't the behaviour of a guy trying to cover anything up.

Those of us who loudly opposed the creation of Paul Martin's sponsorship inquiry did so because we felt that, one, there was nothing Justice John Gomery could do that the Mounties couldn't do better, or weren't doing already. Two, the inquiry's terms of reference were rigged to exclude scrutiny of polling, which was where Martin's pals had made millions. Three, the inquiry's rules of evidence would open the door to an avalanche of unproven hearsay and innuendo. We were right. The result? The reputation of federalism took a serious beating. People became even more cynical about Canada. In 2007, Quebec separatists and so-called autonomists seized the balance of power in Quebec's National Assembly. And no one seems to be willing to speak up for Canada anymore.

Cast your imagination ahead, then, to the night that will inevitably come, when we Canadians are awaiting the result of another referendum vote. And as the results trickle in, long into the night — and as we all once again contemplate the economic, legal, social, and political chaos that will immediately flow from a separatist win — ask yourself one question: in the year 2005, in an overreaction to misspending in the sponsorship program, should we have stopped promoting Canada in Quebec?

But we did — or, rather, *he* did: Paul Martin. The guy who tried to please everyone, and accomplished nothing in the process. And then Martin did one thing that will forever be associated with his "legacy": he announced a judicial inquiry into the sponsorship program. It didn't matter that the RCMP was already doing a fine job of investigating it, or that the auditor general had done so. It didn't matter that no one was asking for it, apart from the Conservative Party (something they would come to regret, but more on that later). None of that mattered. All that mattered was destroying the reputation of the man whom Paul Martin had succeeded and whom he clearly loathed more than any other. All that mattered was destroying the lives of those who were close to Jean Chrétien, and those who believed in him and his vision of the country.

Which, as it turned out, included me.

JAMES CARVILLE KNOWS ALL ABOUT SCANDALS and witch hunts. For instance, when his friend Bill Clinton was being targeted by partisan opponents — opponents who were spending untold millions to turn a lapse in judgment into an impeachment offence — Carville didn't do what lots of other political people do in similar circumstances. He didn't run for cover and pretend that he never knew Clinton. He didn't hide from the media. He didn't go mute.

On the contrary: James Carville got louder, and prouder, about Bill Clinton. He did interviews. He got busy, like any good war roomer should. For starters, he admitted his friend had made a mistake with a White House intern, sure. But he also started hitting back, hard. He got on TV and told the truth about what was *really* going on: namely, that the Republicans and the Clinton-hating conservative media were trying to turn the personal into the political, trying to transform sex into an impeachable offence. Throughout this period, I observed what Carville was doing very carefully. I took notes, even. His handle-scandal strategy worked — and the proof of that was found in polling. The vast majority of Americans agreed with the essence of what Carville was saying. At the height of the scandal, a Pew Research Center poll found that, even among Republicans, only 36 percent saw the controversy as very important, and only 33 percent were following it very closely. Clinton's approval ratings went up, not down. And fully 60 percent of Americans said they'd be satisfied to put an end to the controversy if Clinton were to tell the American public that he had had a fling with Monica Lewinsky but lied about it to protect his family.

Around that time, I got on the phone and spoke to Carville. I told him about the latest partisan attempt to destroy *my* friend Jean Chrétien, which bore remarkable similarities (minus the sex) to the partisan attempt to destroy *his* friend Bill Clinton. Said Carville, "They made a mistake. You need to *politicize* your political differences, not *criminalize* them. You turn people off if you go too far. Voters aren't stupid, you know?"

Those words — more than any other — made clear what I had to do, as the hysteria about the sponsorship scandal started to grow throughout 2004 and 2005. The sponsorship inquisition wasn't legal — it was political and personal. Unlike many of Chrétien's friends, and contrary to the advice I received from many folks, I would *not* go into hiding, cloistered with lawyers (who get paid $600 an hour to tell you to say "no comment"). Unlike many of Chrétien's former caucus colleagues, I would not pretend that I had never known the guy. I would not go mute. That stuff *never* works. When a so-called scandal is raging, saying "no comment" *never, ever* works.

Instead, I would do what James Carville had done. And, right off the top, let me make crystal clear that I didn't ask Chrétien's permission, or his lawyers', or anyone else's. Nobody paid me. I just did it. And I'm glad I did.

I figured I shouldn't bother trying to change the minds of the people who lived in Ottawa (most of them had already made up their minds). I would try and influence news coverage, to change the minds of people who lived elsewhere (most of them had a lingering fondness for Chrétien, and were suspicious that Martin was out to hurt the man he despised so much). Only former Bush speech writer David Frum — with whom I often disagree, but whom I have come to know and like — clued in to what I was up to. In a column he penned at the time, Frum called me "the James Carville of Canadian politics," which was rather nice of him, but not very accurate. What *was* accurate was Frum's observation that I had stolen a page from Carville's book, and was going after Paul Martin, John Gomery, and the other Chrétien-haters in the way that Carville had gone after Ken Starr and the Clinton-haters in Congress and the news media. Handle the scandal: Fight back, don't leave it to the lawyers, and — most of all — attack the attackers. Make them look like a multi-million-dollar, mean, extreme smear machine. Which they were.

"Warren Kinsella [is] belting out old hits from the Clinton impeachment songbook. There's the campaign of denigration against the investigator: 'Gomery Pyle' as Kinsella calls him," wrote Frum. "There's the accusations of bias against everyone in sight … There are the incessant complaints about cost … And of course, there are the insinuations of political conspiracy against poor little us — not a right-wing conspiracy this time, but nonetheless still vast … Will these time-tested tactics work?"

I certainly hoped so. The time-tested tools at my disposal were my mouth (for radio and TV and newspaper interviews) and my index fingers (for the typing of pro-Chrétien op-eds, mainly for the *National Post*, which genially printed every single one). And I also had something else in my tactical toolbox, over which I had complete control and which I didn't need to run past a scandal-loving media gatekeeper. I had my website, which some called a weblog, or a blog, but which I called (and still call) a website. Far beyond my expectations, or anyone else's, the blog became a key part of everything I did about sponsorship, Chrétien, and the out-of-control, wildly unfair, plainly partisan Gomery commission. When the slime-Chrétien operation was at its height, reporters were telling me that more people were reading *my* take on the Gomery circus than *their* news stories. (Hell, when Gomery was wrapping up, I was regularly registering more than a hundred thousand hits a day on the site.)

Did it work? Well, as columnist John Ivison wrote in the *National Post*: "Kinsella has one of the most popular weblogs in the blogosphere. Every day, thousands tune into Kinsella's latest thoughts on the political issues of the day, which almost exclusively revolve around abusing the Martin wing of the Liberal Party — which he fought for a decade as a loyal Chrétien advisor — and bashing what he has christened the Gomery Pyle Commission." Though John might have meant it as a criticism, I took this part of his column as a compliment: "[On his blog, Kinsella] has no use for rapier wit — he much prefers to take a two-handed broadsword to his victims." True enough!

I had started the website in 1998 or so, at the urging of some Jewish friends. They had noted that assorted white supremacists, anti-Semites, and far-right kooks who despised me — such as Holocaust deniers David Irving and Ernst Zundel, the latter of whom I had taken to task as a journalist and in a book I had written about the racist right called *Web of Hate* — were smearing me on a regular basis. My friends suggested I put together my own website to counter the online ravings of the haters. I was a bit intimidated by the technological challenge, at first. Soon enough, however, I learned it wasn't all that difficult to get a website going — and, with the invaluable help of my brother Lorne and his best friend, Eric Johnson, my "daily musings" started to get read by many more people than I had ever imagined possible. Though he meant it as a put-down, author Peter C. Newman, a member of the Chrétien-hating commetariat later observed that, on-line, "Warren Kinsella can have an effect on as many Canadians as the *New York Times*." Not quite, but there was no doubt that a blog could have an impact, if done right.

So I got to work. Because I love them, and because they're a lot more fun to read, I have put together the main elements of my one-man media/blog effort as a top ten list. And I've used the sponsorship mess, and the resulting Gomery Pyle Show, as my case study.

You can call it Kinsella's Handle Scandal Manual. If it'll work for Gomery, kids, it'll work for you!

Kinsella's Handle Scandal Manual

Don't Get Mad, Get Even!
When trying to survive a scandal, strategies don't matter so much. Tactics don't matter so much, either. What matters most is you. If you look guilty, if you look worried, you're screwed. That's what counts the most, as you handle scandal.

That said, here are the facts. A Cape Breton Liberal MP, David Dingwall, was named Canada's Minister of Public Works in November 1993. Because Dingwall and I were friendly, and because the Prime Minister's Office (PMO) wanted me there, I was made Dingwall's executive assistant from November 1994 until January 1996. In due course, he got shuffled off to Health Canada. Since I was fed up with government — and, particularly, everyone's apparent willingness to tolerate Paul Martin's thugs, even three of the top advisors to Chrétien — I decided to get back to the real world. My wife and then-infant daughter and I moved to British Columbia in February 1996, where I took up a job at a PR firm (not necessarily "the real world," on either count, but it would do).

The sponsorship program, says Canada's auditor general, was cooked up by Public Works' Communications Co-ordination Services Branch after Dingwall and I left, in November 1997, and it ran until 2001. Pretty soon after that, stories started emerging that the Quebec advertising agencies involved in the sponsorship program had been paid millions to do little or no work. The media came to call them "Liberal-friendly" ad agencies, but I — as one of the people who had earlier slashed millions out of the federal ad budget — had never heard of, let alone met, any of these so-called Liberal-friendly executives. There were even rumours about kickbacks to the Quebec branch of the Liberal Party. It was a big, stinking mess; it was a scandal. Chrétien called in the auditor general and then the Mounties.

That's the whole sponsorship thing, in 130 words or less. Next up: the hobby farmer Paul Martin picked to get to the bottom of the whole sordid affair.

Justice John Gomery, a self-described hobby farmer from Westmount, seemed like a nice enough fellow. Having been on the bench for quite a few years, he knew all of the tricks of the judge trade: chumming it up with the army of legal counsel in attendance every day for the inquiry's hearings, radiating wisdom and beneficence, hamming it up for the media, warmly greeting every new witness. He was good at that stuff. I'll give him that much.

But here's the thing: after giving media interviews wherein he commented on the evidence before the evidence was all in; after retaining the best friend of the Chrétien-loathing Brian Mulroney to be lead commission counsel; after hiring his daughter's law firm, sole-source, against the advice of the Department of Justice; after spending nearly $100 million to investigate a program whose annual cost was far less than that; after making all sorts of un-judgelike comments (viz., calling Canadians "ignorant" when his commission was getting started and not as many were paying attention, and calling Jean Chrétien "small-town cheap" before the former prime minister had even taken the stand in his own defence); after all that, John Gomery was pretty universally regarded as a bit of a disaster. Nice guy, maybe, but not the right guy to lead a commission of inquiry.

In fairness to Paul Martin, too, the Westmount hobby farmer wasn't his first choice. A bunch of other learned jurists had turned him down. He was in a rush to smear Jean Chrétien, however, and Justice Gomery would have to do. Inquisition time!

Martin's objective, allegedly, was his promised ethical cleansing of the debauched, depraved, demoralized houses of ill repute that were Jean Chrétien's government and the Quebec branch of the federal Liberal Party. (You know, the government and party of which Paul had been alleged to be a prominent part.) Martin's assistants — who always spoke under the cloak of anonymity, because they were cowards, and because it made defamation a lot simpler — gave media interviews describing the sponsorship program's national unity fund as "a honey pot," and asserted that good old Paul Martin had known nothing, absolutely nothing, of its existence. Shortly afterwards, we learned that, one, Martin, in fact, knew all about the fund; two, he lobbied for sponsorship projects in Quebec; and three, he personally corresponded with at least one of the ad executives was at the centre of the controversy. Interesting, that.

None of us Chrétienites hated Martin or Gomery, particularly, but nor did we like them all that much either. Still, every once in a while, I would get really, really mad about Martin and Gomery and what they did in 2005 and 2006. Their legacy wasn't a happy one: destroying the name of federalism in the province of Quebec; providing lots of ammunition for the separatists at the time of the next referendum; ruining the reputations of dozens of innocent people; and, worst of all, ensuring that millions of voters are even more cynical about political institutions than ever before. There weren't words, really, to describe the nature and size of Martin's bullshit. For guys like me, it was easy to get mad about it all.

But we — me in particular — resolved to keep our cool. Be passionate and tough as James Carville had been, sure, but don't lose your temper. Don't let them see you sweat. In any scandal, your demeanour is key.

Make *them* angry, instead. Make *them* sweat. So I, we, tried to do that. Did it work? Some say it did: Gomery's press people released a book about the inquiry days after it finished hearing evidence. In it, Gomery is quoted hissing that I was "a shill" who was "highly inexperienced" at politics. And so on, and so on.

Coming from the Westmount hobby farmer, I took that as the highest form of compliment. And it told me something else: *we had gotten under his skin.* We had done to him what he had sought to do to us. That's point number one in Kinsella's Handle Scandal Manual: be passionate and relentless and tough. But don't *ever* let them see you sweat!

Magnify Mistakes, Misspending, and Misstatements!
When someone is out to magnify your mistakes, misspending, and misstatements — and we all have 'em, at one time or another — then you

need to return the favour. It's the polite thing to do. It's the smart thing to do, as well.

Now, was the sponsorship program a bona fide scandal? I guess so, sure. But when I was in the midst of defending my friend Chrétien, I never referred to sponsorship as a "scandal." Never would I validate our adversaries' central thesis with the careless use of language.

What was it, then? The sponsorship inquiry was (allegedly) all about investigating mistakes that had been made by bureaucrats and politicians. It was all about (ostensibly) probing the misspending that had happened under The Other Guy's watch. If it could highlight some terrible things that The Other Guy had said, so much the better.

Using my wee website, I made that my mandate, too. Every single day — and sometimes up to a dozen times a day — I would post stuff I had come across in the morning paper, or on the Canadian Press wire service, or that was sent to me by a hardy, fearless charter member of the pro-Chrétien club. My objective was simple: tag the Gomery Pyle Commission (as we called it), and the woolly-headed Martin regime (as it was), with the very things they were trying to lay at *our* doorstep. What's good for the goose is good for the gander, as one of Martin's more rebarbative cabinet ministers often liked to say. I agreed.

Given that I was seeking to make Gomery and Martin look as bad as I possibly could, it was important that I not be the sole source of the allegations about mistakes, misspending, and misstatements. That stuff had to mainly come from others. Early on, the media became my best friend in this regard.

In January 2005, for example, Daniel LeBlanc — the dogged *Globe and Mail* guy who had been on top of the sponsorship mess from the start — recognized that something was, well, not quite right with the headline-hungry hobby farmer. LeBlanc wrote, for instance, that Gomery's past "musings on evidence [got the] judge in hot water." He noted, "Gomery always had a politically incorrect tongue." He wrote that, previously, the provincial Court of Appeal had "chastised him for his 'gratuitous' outburst and 'mood swing.'" He added that "in a move that even his supporters acknowledge was maladroit, Judge Gomery [has] decided to go beyond generalities and spoke to the media about some of the evidence before him."

The most revealing part of LeBlanc's story, however, was to become very, very helpful, in the weeks and months ahead. As LeBlanc noted, "lawyers, however, are incensed by Judge Gomery's attitude and are concerned that his final report will not be objective. Fear is that he has already shown that he likes media attention, and that his conclusions on the sponsorship program could be unnecessarily sensational."

Not objective, eh? Thought so. Likes media attention, eh? I've known plenty of politicians like that, too. No matter how cautious they are — no matter how well trained by media handlers — their ego inevitably trips them up. They always end up looking bad. Bingo.

So I used the website, and every media interview, to shine a bright light on anything that buttressed the impression that Gomery was making loads of mistakes, and spending loads of public money, and saying loads of inappropriate stuff. I used the blog and the mainstream media to suggest that Gomery was an egocentric, sensationalistic, partisan media hound. Maybe he was, maybe he wasn't. I'm not a shrink, so that wasn't my job. My job, as I saw it, was to ensure that as many people as possible *thought* that he *might* be.

Gomery made it easy for me, starting in December 2004, with his infamous and ill-advised media interviews. He, and the media, provided plenty of incriminating evidence. The dean of the Ottawa Parliamentary Press Gallery, the *Sun*'s Doug Fisher, called for Gomery's removal early in 2005. He's got "loose lips," wrote Fisher in a chillingly accurate column; he's "unfair and glib"; and, if he didn't go, Fisher concluded, then "his eventual report will not be respected." A Liberal-hating conservative columnist, Clare Hoy, wrote that Gomery's remarks were "shockingly inappropriate." Added Hoy, "Gomery has harmed both himself and the inquiry process. And the worst part is that if he stays the course and ultimately confirms what we all suspect, he's handed the Liberals an opportunity to claim the process was stacked against them. Now that would really be annoying."

Hoy focused on another important point: "Perception being reality, why would Gomery have hired an '80s-era PC partisan, Bernard Roy, as commission counsel? Roy was a schoolmate of former Tory prime minister Brian Mulroney. He helped Mulroney get his first legal job, was best man at Mulroney's wedding, became Mulroney's principal secretary and himself was embroiled in a few Quebec-centred patronage controversies during the Tory regime."

Other respected pundits said the same sort of stuff, and I made certain that as many people as possible knew it. I didn't need to say anything on my own, particularly. I just needed to act as an anti-Gomery, anti-Martin echo chamber, and I knew it would get picked up. Some might suspect I was doing Chrétien's bidding, of course, but I again assure you that I wasn't. As with Carville and Clinton, Chrétien was ticked with me once or twice (and his lawyers more than that). But he and his family quietly appreciated that I was in their corner, trying to protect the guy I considered the best prime minister Canada ever had. They didn't tell me what to do, but they didn't tell me to stop, either.

So I continued to be an on-line echo chamber, highlighting and magnifying every bit of Gomery criticism I could find. The *Citizen*'s Susan Riley: "[Gomery has been] most un-judgelike (if not injudicious) … now it is Gomery's turn to sound defensive." My *Post* colleague Don Martin, who was the first guy to nail Gomery in an interview: "[Gomery inserted] foot in mouth … sounding very unlike a judge … there's no denying Gomery was guilty of shooting from the lip before his judicial brain was loaded … No person sitting in neutral judgment should venture public opinion on matters still being heard under oath. Gomery's not totally impartial … [he has] some bias." The *Globe*'s veteran columnist, Jeff Simpson: "Before Christmas, Judge Gomery unburdened himself in media interviews on certain evidence and witnesses he had already heard that left other judges and experienced lawyers slack-jawed … [Gomery] has already damaged his inquiry's credibility." He should resign, right?

I, however, secretly did not want Gomery to go. His loose lips, his blatant unfairness, and his glibness were our secret weapons. He was his own worst enemy. I wanted people to know that — as Hoy had written — the process "was stacked against" my friend Jean Chrétien. Gomery, more than anyone else, was helping to facilitate that impression.

Being way smarter than me, Chrétien's savvy Ottawa lawyer, David Scott, wasn't so sure. After a lot of internal debate, Scott appeared before Gomery in January 2005 to urge Gomery to return to his hobby farm. Said Scott, looking Gomery right in the eye, "Your remarks to the press were unprecedented … You have commented on the evidence, made observations of a political nature and stated that you 'have nothing to lose' and 'really don't give a damn what they think' because you 'have no ambitions' and are going to retire soon.'" It was, as Scott said, a "matter of grave concern." Gomery didn't look too happy. He sat in his big judge chair and glared down at Scott.

Scott didn't back down. The guy was fearless. "You have nonetheless reached conclusions of fact or drawn inferences from the facts before the evidence is complete ... you have closed your mind." Scott reminded Gomery that, in a December 2004 interview in the *Ottawa Citizen*, he had said, "this was a government program which was run in a catastrophically bad way."

That wasn't all, said Scott. In an interview in the *Globe* in the same week, Gomery had already dismissed some of the testimony before him, sniffing that "judges hate being lied to" — implying that he had been lied to already, but without telling us by whom. He told the *Globe* that his report would be "very harmful" to some unidentified people. He said he had "the best seat in the house for the best show in town" and that there was lots of "juicy stuff" to come. And he even played amateur political scientist, observing that the report "might have more consequences for a minority government than for a majority government."

Scott said to Gomery, "It is not only not possible to justify these statements from a fairness standpoint, but your intentional public airing of them casts serious doubt upon the objectivity of the process." Ouch!

As I had hoped and expected, a furious-sounding Gomery later refused to remove himself. I was delighted. The judicial loose cannon would continue to fire away — at himself!

When it came to misstatements, then, I had plenty to post on my website — and most of them came from Gomery's own mouth. But what about misspending? Since the sponsorship mess was all about misspending, it was vital that I unearth any evidence I could find that Gomery was misspending too. I didn't have far to look.

Let's put it this way: to say that Gomery Pyle spent taxpayer money like a drunken sailor would be to sully the fine reputation of drunken sailors everywhere. Gomery wasn't just biased; he was also costing taxpayers untold millions. When I first eyeballed the number of lawyers at the commission, I did some quick math, multiplying the number of Armani suits by their big-city law firm hourly rates. Then, as I wrote on my website as the commission got underway, "Did you hear that sound, yesterday? It was the sound of a big, fat, shiny golden apple landing on the heads of a number of gargantuan Canadian law firms. Day after day of hearings! Full, or near-full, hourly rates! Millions of documents to read and re-read! Yahoo! The Gomery gravy train has arrived!" I predicated the sponsorship inquisition would cost more than the program it was investigating. And it did.

Not long afterwards, one CTV report, which I dutifully mentioned about a thousand times, discovered that the cost of the inquiry was getting darned close to $100 million. Documents obtained by *CTV News*, in fact, showed that the legal fees for Gomery's inquisitors were chewing up millions upon millions. They were out of control. Lead counsel Bernard Roy, who was Brian Mulroney's best friend and the best man at his wedding — which was, as my blogger pal Dan "Calgary Grit" Arnold hilariously observed, like "having Jerry Falwell tried by Spongebob Squarepants" — was getting close to $1 million. His co-counsel, Bay Street lawyer and ardent Paul Martin fan Neil Finkelstein, had already broken the $1 million ceiling, CTV found. And their associate counsel, some Martin-loving guy named Guy Cournoyer, was also getting close to a million bucks.

What did that all mean? Well, it meant that Gomery was already costing four or five times what the U.S. 9/11 commission had cost. And it meant the Gomery commission was costing four or five times the annual cost of running the sponsorship program itself. When people heard that, I figured, taxpayers' blood would start boiling anew. So I made sure they heard it — over and over and over. Not very "small-town cheap," was it? Nope. More Westmount-sized expensive, you might say.

In magnifying Gomery's mistakes and whatnot, I couldn't just rely upon others all the time. I had to occasionally do some investigative reporting of my own and create a bit of my own news. So on one occasion, I wrote a letter to Gomery's flaks, asking:

> Why did Judge Gomery give a sole-source, multi-million-dollar contract to the Ogilvy Renault law firm? Was he not advised by the Department of Justice not do so, given that his own daughter was a partner there?

Why didn't he disclose this apparent conflict?

Why did he also give non-competitive, sole-source contracts worth millions of dollars to a forensic accounting firm, a transcription service, and an anti-Chrétien PR [man] — along with sinecures to partisan critics of Jean Chrétien? Didn't he realize that was wrong?

Given the fact that he was ostensibly presiding over a judicial probe into contracting irregularities, shouldn't Gomery ensure that every contract issued by his commission — every red cent — was competitive, transparent and cost-effective? What was his explanation for doing the very thing he's supposed to be preventing?

Not many lawyers (as I supposedly am) will express themselves like that to a judge (as Gomery claims to be). But, as I told my own lawyer and friend Clay Ruby, the Gomery Circus had long since stopped being about the law and politics. It was about politics. I figured Gomery wouldn't reply, and I was right. One of his army of press manipulators wrote back, saying they would respond "in due course."

But, thankfully, they never did. So I made sure a dozen reporters heard about that. And, when they reported about what I'd been seeking, I blogged about what they had reported. And so it went — on and on and on, for months. You get the picture.

Hypocrites Always Deserve What They Get!
People in glass houses … well, you know. Everyone knows that one. It's a Biblical admonition that has stood the test of time. And, when it comes the Handle Scandal Manual, truer words have seldom been spoken.

People, you see, hate hypocrites. Hate 'em. Like they say in the Gospel of Matthew: when The End comes, and God is evaluating who is naughty and who is nice, hypocrites will always "receive a greater damnation." Amen to that.

With the Gomery commission, and the Martin administration, hypocrisy was always in abundant supply. Indeed: rank, bald-faced hypocrisy was practically the coin of the realm during the blessedly short Martin era. I knew, and we knew, that if we highlighted the Gomery-

Martin hypocrisy, it would serve to undermine their mission to destroy Jean Chrétien. That's how it is in every case of scandal, real or perceived — if you nail your accuser with the same stuff he's flinging at you, he can't ever win. Expose hypocrisy, whenever and wherever possible.

So, for example, I worked doggedly to expose the fact that Justice Gomery had, early on, ordered that the law firm of Ogilvy Renault be retained as his commission counsel.

In and of itself, there's nothing scandalous about that. It's a great law firm. I may even have a relative who worked there, and I think I applied there for an articling position once. The problem wasn't just that Gomery proposed to hire Brian Mulroney's former chief of staff, the aforementioned Bernard Roy, to be his lead commission counsel. The problem wasn't just that Mulroney still worked there. The big, big problem was that Gomery's daughter, Sally, worked there. And, as a partner, any of the federal boodle Ogilvy Renault acquired during the inquiry would go, at least in part, to Gomery's daughter. Wasn't that a wee bit of a conflict of interest? Wasn't the sort of thing that Gomery was supposed to be investigating? As I observed more than once on my website, not even Chuck Guité was accused of flipping a million-dollar, sole-sourced contract to his daughter!

So I marketed that bit of news relentlessly throughout the blogosphere and the media. At first, I had few takers. No surprise there: as I wrote in Lesson Three, the media love scandal. They love it when the lions get thrown another Christian; conflict has always been more fun to write about than its opposite. In the sponsorship context, the lion was Justice Gomery, and the Christians were the Chrétien folks. The media, having decided who was the bad guy and who was the good guy, didn't want to revisit the assignment of roles. It would require too much work — and, even worse, perhaps even an apology to the public.

Ditto the bloggers. Most of them were angry white conservative males, who saw the Gomery inquiry as their best shot at electing an angry white conservative government. I had warned some of them, early on, that the Martin cabal had rigged the inquiry's terms of reference to exclude any scrutiny of their own wrongdoing — and that the main recommendations in commission's report had been cooked up long in advance, too. But the bloggers wouldn't listen. To them, the Westmount hobby farmer was their St. George, slaying the twin-headed dragon of corrupt French-Canadian liberalism. Sigh.

Eventually, we located a journalist who knew a stinker when he saw one. It was *Le Soleil's* Michel Vastel. In February 2005, Vastel wrote, "[Was] the choice of Bernard Roy as lead commission counsel by Judge Gomery, aimed at assisting the career of his daughter, who works in the same law firm as Mr. Roy? Ignoble, indeed, but unfortunately true!"

True indeed. Martin, meanwhile, wasn't much better than his fellow Westmount resident. Throughout 2004, Martin had perfected a political Sergeant Schultz routine, professing to have seen, heard, and known nothing about the sponsorship program and anyone who was involved in it. Then, in October 2004, a letter surfaced — dated April 2001 — in which Martin had, on his official letterhead, extended birthday greetings to the adman, helpfully adding a cheery handwritten postscript. As even Gomery was later forced to admit, the ad guy had been engaged in dealings that "were at best dubious and at worst unethical."

When someone is chasing a scandal, they have to be above reproach, in every way. The second they do the very thing they are investigating — the moment they are hypocritical — you've got 'em. They're done like dinner.

Mock 'Em, Sock 'Em, Rock 'Em!

As indicated earlier, you shouldn't be afraid of the scandalmongers. Easier said than done, I know, but it's crucial that you respond — quickly, factually — to their every allegation. And, moreover, that you do it with a big smile.

December 17, 2004: there it was, in black and white, on page five of the *Globe and Mail*. After only four months of hearings — and while the sponsorship inquiry was *still actually underway* and my friend Chrétien had yet to be given an opportunity to defend his good name — Justice Gomery decided to give an interview. The first sentence in Dan LeBlanc's 670-word news story read as follows: "Two things stuck in Mr. Justice John Gomery's craw in four months of hearings into the sponsorship scandal: lying witnesses and former prime minister Jean Chrétien's personalized golf balls."

That's what it said. This guy was a judge and a lawyer, and he was saying stuff like this, in the fifth paragraph: "It's such a disappointment that the prime minister of Canada would allow his name to be put on golf balls to be used at golf tournaments. That's really small-town cheap, you know, free golf balls." Pardon my French, but that's a fucking quote, folks.

Small-town cheap! He had called Chrétien small-town cheap! Within minutes of the *Globe* hitting the streets, my phone and BlackBerry started ringing. Political folks, who are generally surprised by nothing, were astounded. And lawyers I know — and even one retired judge — told me they had never seen anything like that before, coming (as it did) from a judge in the middle of a legal hearing that would have serious implications for the reputations and personal liberty of many, many people. One of them even suggested that someone should consider taking Gomery to the Canadian Judicial Council, where Gomery would almost certainly be censured. He referred me to Section 65 of *The Judges Act*: Gomery, he said, had arguably "been placed, by his conduct or otherwise, in a position incompatible with the due execution of [his] office."

I agreed, but even at that stage, some Machiavellian Chrétien types were starting to suspect that Gomery might turn out to be quite useful, just as Ken Starr's missteps had been useful to James Carville. When a few more interviews took place, Chrétien's lawyer asked Gomery to recuse himself. To the surprise of no one, he wouldn't. But did we forget it? No way. Not a chance. You don't say something like that about the Little Guy from Shawinigan and get away with it.

In the first week of February, I got together with one of my best friends, former fellow Chrétien staffer Charlie Angelakos. We talked about Chrétien's much-anticipated appearance before Gomery. We talked on the phone with Chrétien's legendary executive assistant, Bruce Hartley. We talked to some other folks, too, but I don't plan on revealing their names, or any of the salacious details. Suffice to say that Angelakos flew up to Ottawa before Chrétien was slated to appear. He carried his overnight bag, and something else, too.

The best way to deal with a political adversary like John Gomery — because that's what he was, and none of us had a doubt about that anymore — is to mock them. When battling an allegation of scandal, humour is the best strategy. That, and an ability to fire a shot right up the middle.

So I'm going to take a shot in the dark — a long one, using a three-iron — and say that this exchange, coming at the end of Chrétien's turn on the stand at the Gomery Circus, represents one of the best performances in recent Canadian political history. And, simultaneously, I submit that it was the moment where the good guy (Jean Chrétien) had decisively clobbered the bad guys (Gomery and Martin). It began as Chrétien reached into his briefcase, while he was being questioned by his own lawyer, David Scott.

MR. SCOTT:	And where did those golf balls come from?
MR. CHRÉTIEN:	You know, what happened is … [I] have to explain to the Commission. When we are travelling abroad, social things [happen] and we gave little gifts or received little gifts, and at the beginning in '94, I received golf balls from … the President of the United States, and I received many. They were giving the same balls to the bodyguards who were with me and so on as a courtesy thing, as a souvenir. So we decided that we had to do the same thing, and so we had — somebody said … We should have balls with your name on it.
MR. SCOTT:	All right. Now, these golf balls that we see in the photographs of which there are many remaining, Exhibit JC-3, were those golf balls that were given out in your capacity as the Prime Minister to, for you have given examples of, officials of other countries?
MR. CHRÉTIEN:	Yes. It was not used for the unity file. When the government — when the Prime Minister or any minister had some things to buy, the buyer for the government is the Department of Supply and Services. So we have to request there, even the Prime Minister, to buy for us.
MR. SCOTT:	All right. So were any of these golf balls given out at your own golf tournament …
MR. CHRÉTIEN:	Never.
MR. SCOTT:	… the fundraiser for the Liberal Party?

MR. CHRÉTIEN: Never.

MR. SCOTT: And were golf balls …

MR. CHRÉTIEN: Not these balls. There were some given …

MR. SCOTT: All right. Who paid for those?

MR. CHRÉTIEN: … or caps given in my riding.

MR. SCOTT: And who paid for those?

MR. CHRÉTIEN: But we paid for it. The association paid for it.

MR. SCOTT: All right. Come back to these golf balls then that are in the photograph. You said you got golf balls from others.

MR. CHRÉTIEN: Yes.

MR. SCOTT: Who did you get them from, Mr. Chrétien? Do you have some examples?

[Lots of laughter. Reporters were laughing, and lawyers, too. Chrétien reached into his bag to extract more golf balls. Gomery was flushed, and he looked like his head was about to explode.]

MR. CHRÉTIEN: Yes, yes. I have a ball here with the seal of the President of the United States and signed by a Texan town Crawford, Texas, George W. Bush … with the seal of the presidency, and his name signed. Here, I have one from a small town-guy, I guess, from Manila, Philippines, President Ramos, plus the flag of his country. It is very common. I have one here by a very well-known group, Ogilvy Renault. You know them? Mr. Roy and Mr. Mulroney and Mademoiselle [Sally] Gomery are all members of that firm. I cannot call them small town [or] call them Westmount cheap. It would be an oxymoron.

[Lots more laughter.]

MR. SCOTT: *[barely able to keep his composure]*:All right. Mr. Chrétien, did you receive those golf balls from the persons you have identified?

MR. CHRÉTIEN: Yes. Only one that was given to me by another; it is from George W. Bush. The others I received them from them.

234 | The War Room

MR. SCOTT:	And did you give them golf balls with the maple leaf and your signature on it?
MR. CHRÉTIEN:	Yes, and I gave them to their bodyguards and/or their partners who were playing golf with us.
MR. SCOTT:	Thank you very much, Mr. Commissioner.
THE COMMISSIONER:	Thank you, Mr. Scott. Is that all for the witness? Thank you, Mr. Chrétien.
MR. CHRÉTIEN:	Thank you, Mr. Commissioner.

His face scarlet, Gomery scuttled out of the room with his minions and well-paid lawyers. The whole thing took just a few minutes, but it was the end of the Gomery commission, pretty much. Chrétien had won. It was all that average folks would remember. I immediately started posting on my website the stuff that reporters were saying as Chrétien strolled out of the inquiry, everyone trying to shake his hand, some even asking for autographs. The CBC's Don Newman declared, "That was a grand-slam home run." Another CBC guy, Keith Boag — never a Chrétien fan — said, "It was brilliant … it restored dignity." And Canadian Press reported within minutes that "it made for superb political theatre." I blogged every word, and then blogged about it when they wrote about my blogging.

The next day, it was the same on the front page of every newspaper. Inside, too. In the *Post*, Adam Radwanski wrote, "Count on Jean Chrétien … to remind Canadians of why they miss him … the fighter almost always wins." His *Post* colleague John Ivison: "[Chrétien] was secretly packing the equivalent of a Winchester rifle in his briefcase … pulling off an act of revenge that will have earned him grudging respect, even from those who wouldn't give him the parsley off their fish … As Gomery glowered above him, Chrétien completed the humiliation." Bruce Garvey, also in the *Post*: "There is no smoking gun. Nor will there be one of those seminal moments of political theatre that destroys careers and reputations … No, this Gomery inquiry is dreary, plodding fare indeed, enlivened only by Jean Chrétien's briefcase full of presidential golf balls with small-town connections."

And that was just one newspaper, and a conservative one to boot! It was the same everywhere else. Lawrence Martin, who spent years trying to peddle flimsy Chrétien "scandals," in the *Globe*: "CHRÉTIEN STICKS IT TO 'EM ONCE AGAIN … Nothing stops the iron man … Not only does he elude his tormentors, he often ends up sticking it to them, as well." Margaret Wente, also in the *Globe*: "Jean Chrétien has more balls than anyone … for those who want Mr. Chrétien to pay, I'm afraid they're doomed to disappointment." And, in a news story by the same paper's Jane Taber and Campbell Clark: "MARTIN AND MPs APPLAUD CHRÉTIEN TESTIMONY … Prime Minister Paul Martin led a rousing ovation at caucus yesterday for Jean Chrétien … the Prime Minister's support was echoed by some of his MPs as they emerged from the morning caucus meeting. Caucus chairman Andy Savoy told reporters that Mr. Chrétien was a 'small-town guy who opened a big-town can of whoop-ass on his detractors.'" (Later, typically, Martin denied having led an ovation. And people wondered why Charlie Angelakos had tagged Martin as "Mr. Dithers.")

The *Sun*: "[A] ballsy performance … he stole the show." The *Ottawa Citizen*'s Susan Riley: "So much for small-town cheap." The *Edmonton Journal*'s Alan Kellogg: "Count out the little guy from Shawinigan at your peril … the legendary political champ reminded us of the protean chops he's possessed all along." The *Globe*'s Campbell Clark: "Remarkable." Jane Taber, again: "[Chrétien] provided the knockout punch of the sponsorship inquiry … The inquiry lawyers were stunned … the reporters laughed … Mr. Chrétien had just provided the best political theatre Ottawa has seen this season." The *Toronto Star*'s Les Whittington: "Jean Chrétien teed off on Justice John Gomery with a wicked shot … it all built to the climactic flourish, a golf ball emblazoned with the name of the law firm Ogilvy Renault — the same Montreal law firm, Chrétien delighted in pointing out, that is home to chief commission counsel Bernard Roy, former Prime Minister Brian Mulroney and Gomery's daughter, Sally … Gomery stared at Chrétien stone-faced during the golf ball display."

My personal favourite came from Susan Delacourt, a *Toronto Star* scribbler who flat-out adored the Martin people and had never disguised her contempt for the Chrétien folks, and me in particular. Wrote Delacourt, "[Chrétien] launched several well-aimed shots over the day yesterday at commissioner John Gomery and the lead counsel, Bernard Roy … sources say several Liberal MPs were jubilant as they watched

Chrétien's testimony, saying he saved the Liberal brand, and whispered they wished Prime Minister Paul Martin could perform that way."

Chrétien won because he wasn't afraid to hit back, hard — and because he did it all in a funny, memorable way. Gomery and Martin never recovered.

Tell the Truth and Take Responsibility!
Don't lie! Don't fib! And when the other guy tells a bald-faced whopper — when he refuses to take responsibility for his own mistakes and misspending and misstatements — call him on it. Go after him. But don't emulate him.

After he created the Gomery Pyle Commission, you see, and after the Liberal Party immediately started to gush voter support, the hapless Paul Martin and his small circle of goons recognized that they had made one of the biggest mistakes in political history. Running around Canada like a headless chicken, shrieking about how the political party you happen to lead is corrupt, is — surprise, surprise — really bad strategy. Go figure.

Ipso facto, they needed to find someone to blame about not just sponsorship but, now, the resulting loss in public confidence, too. Three guesses whom they picked, and the first two don't count.
Jean Chrétien, c'mon down!
Martin's toadies started telling media supplicants — anonymously, naturally — that Jean Chrétien had actually *timed* his retirement to avoid being around when the manure hit the proverbial air conditioning device. That is, Chrétien knew that the auditor general's report was going to be bad, bad, bad, and he needed to get out of town before it hit the streets. Uh-huh. Sure.

The problem with this bit of spin was that, like most things said by top Martinites, it just wasn't true. It was bullshit. Once again (and as history records), Chrétien had called in the cops. Those same police investigations had been going on for *two years* before he retired — and, not to put too a fine point on it, the Liberal Party had been polling at about 55 percent for most of that period. Remember this: what kills you with the public, mostly, isn't a scandal. It's how you *react* to the scandal. To recall the lesson of Watergate — it's rarely the break-in, it's usually the cover-up. Jean Chrétien did all that could reasonably be expected of him: he called in the auditors, he called in the police, he kept his cool, he offered to take the heat. People approved of that.

Paul Martin, meanwhile, blamed everyone else but the guy in the bathroom mirror. He tried to cover up. No one ever approves of *that*.

As one of his guys, I knew that Jean Chrétien had met with Paul Martin in the fall of 2003 and offered to stick around and take the sponsorship heat. The offer was also made to his swaggering, pompous inner circle. As the clerk of the Privy Council said, under oath, at the Gomery Circus, "[The offer] was transmitted to Mr. Martin's people. There was no response."

The Martin cabal wanted Chrétien out before the end of 2003, so that they could start their glorious hundred-year reign at the start of 2004. And they were pompous enough to believe their blame-Chrétien "strategy" could work. As the *Winnipeg Free Press* reported at the time: "Martin has no one to blame but himself. Chrétien originally planned to retire in February 2004, but Martin's cabal pushed him from office in December 2003. Had Chrétien stayed, he would have retired under a cloud, with Martin riding in on his white horse to clean up the mess. But Martin's overeagerness for office did him in." Exactly.

Unlike Paul Martin, however, Jean Chrétien was a real leader. As Harry Truman said, Chrétien knew that the buck stopped on his desk. He was prepared to take the heat. For example, before he fired a few metaphorical golf balls at Justice Gomery's gleaming pate, Chrétien read a long prepared statement. He told the truth, and he took responsibility for his own mistakes. Unlike Paul Martin, he didn't try to pin it on bureaucrats, political colleagues or his former boss. Unlike Paul Martin, he didn't deny any knowledge of the sponsorship program — in fact, he defended it.

"Sponsorship is much more than just billboards, flags and word marks. It is involvement with organizers of community events, people who are often opinion leaders in their communities, letting them know that there is also a Government of Canada that relates directly to citizens, that the Government of Canada does more than just collect taxes while the Québec government delivers programs," Chrétien said. "This type of federal presence amongst community leaders was part and parcel of our overall strategy. That is why we committed to spending a significant amount of money every year to be part of community events. And we did not restrict the program to Québec because the Government of Canada should be present in communities across the country."

Were mistakes made? Did he bear any responsibility for those mistakes? Chrétien didn't flinch. "I regret any mistakes that might have been made in the course of this program, or any other government program. As Prime Minister, I take ultimate responsibility for everything good and everything bad that happens in the government. Those mistakes that were made in good faith can be excused. Any that were made in bad faith are inexcusable. If some people acted in bad faith for personal gain, they betrayed the Prime Minister, the government and the country. They should be identified and punished, subject, of course, to due process of law." He paused. "But there is absolutely no doubt in my mind that it would have been a totally unforgivable mistake to leave the field of sponsorship of community events in Québec to the Parti Québecois government alone."

See, Paul? That's called telling the truth and taking responsibility. If you had done that at the start, you'd still be prime minister right now.

Motives Matter!

As in murder mysteries, so too in Kinsella's Handle Scandal Manual: motives matter. Motives count. With any scandal — with any noun, post-Watergate, to which people attach the suffix "gate," in fact — people want to be assured that justice and truth are the ultimate goal. Not vengeance and partisan chicanery. In my view, people want to know why someone is chasing a scandal. Is it because they have to — or because they *want* to?

In the case of Paul Martin, the answer was self-evident. He clearly disliked Chrétien, and he was almost certainly using the Gomery commission as camouflage for his political agenda. Ulterior motives were everywhere to be found, in those bad old days, and they mostly originated with the Martinites.

Here's how the Martin camp went about healing the divisions created by their decade-long effort to oust a sitting prime minister. Here's how they sought to build a good working relationship with the public service. Here's what Gomery was *really* about.

CanWest News Service, February 12, 2004: "The Chrétien government concealed 'criminal' wrongdoing in the Quebec sponsorship scandal from Cabinet ministers, including Paul Martin, according to the

Prime Minister's senior advisors, who blame the fiasco on Jean Chrétien … 'This public inquiry is going to pin it all on them.'"

Toronto Star, February 13, 2004: "Privately, Martin's advisers say Chrétien's approach was more of the old-school, favours and patronage system."

Canadian Press, February 22, 2004: "The hunt for culpable parties in the federal sponsorship scandal will extend to the uppermost reaches of the public service, says a highly placed Liberal official."

Canadian Press, February 13, 2004: "Shadowy political forces were at work in the federal sponsorship scandal, Prime Minister Paul Martin said Thursday … For the first time, Martin laid the blame not only on a small group of bureaucrats — 'Let's call them the mechanics in all this' — but on their political masters."

Vancouver Sun, February 28, 2004: "Martin argued Friday that the sponsorship scandal was partly the result of the enormous powers wielded by the Prime Minister's Office, and he vowed to dilute that clout."

And so on. There are plenty of other examples we could cite, sadly, but this book is already long enough. In the view of not a few people, Martin's quest wasn't getting at the truth, or bringing wrongdoers to justice, or anything like that. (The RCMP was already doing all of that stuff anyway, and doing it better and cheaper, too.)

As was well known by everyone in Canada, Paul Martin had always despised Jean Chrétien. That fact, plus the suspicion that the Gomery commission's terms of reference had been rigged to protect Martin and his cronies — along with the anonymous commentary helpfully supplied by Martin's own PMO staff about the ultimate objective (ie. the public inquiry is going to "pin it all on them") — combined to leave no doubt about Paul Martin's true motive. None of it was even debatable.

John Gomery, the amiable hobby farmer from Westmount, was less easy to associate with impure motives, however. That required some work. Gomery hadn't been lusting after Jean Chrétien's job for a decade, like Paul Martin had been. He didn't oppose some key Chrétien policy, as far as anyone was aware. Chrétien had never said anything mean about Gomery, or vice versa. How, then, to make the case that the latter was out to destroy the former? With Martin, easy; with Gomery, not so much.

The best clue was found in that early 2004 Daniel LeBlanc analysis in the *Globe*. Gomery had a country-sized ego, LeBlanc revealed, and he clearly loved all the attention he was getting in his new role, as the Ken Starr of the north. He was profoundly grateful for the opportunity Paul Martin had given him — and, at all relevant times, he was not willing to challenge the conventional wisdom then prevailing in Ottawa. At all relevant times, pretty much everyone — the dumb Conservatives, the dumb Bloc, the dumb NDP, and the dumb Martin Liberals — were all eager to associate Jean Chrétien's name with scandal. Why was that dumb? Let me answer that question with another question: how was it in any way strategic for the Opposition parties to run down the private citizen named Jean Chrétien? Last time anyone checked, circa 2004, his name hadn't been on a ballot since 2000. And, um, Martin's was.

Gomery, meanwhile, wasn't all that interested in stopping the lynch mob. If at all possible, he wanted to grab a pitchfork and join in on the fun. It would ensure more media coverage, after all.

I was befuddled, and a senior lawyer pal provided some useful analysis. "I've appeared before these kinds of guys many times at commissions and inquiries," said the lawyer friend. "They've been labouring in obscurity for years, rendering judgments that no one reads or cares about, and all of sudden they are rock stars, and they love it. It feeds their ego like you wouldn't believe. They start saying more and more provocative stuff, because it gets them more and more media and political attention. For some of them, it's the highlight of their careers."

So Gomery, in search of said attention, did all he could to attract it. He craved headlines; he would say all sorts of things to get them. For instance, in October 2004, Gomery permitted lawyers to make unsubstantiated allegations of alcoholism about a Liberal aide who had passed away a few days earlier and obviously could not defend himself. It was utterly, thoroughly disgraceful. As I wrote on the website at the time, "Even Ken Starr did not do that. Is there any decency left?"

A few months later, in February 2005, Gomery went after a friend of mine, former PMO staffer Jean Carle. Acting as his own legal counsel, in effect, Gomery castigated a sponsorship that had been linked to a Crown corporation that Carle had worked at. Looking at Carle, Gomery said, "If this was about drugs, we'd call it money laundering. Don't you agree?"

Money laundering! Drug dealing! Why didn't he accuse us of serial murder, rape, and the Munich Pact, while he was at it?

But there was more to come, all of it making plain that Gomery had abandoned any pretence of fairness or even-handedness. In the fall of 2005, Gomery convened what he innocuously called roundtables, and invited sworn Chrétien adversaries and/or political opponents to attend and give him advice about what should be in his report — former Conservative politicians and advisors such as Barbara McDougall, Patrick Boyer, Derek Burney, John Crosbie, Roch Bolduc, and John Fraser. He even invited Rod Love, the campaign manager to Stockwell Day, the guy Jean Chrétien wiped the floor with in 2000. "What next?" I wrote on the website. "Brian Mulroney? ... Oops, sorry. They already had Mulroney's best man and Chief of Staff acting as lead commission counsel, didn't they?"

Now, don't get me wrong: Fraser is a kindly man, Boyer's respectable, McDougall's a nice lady. Bolduc was at that point a Conservative fundraiser. But, um, they were all Tories! For example: asking Norman Spector to be a participant in a roundtable? Spector, who had been Mulroney's chief of staff after Roy, and who viscerally detested Chrétien (and me), declaring that the former Liberal leader had "devised a massive propaganda campaign, the sponsorship program ... [that] is his true legacy on national unity." Anticipating criticism of the type I was throwing his way, Gomery apparently figured he needed a "Liberal" advisor, too, so he signed up Raymond Garneau. As some may recall, Garneau was the insurance salesman who called on Jean Chrétien to resign in 2002. Gomery, however, made him the chairman of the advisory panel to the commission that was investigating Chrétien. Sound fair to you?

Me neither. The whole thing was crazy. It was farcical. And, as things turned out, Canadians also thought it all stunk to high heaven, too. Handle Scandal Manual rule of thumb: always try and figure out a scandalmonger's motives. And, if their motives are impure — as the motives of Martin and Gomery inarguably were — tell everyone in the vicinity.

It'll work for you, because — contrary to what Martin, Gomery, Spector, Roy, and their ilk believed — most people are fair. They know bullshit when they see it.

Expose the Bullies!

Nobody likes bullies much. That's what we call a truism. And when you are being accused of scandalous behaviour by a thug, that's what we call a good day.

One day in May 2005, as I recall, was a good day. I thought I could hear much tut-tutting north of the Queensway, in the nation's capital. Some Grits were miffed that Conservative Party Leader Stephen Harper had been (justly) angry that the Paul Martin regime had been delaying a confidence vote — delaying it in such a way that it adversely affected the health of two Conservative MPs then undergoing cancer treatment. In high dudgeon, the Martinettes were immediately thereafter on a full media campaign, talking points in hand, all soberly declaring Harper's allegation "low," and so on. Was it?

Well, no, actually, it wasn't. The Martin cabal cared about one thing — power. Getting it, keeping it. For example, I recall one Friday evening a few years back, when I almost quit the Liberal Party of Canada. It was the night that the Martin cabal took over the riding association of former British Columbia cabinet minister Herb Dhaliwal, knowing that Dhaliwal was out of the country and that his wife was dying of cancer. I had witnessed a lot political thuggery in my day, to be sure, but I had never before seen anything as disgusting, and as inhuman, as that. It was only a friend in Ottawa who talked me out of quitting. (I quit later, when the Martin brain trust called the Chrétien folks "criminals," and when they started recruiting separatists as candidates.)

The bullying of Herb Dhaliwal has become the stuff of legend within the Liberal Party of Canada. Read this snippet from a newspaper piece by Paul Martin's official biographer, John Gray. "On television, [Paul Martin] gives the sad impression of a desperate man on a high wire who suddenly realizes that in the big job there is no safety net. It was always said of Mr. Martin that he loved public policy but hated politics. That may be the happiest explanation of the crudeness of his leadership campaign, where the only art was shooting the enemy wounded," Gray noted. "He shrugged Sheila Copps out of politics and *allowed his lieutenants to hijack the riding of a cabinet colleague whose wife was dying of cancer.* The people who won him the leadership were skilled in the craft of regicide, but governance was not in their curriculum vitae. Yet those are the people who are now his aides and advisers in government."

Even before Paul Martin became prime minister, he and his entourage had been acquiring an unhelpful reputation for being bullies. Enter the name "Paul Martin" and the words "thug" or "bully" in a news search engine, as I did, and you'll get nearly a thousand news stories. It's not very scientific, admittedly, but I can tell you that the perception was widespread, within the Liberal Party and without. The Martin folks would stop at nothing to seize power.

In fairness to Justice Gomery, I don't think he necessarily bullied witnesses or the people he disliked. But it was enough that he was seen as too closely aligned with the bullying, thuggish Martin gang.

Throughout 2004 and 2005, the exiled Chrétien team would tell the media — on the record, too — all about the latest bit of Martinite thuggishness. Why were they bullies? To this day, I truly do not know. Perhaps they thought they were being decisive. Perhaps they simply enjoyed it. Whatever the case, they never shook the public impression that they were swaggering yobs — and that Justice Gomery was there to do their bidding.

Get and Keep the People on Your Side!
When fighting a scandal, does public opinion matter? Let's put it this way: Is the pope Catholic? Does a bear shit in the woods? Does a one-legged duck swim in circles? Is a frog's ass watertight? Does a one-legged pope with a watertight ass shit in circles in the woods? Well, yes!

In or about February 2005, polling was concluding that a majority of Canadians thought the Gomery Pyle Show wasn't going to find out anything. A whack of Canadians thought its $80 million (and counting) price tag was obscenely high. And a huge number — bigger even in Quebec, where they were paying the closest attention — thought Justice Gomery was clearly biased against Jean Chrétien and had already written his final report.

For Paul Martin, things hadn't turned out all that well, either. In the spring of 2005, the *Globe* published a big poll showing that the federal Conservatives were ahead of the Liberals. But, as the *Globe* put it, "the most stunning finding shows that 61 per cent of Canadians surveyed believe the prime minister is the federal political leader most likely to tell a lie if it would help him politically. Only 26 per cent believe that of Conservative Leader Stephen Harper."

This was my favourite part: "When asked which party leader is the most hypocritical, 54 per cent chose Mr. Martin, compared to 29 per cent for Mr. Harper. In a similar vein, 63 per cent thought Mr. Martin the most dishonest, compared with 20 per cent for Mr. Harper."

Our objective, my objective, has never been to change the minds of the media or the "thinking" of officialdom. The objective has been — through the media (if possible) and through websites (if necessary) — to capture the support of Joe and Jane Frontporch, and to keep it.

With Jean Chrétien, the assignment was comparatively easy. As I said to him more than once during the Gomery ordeal, "Do you think that they can hurt, over forty weeks, the reputation you built over forty years? Not a chance. It didn't work with Clinton, it won't work with you."

Get the people, and keep the people. If you have the people, what the inquisitors and prosecutors say is immaterial. Always.

Hit 'Em Hard, Hit 'Em Fast, Hit 'Em Often!
In a twenty-four-hour-a-day, seven-day-a-week, five-hundred-channel media universe, as James Carville says, speed kills — your opponent. When combatting a scandal, you have to be faster and tougher than you've ever been. You have to hit your opponent, over and over and over.

So, when I was going after Gomery day after day after day, did he get angry with me? Did he react? Did he care?

To be honest, I didn't know. Gomery kept his cool, mainly, which I grudgingly admired. But then, in the spring of 2006, something called *Inside Gomery* hit the bookstores — and we learned that we *had* been getting through. Gomery and his army of lawyers and advisors *had* been feeling the punches.

Between the swaths of preening vanity and ham-fisted prose contained in the puny book — written about the famous Quebec jurist by his obliging press flak, Francois Perreault — there were a handful of revealing details.

One came midway through the slender booklet and described the day in February 2005 when Jean Chrétien arrived at the Gomery commission to testify. Surrounded by "an entourage of lawyers and cronies,"

Perreault sneered, and "looking extremely pleased with himself," the former prime minister "ripped a marker" from the hands of "a bold spectator" and, "unable to restrain himself," autographed the man's forehead.

"Appalling," Perreault wrote. "Chrétien's coterie guffawed as one man."

But here's the thing, as I later informed Perreault in the pages of the *National Post*: The "bold spectator" was a comedian from CBC's *This Hour Has 22 Minutes*. If Perreault had been physically present to witness the encounter, done for laughs on both sides, he would have known that. But he wasn't.

Reading *Inside Gomery*, one almost gets the impression that the Westmount hobby farmer and his friend Perreault weren't actually physically present for quite a lot of the $100-million, two-year-long sponsorship inquiry. Much of the book was like that, as I discovered, but that wasn't its biggest problem. Its most serious problem was that *Inside Gomery* represented a huge conflict of interest — for three main reasons.

One, Gomery permitted Perreault to pocket the proceeds of the French and English editions of his booklet, even though his PR underling had already received approximately $250,000 in public monies in a contract awarded without competition. Two, Gomery and Perreault advanced the book scheme while the Gomery commission was still underway and receiving legal submissions. Three, Gomery actually encouraged Perreault to write the book despite a confidentiality agreement signed by the former Quebec journalist.

Perreault, *La Presse* reported when the story first broke, wrote his book on the taxpayers' dime, whilst the commission was still hearing evidence, and for personal profit. When a sharp reporter confronted him with rumours about those things, Perreault prevaricated. To pen such a tome would be akin to "insider trading," he said. Agreed. But he did it anyway, and with John Gomery's blessing and participation.

That Perreault would be involved in such an appalling lapse in judgment was unsurprising (it mirrored the judgment of his boss, after all). Some of the critical statements he had made to reporters about Jean Chrétien would come to form part of Chrétien's federal court case documenting Gomery's bias. And, in March 2005, the communications firm Weber Shandwick — which had named Perreault executive vice-president, business development in 2004 — quietly removed the Gomery spokesman from its payroll.

So, had we — and I — gotten under Gomery's skin? Had the Handle Scandal campaign worked? Well, in one key passage, Perreault documents Gomery as actually saying that Chrétien's sworn testimony was a "vaudeville show." (If that wasn't what lawyers call a reasonable apprehension of bias, nothing is.)

But on me and my little blog campaign? On me, Perreault — with Gomery's approval and apparent participation —wrote practically *a whole chapter*!

In the chapter titled "Cyberbattle in the Blogosphere," Perreault opened with the observation that "blogging is the equivalent of communicating by word of mouth, only it's all conducted on the Internet." Got that? Blogs, Gomery's new media expert wrote, are useful in spreading "misinformation." Oh really? Is that so?

"As a Liberal activist, Warren Kinsella was obsessed with waging war against the Gomery Commission and all those who represented it," Perreault wrote. "Little known beyond Parliament Hill, he had been an executive assistant to Public Works Minister David Dingwall before moving to Prime Minister Chrétien's office."

Um, flat-out, 100 percent *wrong*, and it was only the second paragraph! I worked for Chrétien when we were in *Opposition*, and then for Dingwall when we got into *government*. (Was I "little known?" I guess so — but it's rather *odd* writing close to a whole chapter about me, then, ain't it?)

Perreault's next error came in the very next sentence. He pronounced that "this party militant had played a modest supporting role in the sponsorship [program]" — when, in fact, the program didn't even come into existence until nearly two years after I left government. But there was more.

"From the start of the commission proceedings, Kinsella turned his website into a forum for nasty gossip," Perreault sniffed. "He peppered the media and other public-opinion makers with emails that attempted to put John Gomery himself on trial." (Well, that much was true. Guilty as charged.)

Perreault goes on and on like that, for page after page. It was pretty boring. One thing was clear, however. Perreault and his boss didn't like me one bit — which upsets me a great deal, as you can well imagine. I was, in Perreault and Gomery's view, "in-house webmaster" for assorted "partisan ex-hack[s] from the old Liberal regime." I posted "propaganda" on my website. I was a "zealot." Et cetera, et cetera. You get the picture.

What did it all signify, given that Perreault's book sold about a dozen copies, outside of his immediate family? Not much, admittedly. By the time his self-mandating, self-financing, out-of-control political inquisition sputtered to a close at the end of 2005, the public didn't care about the Westmount hobby farmer anymore, or his press flak, or his press flak's forgettable booklet. They were irrelevant.

For me, however, it was noteworthy that Gomery and his well-paid supplicants had noticed what I had been doing, and that they had been pissed off about it. As Perreault himself admitted, reporters and bloggers would "plunder" my website, looking for "catchy lines" and "download[ing] their song sheet." Then, he said, "many political commentators" would repeat my lines and point of view.

Did the anti-Gomery campaign work? No less than the Westmount hobby farmer said that it had.

Sponsorships Work!
And not only do sponsorships work, it's possible to survive massive sponsorship-related scandalmongering, too.

You get yourself, and your organization, through a scandal crisis by keeping your cool. By magnifying the mistakes of the other side. By exposing the hypocrisy and ulterior motives of bullies. By hitting back hard, and by using humour. By telling the truth, and taking responsibility for your own screw-ups. By keeping the confidence of ordinary people.

You get through to the other side with the Handle Scandal Manual!

Get Modern!

M ODERN *SCHMODERN.*

What the hell are these blog things? And Facebook? And MySpace? And YouTube? And Flickr? And podcasting? And "citizen media?" And, while we're on the subject, does this World Wide Web thing really amount to a hill of beans, Virginia?

I mean, should any self-respecting war room warrior really *care* about any of this stuff?

Well, first things first. Definitions are important, and — in case you are wondering — so too are blogs. In a poll they did a couple of years back, my pals at the respected Ipsos-Reid agency attempted to define these wildly popular weblogs, or blogs. Their take: "Web pages with minimal to no external editing, providing online commentary, that are periodically updated and presented in reverse chronological order, with hyperlinks to other online sources. [Respondents] were further told that blogs could function as personal diaries, technical advice columns, sports chat, celebrity gossip, political commentary, or all of the above." Sounds about right.

Me, I have a simpler definition. I agree with what someone else once called the Internet — namely, it's "a vanity press for the deranged." Some days, that sums it up, pretty much.

War rooms and the things that war rooms do — paid and unpaid media, quick response, opposition research, quick response, handling scandal, and so on — are all about effective communications. For any war room warrior, to paraphrase the *Cool Hand Luke* axiom, a failure to communicate is fatal. Effective communications are mission critical. In my experience, there are two types of communication failures: human and technological. During any campaign, human failures aren't merely probable, they're positively inevitable. But technological lapses, while also sometimes unavoidable, shouldn't be happening as often. They're avoidable.

The modern media environment is digital, difficult, and double-quick. To survive in it — to thrive in it — you need to be modern, too. It's essential. And that is why war room warriors have embraced the Internet and its progeny with a vengeance. Blogs in particular.

But why, you ask? And, while we are on the subject, who are the guys behind these blogs and the like? (And they mainly *are* guys, too, regrettably.) Well, a 2004 MIT study looked at five hundred bloggers in nearly forty countries and found that nearly 65 percent were male, and that about 60 percent had a college or university education. Nearly 80 percent were white, and most of them were pretty young, with the vast majority landing somewhere between the ages of twenty-one and forty. Most of them had been at the blogging game for a couple of years (some less, some more). Okay: So there's a bunch of well-educated young white guys wearing jammies, pecking away at computers in their mothers' basement. So what? Does anyone actually admit to reading what these *pyjamahadeen* are writing? Does anyone *care*? Well, um, *yes*, according to Ipsos-Reid's pulse-takers. In their aforementioned 2005 study, they found that blogs seem to be most popular among those with high household incomes ($60,000 or more), men (48 percent, versus 35 percent among women), younger adults, and — again — those with post-secondary education. A marketer's (or a politician's, or a war roomer's) dream constituency: educated, affluent, engaged. And it's growing all the time.

But it gets even *more* fascinating, fellow Luddites. The Ipsos-Reid agency concluded that about half of the folks who are on-line have read blogs. Among those who have read 'em, an incredible 60 percent believed blogs influenced public opinion, and 40 percent thought they helped to shape mainstream media, politics, and public policy, too. Another 40 percent described blogger content as "accurate," and fully half said they trusted the content of these websites either somewhat or a lot.

Why is any of that a big deal? Simple: because pollsters have also concluded that the mainstream media don't have that kind of popularity anymore. Because the traditional news media are being read, or viewed, less and less. And because the old-fashioned media — newspapers, radio, TV — just aren't considered all that trustworthy anymore. Meanwhile so-called new media continues to grow by proverbial leaps and bounds, and is seen as more trustworthy and reliable.

A big 2005 Pew Research Center study tracked the views of more than 2,200 on-line Americans throughout the 2004 U.S. election campaign. Its findings are surprising, perhaps astonishing. From 1992 to 2004, network television news went down nearly 20 percent — from 55 percent to 36 percent — as a "primary news source." Newspapers, in the same time frame, plummeted from 57 percent to 39 percent. Magazines, from 11 percent to 3 percent or less. The Internet, meanwhile, wasn't even a factor in 1992 — it barely existed. But by 2004, nearly 20 percent of Pew's respondents were saying the Internet was their primary news source.

Meanwhile, half of Internet users — and nearly 60 percent of those who got their political news on-line — agreed "the Internet has raised the overall quality of public debate." Most of the folks who pick up their political news on-line do so because it's more convenient than the old ways of getting news, Pew found. But the study also found that millions of citizens find the Internet — and blogs, in particular — give them information and opinion they simply don't get from TV, newspapers, or radio. One of the many ironies, here, is that citizen media and Internet-based advocacy — in a blog, in a podcast, on one of the social networking sites like Facebook — is, like diary-writing, essentially a personal activity. It wasn't conceived to be a competitor to the mainstream media (although, in some respects, it's turned out that way). Some bloggers write about

their lives (usually under a pen name) in an intensely personal way —
saying things on-line they would *never* say to friends and family. While
they often secretly wish they had as much influence as mainstream
media people, most sensible bloggers know that they don't. With very
few exceptions, no *single* blogging voice can have a noticeable political,
economic, or social impact.

Why? Well, for starters, because there are simply way too many blogs
out there. Technorati, the helpful web service that tracks blogs, estimates
there are more than 60 million worldwide, and with a new one being created every second or so. In a media environment as crowded as that one,
getting noticed is virtually impossible.

But there's another reason why blogs, bloggers, and the like are unable to change the march of history in the way that the traditional, mainstream media sometimes do — and it's because the new citizen media
is *horizontal*, not *vertical*. That is, blogs and their ilk form an anarchic,
leaderless, disputatious media community. They don't organize themselves in the way that corporations or unions or governments do. They're
not hierarchical. On their own, they don't possess the agenda-setting
clout of, say, a network TV news anchor. Working together, however
— working as a unified, organized community, which is usually a lot
easier to say than to do — bloggers can actually topple a network TV
news anchor. (Ask Dan Rather.) The advent of citizen media — because
that's what it truly *is*, average citizens seeking to contribute to, offset,
or even replace the traditional corporate media — is arguably the third
great communications revolution (the first being the development of the
Gutenberg printing press, the second being the popularization of television as a mass medium). Mainstream media folks who sniff that it's a
fad, or unimportant, are just plain wrong, in my opinion. To me, they
sound an awful lot like dinosaurs dismissing the possibility of the Ice
Age. They just don't get it.

They should; they need to. (Smart war room warriors certainly have.)
Citizen media is changing politics, business, and social interaction. It has
the potential to change everything.

Don't just take my word for it. Ask Bill Clinton. He knows.

THE BIGGEST POLITICAL STORY of the nineties arrived in the early morning hours of Sunday, January 18, 1998. It did not appear on the front pages of the *Washington Post*, or the *New York Times*, or the *Globe and Mail*. Nope, it first appeared on the Internet. The story was written on a battered old 486 computer in a dingy apartment in a part of Hollywood not often visited by tourists. Here is what it said:

NEWSWEEK KILLS STORY ON WHITE HOUSE
INTERN

BLOCKBUSTER REPORT: 23-YEAR OLD, FORMER
WHITE HOUSE INTERN, SEX RELATIONSHIP
WITH PRESIDENT

World Exclusive
Must Credit the DRUDGE REPORT

At the last minute, at 6 p.m. on Saturday evening, NEWSWEEK magazine killed a story that was destined to shake official Washington to its foundation: A White House intern carried on a sexual affair with the President of the United States!

The DRUDGE REPORT has learned that reporter Michael Isikoff developed the story of his career, only to have it spiked by top NEWSWEEK suits hours before publication. A young woman, 23, sexually involved with the love of her life, the President of the United States, since she was a 21-year-old intern at the White House. She was a frequent visitor to a small study just off the Oval Office where she claims to have indulged the president's sexual preference. Reports of the relationship spread in White House quarters and she was moved to a job at the Pentagon, where she worked until last week.

The young intern wrote long love letters to President Clinton, which she delivered through a delivery service. She was a frequent visitor at the White House after

midnight, where she checked in the WAVE logs as visiting a secretary named Betty Curry, 57.

The DRUDGE REPORT has learned that tapes of
intimate phone conversations exist.

The relationship between the president and the
young woman became strained when the president believed that the young woman was bragging to others
about the affair. NEWSWEEK and Isikoff were planning to name the woman. Word of the story's impeding
[sic] release caused blind chaos in media circles; TIME
magazine spent Saturday scrambling for its own version
of the story, the DRUDGE REPORT has learned....

Not so long afterwards, Lucianne Goldberg lets loose with a throaty
laugh, thickened by too much coffee and too many years of Marlboro
Lights (smoked using an 18-carat Dunhill holder from Harrods, no less).
She has just been asked whether there is any chance that the Internet
posting by her "very good friend" Matt Drudge on January 18, 1998 —
about a president of the United States having a tawdry affair with a naive
young White House intern, and the history that it helped to create —
will be repeated again anytime soon. "That was a huge, huge story," she
says, ensconced in her West Side Manhattan office, where her eponym-
ous website registers hundreds of thousands of hits every week. "I don't
think there'll be anything like it for a long, long time."

Does that mean that people in politics have learned their lesson?
That they will be wary, now that the Internet is available to punish them
for earthly indiscretions? Goldberg finds that one particularly funny. She
howls with laughter. "Listen, sweetheart, people in politics are never going to change," says the woman who, along with Monica Lewinsky, very
nearly toppled a president. "They're still having affairs, they're still steal-
ing money. But it's the speed of the thing. It's a fact: with the Internet, we
can get it on a website and out to a million people in three seconds. And
Matt can get it out to more people than that!"

Lucianne Goldberg, a.k.a. Lucianne Steinberger, a.k.a. Lucy Cum-
mings, is like that. She's a bit of a bullshitter, like everyone else in politics, but she's not entirely without charm. Brash, tough, outspoken, she is

not one for nuance, or equivocation. She speaks entirely in pithy quotes, all the time. Making use of a mix of Matt Drudge, the Internet, and a sordid political scandal, Goldberg took on a very popular (and powerful) president. That president narrowly escaped impeachment in the U.S. Senate, imperilled his marriage and most probably helped to defeat his Democratic Party successor, Al Gore. But Lucianne Goldberg is still standing, and still smiling — even prospering.

Before the Internet, and before what became known as Zippergate, Goldberg had previously achieved distinction for authoring a few novels of the steamy variety, such as *Madame Cleo's Girls*, which was about a trio of top-rung prostitutes ("Chick stuff," she calls it). She also ghost-authored a few books for others. But what Goldberg knew most of all was her way around the scandal circuit. Born in 1935 in Boston, raised near Washington, she was the daughter of a government physicist. When she got old enough to write, she offered what she likes to call "the dish" in a gossip column for a local paper. She even worked on the presidential campaigns of John F. Kennedy and Lyndon B. Johnson, and alleges that Johnson tweaked her nipples in a White House elevator. Uh-huh.

And then, somewhere along the way, she became a Republican. Tall, buxom, and quick-witted, Goldberg became an actual bona fide spy on behalf of Richard Nixon's dark 1972 campaign for president. Goldberg was the Nixon campaign's mole on the campaign plane of Democratic candidate George McGovern. Working under the guise of a reporter for something called the Women's News Service, Goldberg filed dozens of reports on supposed McGovern staff shenanigans to her infamous boss, Washington lawyer Murray Chotiner. She was paid $1,000 a week for her spy work, plus $12,000 for expenses; her code name was Chapman's Friend, and even Richard Nixon can be heard using that appellation in the White House tapes. Thirty of her salacious reports, dictated to a secretary at Chotiner's firm, can now be found at the U.S. National Archives. Later, she described herself as "a human tape recorder" for Richard Nixon's campaign, capturing every detail she could, for maximum political damage.

Many years later, using some new technology and a new set of facts, she did it all over again. This time, her target was Bill Clinton, and her chosen technology was the World Wide Web.

Goldberg had known Linda Tripp, a non-political staffer at the White House, since the summer of 1996. They met because Tripp had been the last person to see White House counsel Vincent Foster alive. Foster, a close friend of the Clintons, had died by his own hand, but right-wing conspiracy theorists insisted it was a homicide. At first, Goldberg wanted Tripp to act as a source for a book about Foster's death; as the two got to know each other, Goldberg thought Tripp might be able to do a White House exposé herself. A single mother living in Maryland, Tripp had worked under the George Bush and Bill Clinton administrations in a variety of positions and knew many of the relevant political players. But Goldberg eventually concluded that Tripp could not write, and Tripp was afraid that she would lose her job. They agreed to put the project on the back burner.

A year went by. In the fall of 1997, Tripp told Goldberg an extraordinary story: a reporter from *Newsweek*, Michael Isikoff, following up on tips from his own sources, one of them Goldberg herself, had contacted Tripp to question her about a young woman Tripp knew. The young woman was having sexual liaisons in the Oval Office with the president of the United States (then under a number of investigations by conservative Independent Counsel Kenneth Starr). Tripp wanted Goldberg's advice about what to do.

Certain of two things — one, that Linda Tripp would eventually be called to testify about her Pentagon friend Monica Lewinsky and, two, that no one would believe her testimony — Goldberg decided to push Tripp to tape her telephone conversations with Lewinsky. Otherwise, she said, the Clinton "machine" would destroy Tripp and her family. Tripp apparently accepted Goldberg's advice; she started to secretly tape Lewinsky's recollections about her affair with the president of the United States.

Goldberg arranged for Isikoff and Tripp to meet again. The *Newsweek* reporter sat stone-faced as the two women told him that they possessed tapes of Lewinsky's recollections. In the days that followed, lawyers representing Kenneth Starr targeted Goldberg, Tripp, and Lewinsky, seeking confirmation of the affair with Clinton. Tripp, for one, was terrified; so too Lewinsky. Goldberg started calling around for lawyers willing to represent her friend Linda.

As Isikoff was preparing to go to print with his story about the affair — and Kenneth Starr's investigators were scrambling to beat Isikoff with evidence they could possibly use in a prosecution of Bill Clinton for something, anything — Goldberg received a call from Matt Drudge. A former paperboy and 7-Eleven shelf stocker, Drudge was in his thirties and running a website out of his basement apartment in Hollywood. His father had bought the computer for him at Radio Shack. Drudge had no university education and no background in journalism, and it showed. Most days, Drudge was little more than a Republican hack. But he had lots of right-wing friends like Lucianne Goldberg, people who delighted in feeding him gossip. Along with a few links to newspapers and columnists, he posted tidbits on his website, which he called the Drudge Report.

Goldberg has claimed that Drudge had the entire story when he called her at home, around midnight on January 17, 1998. Goldberg says Drudge was seeking confirmation about the Lewinsky story; according to her, she had never spoken to him before. Why Goldberg would so quickly confirm the story to a total stranger named Matt Drudge, a story worth a lot of money in the tabloid press, is suspicious, to say the least. But she insists that she did so because the pair shared a hatred of Bill Clinton. She later told the *Washington Post*, "I wasn't going to lie to [Drudge] … I mean the man had all the information. He'd already written it when he called me. He read me parts of it. It would have been kind of dumb of me to say, 'Huh?'"

Matt Drudge mused about the story for a few hours, and then he posted it on his website. The rest, as they say, is history. The story bearing Monica Lewinsky's name would not have happened at all, says Goldberg, were it not for the wonders of the Internet. "I'll tell you why," she says, lighting another cigarette. "Because it would have gone mainstream and we could not have controlled it. Isikoff had 60 percent of the story. He would have run with it, and the White House and the liberal establishment would have found a way to spin it and it eventually would have died. They would have been able to go with Monica is a bimbo, Monica is a stalker. They were all set to do that, in fact, and they started doing it … They would have been able to co-opt a mainstream newspaper. But they couldn't, if it was squeezed out through the Internet. And that is what happened."

When Drudge's story "squeezed out," as Goldberg puts it, there could be no denying the facts: the Internet had become an integral part of one of the biggest political stories anyone had ever seen. His posting rapidly showed up in countless e-mails, discussion groups, and chat rooms. Mainstream media organizations felt that they could not ignore the story. In time — and not a lot of time, either — more than 2 million people a day were clicking onto Matt Drudge's website to learn the latest about the scandal that gripped the United States for the entirety of 1998. Bill Clinton barely escaped with his political hide, while Drudge got a big book deal and television show. Goldberg got a syndicated radio program and lots of infamy.

As a political communications tool, all agreed: for good or bad, the Internet had arrived.

NOT EVERY INTERNET-BASED POLITICAL EVENT is as big a deal as was the Clinton-Lewinsky mess — but some other big fish have been occasionally reeled in by determined bloggers. In 2006, for instance, Virginia Senator George Allen went down to a richly deserved defeat when he called a non-white Democrat worker a "macaca" — a racist term meaning "monkey." Allen's slur was captured on a cellphone video camera, uploaded to YouTube, and seen by hundreds of thousands of people.

And, in 2002, Republican Senator Trent Lott blew his career to bits when he gave a speech that suggested a wistful longing for racial segregation; liberal bloggers went after him with a vengeance, forcing the mainstream media to cover a story they had previously ignored. In September 2004, conservative bloggers exposed as forgeries documents purporting to be President George W. Bush's Air National Guard records — documents that the powerful *CBS News* anchor Dan Rather had relied upon in a much-seen *60 Minutes* segment. Six months later, Rather announced his early retirement. But the Clinton, Lott, and Rather cases are the exception, not the rule.

Most of the time, in my experience, the Internet has tended to be a useful corrective to the sloppiness or stupidity of assorted lesser mortals, like reporters or mid-level political partisans. Here are just three recent instances in which I played a minor supporting role; there are literally thousands of other such examples, playing themselves out daily in war rooms and campaigns around the globe.

To ensure partisan balance and all that, one story involves a Conservative, one a Liberal, and one a New Democrat. All three deal with the always hot issue of the Middle East (and, full disclosure, I am a Zionist and an ardent defender of Israel). All three case studies make clear how the Internet has become crucially important to any war room — political or not.

The Conservative example starts one evening in August 2006, when CBC's *The National* broadcast a two-minute-long item by respected reporter Christina Lawand. The story was about the governing Conservative party's caucus retreat in Cornwall, Ontario, a prime ministerial press conference, and a protest outside.

Lawand's story was introduced by a solemn news reader, who stated as fact that Stephen Harper's position on the Israel-Hezbollah war was raising "questions" and "criticisms" in Canada. Noting that Harper and his Tory colleagues were meeting a "safe distance away," Lawand filmed a smallish anti-Israel protest. One protester, Elsaadi Daad, deplored the "burning [of] children and killing [of] innocent people." The next shot showed Daad and another woman walking to meet with Foreign Affairs Minister Peter MacKay.

Lawand's news item then immediately cut to the prime minister, standing behind a podium, wearing a blue blazer and an open-necked shirt. Lawand stated that Harper "clearly wasn't swayed" by Daad's pleas. She quoted him saying the following: "I'm not concerned or preoccupied in any way with reactions within individual communities. I think that reaction is very predictable."

The juxtaposition of Daad's emotional prayer for peace and Harper's evidently blithe dismissal of same was jarring. It made Harper seem cold-hearted and callous. It also neatly set up the next part of Lawand's story, which promoted the notion that Harper's Middle East stand was costing his party in Quebec. A pollster was trotted out to say so.

Upon seeing Lawand's report, Conservative blogger Stephen Taylor was pretty pissed off, so he got to work. Using a program found on almost any computer, Taylor put together a seven-minute film containing

260 | The War Room

live feeds of the prime minister's press conference. Taylor's film, found at www.stephentaylor.ca, makes clear that the "individual community" whose reaction had been "very predictable" and with which Harper was not "concerned or preoccupied" was none other than the Canadian *Jewish* community. Precisely the reverse of the impression left by Lawand's story. Pretty unimpressive, to say the least.

Taylor's little film attracted national attention (including in my media column in the *National Post*), and was seen tens of thousands of times. It had a big impact. And — whether a coincidence or not — Christina Lawand left the CBC shortly after Taylor exposed the shortcomings in her story.

The second Middle East–related case study involves Liberals, and also came in August 2006. It centres on a young man named Thomas Hubert — and he was indeed youngish, in his late teens or early twenties — who was a former B.C. New Democrat. Hubert decided to become a B.C. Liberal. Soon enough, he was placed in charge of communications for the Young Liberals in that province, and he became an active supporter of Liberal leadership candidate Gerard Kennedy.

Earlier in August 2006, on a Liberal blog called *Fuddle-Duddle*, Hubert wrote this: "One man's terrorist is another man's freedom fighter. At one point, George Washington was considered a terrorist by the powers that be. History will remember Hezbollah as an organization that stood up to the most vile 'nation' in human history."

Hubert's extremism was not noticed at the time because, one, few people knew he held an official position within the Liberal Party, and two, pro-Hezbollah (or anti-Israel) comments hadn't been all that infrequent in the post-Chrétien Liberal Party, sadly. From interim Liberal leader Bill Graham attacking the prime minister's pro-Israel stance as lacking "nuance" to Liberal associate foreign affairs critic Boris Wrzesnewskyj calling for Hezbollah to lose its designation as a terrorist organization (a designation applied by Jean Chrétien's Liberal government, incidentally), the federal Liberal Party had been walking perilously close to the edge of the abyss, in the view of people like me.

All of which may explain, maybe, why blog enthusiast Thomas Hubert was persuaded to join the federal Liberals in the first place — and why he wrote this in the comments section of influential Liberal activist Jason Cherniak's blog: "The Liberal party is stronger without these violent Zionists in our party. I am glad for them to cease influencing our foreign policy so we are free to promote Canadian values of peace. It amazes me that this community is so absurdly selfish. The only issue that matters to them is the defence of a 'state' that survives on the blood of innocent people. Shameful."

What was "shameful," pretty much every sensible person later agreed, was Hubert's blood-libel anti-Semitism, and more senior Liberals' apparent indifference to same. Not until a few other Grits and pro-Israel bloggers (include, tangentially, me) objected to Hubert's bilious Jew hatred did anything happen. No demands for his resignation. No repudiations by prominent Liberals. Eventually, however, bloggers like Cherniak and Jonathan Ross — plus leadership candidate Scott Brison, to his credit — succeeded in forcing Hubert's resignation. Within a few days, Hubert's anti-Israel website, *The Long Walk*, had gone for one. As in the Taylor-Lawand case, the Hubert controversy became a national news story, and one that saw many Canadian Jews condemning the apparent indifference of the Liberal Party. It, too, had a significant impact.

The third and final case study — this one NDP-related — came a little bit later, in March 2007, but also involves the Middle East. At the centre of the sorry tale was a moron named Robert McClelland (if that is his real name), a blogger in the London area. For years, McClelland has posted some of the most offensive — and stridently anti-Semitic — material in the Canadian blogosphere. He has repeatedly called Israelis "murderers;" he has written that "Jews act like Nazis," and, memorably, titled one post "FUCK THE JEWS."

McClelland had become notorious for his hateful views, and he clearly reveled in it, on his own site and on a much-read group blog called "Blogging Dippers." Despite his clear anti-Semitism, McClelland had somehow been permitted to promote the NDP for a long time. His site featured links to the official NDP website, photos of NDP Leader Jack Layton, and even a tribute to Canadian Socialist icon David Lewis. It had been long believed that he was a sanctioned on-line voice for the NDP.

Until March 2007, that is. One weekend, there was a discussion thread on McClelland's website headlined "When the State starts rounding up my Jewish neighbours, I'll speak up." McClelland's response — which

also caustically referenced me and another Liberal pro-Israel blogger —
was as follows: "Not me ... When next they come for the Jews, I doubt I'll
even be able to muster up a 'what a shame.'" Within twenty-four hours,
the blogosphere had exploded in outrage over McClelland's comments
— and not just from the right, either. On innumerable blogs, pro-NDP
activists demanded that McClelland apologize and withdraw his appalling statements. He petulantly refused.

A day or so later, I was contacted directly by representatives of the
federal NDP. They were appalled by what McClelland had written, they
said — and by the notion that anyone would think McClelland was associated with the NDP. In a letter to the Canadian Jewish Congress, New
Democrat party president Anne McGrath made clear that McClelland's
comments were "highly offensive" and "repugnant." Wrote McGrath: "I
want to assure you that the New Democratic Party of Canada, its provincial sections and local riding associations are not affiliated with Mr.
McClelland and his independently operated blog roll, 'the Blogging Dippers.'" McGrath revealed that her party was at work on developing its
own group blog, one that would better represent its own points of view.
From my perspective, the NDP emerged from the controversy with an
enhanced reputation.

Moral of these cautionary bloggy tales? There are three, actually.
One, a new era is upon us, whether you like it or not. As my fellow *Post*
writer Andrew Coyne has noted elsewhere, reporters like Christina
Lawand have to be much more careful now: There are "20,000 fact-check-
ers" — bloggers and the like — watching everything the mainstream
media do, ready to pounce, ready to object to any factual error, or any bit
of inappropriate editorializing.

Two, as the popularity of blogs and their ilk have exploded, many
corporations and political parties have scrambled to ensure their presence in the so-called blogosphere. But they have not been as watchful
as they should be — and certainly not as watchful as the New Democrats were in the McClelland case. More and more, reputations are being
shaped on-line.

Three, what gets written on-line — what *happens* on-line — can have
profound consequences for citizens, organizations, governments, companies, and campaigns. For everyone, in short — and particularly for

misinformed youngsters like Thomas Hubert. In fact, most war room activity — and a significant chunk of campaign activity — now takes place on-line.

It's a new era — and, like I say, it's time to get modern.

THE INTERNET IS A CAMPAIGNER'S BEST NEW FRIEND — assisting us in getting information out quickly, widely, and cheaply. That's so obvious, it barely merits saying.

In innumerable political campaigns around the globe, the Internet is now used to do opposition research and to communicate with voters and candidates. It is everywhere. In the mid-1990s, national campaigns in the United States, Canada, and Europe made some limited use of websites; for the most part, however, the sites were novelties, and not many political folks took the new technology very seriously. Until the wrestler from Minnesota neck-scissored his way onto the national political scene, that is.

In early 1998, around the same time that a Republican fartcatcher named Matt Drudge was using the Internet to change history, a former professional wrestler named Jesse Ventura decided to enter the gubernatorial race in Minnesota for Ross Perot's Reform Party. A more improbable, and unlikely, candidate you could not find, folks. But one of the first things Ventura did was to register a website, at www.jesseventura.org, for less than $200.

Phil Madsen, Ventura's webmaster, tells us what happened next. "From the first day, our website purpose was clear; to produce volunteers, money and votes in support of Jesse Ventura ... We set out to build and service a base of on-line supporters from which the volunteers, money and votes would come. Early on, Jesse decided the website would be operated like a cul-de-sac and not a crossroads. The site would not be a place for people to arrive at and then exit via links we provided. Once people entered our site, we wanted them to stay and look around. No links to external websites were provided," he said. "Early in the campaign, users would enter the site and view five to seven pages per visit. As election day approached, and as we added more pages to the site, users viewed nine to eleven pages per visit. We had about 2 million hits on the site from February through November, with about 75 percent coming in the three weeks before and after the election."

The website did what it was supposed to do, but far beyond Ventura's and Madsen's wildest expectations. Ventura's astonishing win, the *New York Times* noted, was "a victory that some attribute to effective use of the Internet as a tool for mobilizing volunteers and voters." Soon every campaign, large or small, wanted a presence on the World Wide Web, and not just to smear people (as Matt Drudge had sought to do with Bill Clinton). Very quickly, campaigns and war rooms saw how the Internet could secure, in great numbers, two highly elusive commodities — people and money.

Sure, the Internet is a great source of information. But one of the biggest advantages the Internet now offers candidates and campaigns, far and above anything else, is money. Lots of it. In the first week or so following the 2000 New Hampshire primary, John McCain raised a then-incredible $2.6 million on the Internet. In all, McCain, whose campaign consulted with Jesse Ventura's webmaster before it got started, raised more than $4.1 million from forty thousand individual donors, not big corporations and lobby groups. While he was still a hot political commodity, McCain's website was attracting money to the tune of about $100,000 a day. Not bad. At that point, more than 10 million Americans had visited the McCain website. McCain's campaign loved web fundraising, and not simply because they were raising a ton of dough. The donated dollars, McCain told the media on his tour at the time, were "clean." That is, almost half came from the wallets and purses of individual citizens who had never before contributed to a campaign; they were not lobbyists. And the fact that donations were paid by credit card was also pretty helpful; that ensured that monies were immediately available for use by the campaign.

After McCain, one of the most successful Internet-based political fundraising efforts came four years later, with Howard Dean's campaign for the U.S. presidency. The former Vermont governor's campaign started out in May 2002 with less than $100,000 and fewer than five hundred volunteers. When he told his mother he was running for president, she told him "it was preposterous, the most ridiculous thing I'd ever heard."

But by the time it all came to a screaming halt in January 2004, Dean's campaign had raised more money than any Democrat in the history of the United States — $60 million. Three-quarters of that figure came in individual donations of about $75 over the Internet.

Conceived by a brilliant Democratic consultant named Joe Trippi — a veteran of campaigns for Ted Kennedy, Walter Mondale, Gary Hart, and Dick Gephardt — the centre of Dean's Internet campaign was called "Blog for America," where hundreds of Dean supporters from across America posted comments and updates. Under Trippi's direction as campaign manager, the Dean effort also used the Internet to rally grassroots support, organize meetings (through web services like MeetUp.com), and — more than anything else — fundraise. As Trippi wrote later: "The blogosphere was where we got ideas, feedback, support, money — everything a campaign needs to live."

Why was the Dean Internet effort so wildly successful in the early days of the Democratic primaries? Because, Trippi says, "the Net finally reached maturity." He adds, "The Internet is only just starting to flex its muscles ... I actually think that, four years from now, there will be people looking back at the Dean campaign, thinking how primitive it was compared to the tools that will be available [in the future]. We're only taking the very first steps in using the Net to empower people, to change governance and change the media."

The Internet is an incredible fundraising tool, as McCain and Dean have shown us all (and as my favourite Democratic presidential candidate, Barack Obama, demonstrated again in 2007, raising millions upon millions on-line). But here's an example of what Trippi is talking about when he says the Web can also empower people — the Internet-based campaign against the Multilateral Agreement on Investment (MAI).

Despite the fact that it had no money, despite the fact that it was led by people with no power in the traditional sense, the anti-MAI campaign literally — and I mean *literally* — stopped entire governments in their tracks. Governments! With tanks and soldiers and stuff like that! The powerful, beaten by the powerless, using the Internet. It is an amazing story, and one worth retelling.

A little background: the MAI was one of those things that most average citizens never bother to organize against, simply because they believe they lack the power to get anyone to listen to them. They think it's going to happen, whether they like it or not. The MAI was supported by dozens of developed nations and, ostensibly, was aimed at further liberalizing trade on a global scale. To those many folks opposed to globalization, the MAI was a genuine threat to democracy, human rights, and the environment. On one point, however, both sides agreed: the international Internet campaign against the MAI would prove to be an incredible, and very early, Internet-based political success story.

The anti-MAI drama goes back to 1995, when trade ministers from most of the world's leading industrial economies had been working to hammer out a new worldwide agreement on rules for foreign investment. Among other things, the ministers expected they would be able to conclude an agreement by the end of 1998. They were wrong. Wrong, wrong, wrong.

In political seismological terms, to that point, there had been two major Internet events. One was the leak of the Clinton-Lewinsky affair to Matt Drudge by Lucianne Goldberg. The second was the incredible fundraising successes of John McCain. And the third would be the derailment of 1999's Seattle MAI talks by a few thousand activists who used the Internet to mobilize people in a way that had never been done before. Seattle was memorable for its fierce street battles, certainly, and for televised clips of astonished-looking trade ministers being prevented from getting out of their hotel rooms. But what made the collapse of the MAI so extraordinary, and so unusual, was the role played by the Internet.

For many months before the protestors converged on Seattle, anti-globalization forces had been using homemade websites and mass e-mailing lists to generate a tremendous amount of support for their cause. The Internet was used to do everything from circulating anti-MAI essays to arranging for bed and board for those planning to protest in Seattle. Just one website, www.indymedia.org's "Battle of Seattle," received nearly 2 million hits during the ill-fated trade conference. By Seattle's conclusion, trade ministers flew home with no agreement, but with a keener appreciation for the huge potential political power of the Internet. The anti-MAI groups had won.

Whether you agree with liberalized trade or not, the anti-MAI groups deserve tons of credit for their historic achievement. They opposed the

MAI in a way that was open, transparent, and mostly democratic. (And, before anyone gets upset with me, I concede that on-line manipulation of voters is an unwanted consequence of the Internet's huge growth as a political communications medium — with stuff like web name cyber-squatting, nasty emails, and attack sites. Because websites can be established by anybody possessing a modem, a computer, and a grudge, the possibilities for on-line malfeasance are virtually limitless. I accept that. But the anti-MAI effort wasn't like that; it was, arguably, more democratic than the MAI talks.)

One of the few politicians who have continued to track the anti-globalization effort on the World Wide Web is a former premier of Quebec, Pierre Marc Johnson. Now a lawyer in Montreal, Johnson's impressive curriculum vitae suggests that his views are worth heeding; along with his political successes, Johnson is a medical doctor, a lawyer, and a professor at McGill University. He has been a vice chair of the Prime Minister's National Round Table on the Environment and the Economy, and he has been an advisor to the Secretary-General of the United Nations Conference on Environment and Development. And, at the moment, he believes that the Internet can transform small advocacy groups into political giants. Seattle proved that, he says.

During a discussion in Toronto, Johnson says, "The Internet allows mobilization; it is as simple as that, particularly for persons whose main mode of work is communicating and networking. It is now possible to do it instantly, efficiently and almost at no cost." The men and women he knows well — the ones who were working towards concluding an MAI agreement — were simply flummoxed by the Internet-based lobby, says Johnson. "It was this unbelievable uproar," he recalls. "They got these e-mails. They got messages from constituents, against the MAI. It was powerful — it was *incredibly* powerful."

The failure of Seattle and the failure of the MAI the year before, he writes, were huge political events, and not simply because trade representatives failed in their drive to develop international trade liberalization rules and freer investment provisions:

> The MAI Seattle debacle was partially caused by the surprise effect of the attack. In Seattle, the use of the Net

allowed mobilization of many thousands in the streets. This in turn gave good shots for the six o'clock TV news. [The Internet's] use also allowed for coalitions, common drafting of positions and press communiqués. The best communicators, from the radical end of the spectrum, appropriated for themselves the voices of discontent with the WTO negotiations. The power they unleashed gave the impression of a coherent, cohesive and generalized opposition ... the use of the Net is an instrument of broad mobilization, as long as there is an object to mobilize about.

In Seattle, there was.

Johnson is hesitant to be too critical of the political class, of which he was formerly a very well known member. He gently emphasizes that, even now, "we are all trying to catch up on this stuff." But the fact remains, he says, that politicians, and the people who work for them, are woefully under equipped to deal with the negative implications of Internet activism. "Governments," he says, "are starting to get nervous. They did all of these negotiations [before Seattle] ... and then they ended up being surprised as hell by what happened there."

The moral in all of this, to the likes of Lucianne Goldberg, is simple. The rules of the game have changed. As Goldberg says: "Every political party has their website, sure. But political operatives have figured out that the Web, now, is where they can leak stuff. They know it can get stuff out fast. You don't have to go through the bureaucracy at the *Washington Post* or *Time* magazine or the *New York Times* anymore." She laughs her deep, husky laugh.

"We consider ourselves the new cowboys, you know. We don't have to do anything [political activists] used to have to do. As long as it's checked out, we just let it fly. We don't have to ask anyone's permission, ever again."

WHY HAS THE INTERNET — and its bastard offspring, like blogs, You-Tube, Facebook, Flickr, and so on and so on — become so important? Why have they attracted so many millions pairs of eyeballs, in so little time?

As all of you are painfully aware by now, I love top ten lists. Herewith, and heretofore:

Ten Reasons Why Internet Bloggy Stuff Is Pretty Important

Well, It's Free, Isn't It?
Sure, my little website, www.warrenkinsella.com, gets plenty of mouse clicks. During the 2006 Canadian federal election campaign, for example, it got about 250,000 a day. My pithy response? Big deal. Whatever. My website, like a lot of websites and blogs, gets visitors because it's free, because it's a bit wacky, and, um, because it's free. People *like* things that are free. Bloggers who think they are supplanting the mainstream media should give their tinfoil hats a shake — they get traffic because they are free, mainly. Not because they write Pulitzer Prize–winning stuff.

Many newspapers have responded to the blogger threat in precisely the wrong way. Instead of making content easier to access, like blogs do, a few newspapers have placed some or all of their content behind subscription walls and registration forms and whatnot. That wouldn't be a problem if (a) Internet-age people were in any way patient and (b) Internet-age people believed in paying and/or registering for things online. Neither is true. In the new media environment, everyone is cheap and in a rush: they're used to getting stuff for free, and all in a matter of seconds, too.

If you can get news and commentary for free, why pay for it? It's a question too many newspapers still can't answer.

They're Proudly Biased!
Fair's fair: I don't think the traditional news media are *wrong*, necessarily, to aspire to journalistic objectivity. I just think — like most citizens — that the media are *laughable* when they actually believe it. To put a

fine point on it, "journalistic objectivity" is more than an oxymoron. It's unadulterated bullshit.

Some folks who are smarter than me have put together lists of things to watch for, if you are concerned that a journalist isn't being objective. Are they using misleading definitions and terminology? Is their reporting unbalanced in any way? Do they have opinions disguised as news? Is there a noticeable lack of context? Is there some selective omission going on? Are true facts being used to draw false conclusions? Are the facts being distorted?

If you're like me, you probably can't think of a single news story you've read, seen, or heard — *ever* — that didn't transgress at least one of those rules. And that's the point: do Joe and Jane Frontporch actually believe objectivity is even remotely possible? Um, no, they don't. Gallup, which has been looking at the issue of media bias in the U.S. for thirty-five years, found that the public's confidence in newspapers and television has steadily declined from 54 percent in 1989 to only 28 percent in 2005. A 2007 IPDI/Zogby poll, meanwhile, found the vast majority of American voters believe media bias is alive and well — a whopping 83 percent of them saying the media is biased in one direction or another. Only 11 percent believed the media doesn't take political sides, a recent poll shows.

That is why bloggers, in particular, have been so well-received by smart consumers of news. Bloggers — unlike many traditional, mainstream media — don't even *pretend* they are capable of objectivity. Bloggers, like media theorists such as Walter Lippmann, think that the selection and presentation of "facts" is so fraught with subjectivity, it's absurd to even suggest otherwise. So bloggers revel in bias; they advertise their bias. They are proud of it.

Suggesting that media objectivity is possible is more than wrong — it insults peoples' intelligence. And it's yet another reason why blogs have become so popular in such a short time.

They're Really Easy to Access!
By the end of this decade, the experts tell us, there will be about 1.5 billion personal computers in use worldwide. That's a lot. Literally tons of laptops and desktops will start showing up in places like Russia, China,

and India. That means that, between writing term papers and sending naughty email jokes to friends and authoring important memoranda about widgets, increasingly huge numbers of people will have computers within arm's reach at any given time.

As previously noted, those millions and millions of folks are pressed for time, too. Inventor and toy maker Jim Marggraff's Seven-Second Rule is one, I think, that applies as readily to the web world as it does to toys — to wit, "If the product's art and audio fail to engage the user within seven seconds, the user will never engage." The time limit for getting a human being's attention is seven seconds. After that, they move on. In the World Wide Web, the time limit may be even *shorter* than seven seconds.

Blogs are accessible on two levels, and are immensely successful as a result. One, they're literally ubiquitous. Anyone with access to a computer, anywhere in the world, can find a blog to read in no time at all. Two, blogs are designed to be accessed within seconds — and for free, as well.

Now, try and think of a newspaper or a newscast you can locate, anywhere on Earth, at no cost and within mere moments. Can't, can you? Exactly!

They're the Hegelian Dialectic on Speed!

Well, I can now die and happily go to meet my maker — because I was able to show off by working "Hegelian Dialectic" into a book!

Back in the eighteenth century, as we all know, a smart German fellow named Georg Wilhelm Friedrich Hegel suggested that every proposition (thesis) has an opposite proposition (antithesis) — and that the two sides are hopefully resolved with a happy ending (synthesis). Here's a real-life example: Canadians are weary of Liberal rule, circa 1984 (thesis). Canada makes the terrible, awful, cataclysmic mistake of electing Brian Mulroney (antithesis). Realizing its mistake, Canada achieves supreme social, economic, and political harmony by electing Jean Chrétien for three successive majority terms, commencing in 1993 (synthesis). Something like that.

Blogs, and blog-like stuff, are now valued because they are indeed the Hegelian Dialectic on speed. Anything that happens — any event — will be quickly commented upon, and discussed and debated, in the blogosphere. Any opinion, expressed anywhere, will be rapidly mooted and mulled over and critiqued by bloggers. It's unstoppable, now.

Out of all of that commentary and criticism comes a synthesis of sorts. It is disputatious and messy, sure, but sometimes injustices get redressed on-line, and demagogues get their comeuppance on the Internet. If someone is peddling bullshit or doing something rotten to someone else, they'll get what they deserve in the blogosphere. It's Hegeleian!

They're Populist!

And they're popular, too. The Internet has an astonishing ability to attract volunteers; for example, very early on, Florida governor Jeb Bush picked up more than a thousand campaign workers in 1998 through some very simple on-line recruitment. In the intervening years, campaigns — Howard Dean's in particular — have discovered, to their delight, that the Internet now brings in more volunteers than any other single recruitment method.

Blogs, meanwhile, have added a new dimension: giving voiceless people a voice.

For a long time, you see, free speech advocates (and, as a proud censor who opposes hate propaganda and violent pornography, I'm no free speech advocate) have claimed that there is something called a "marketplace of ideas." That is, that anyone with a point to make can — in a democracy — make it.

That's bullshit, of course. Before the Internet came along, the notion that I or anyone I knew had the means to offset the "ideas" that guys like, say, Larry Flynt propagate in *Hustler* was laughable. It was a joke. How could an average person get noticed, let alone heard, in a landscape dominated by millionaires, governments, corporations, and multinational media behemoths? How could we compete with rich jerks with their own printing presses? We couldn't, not for a long time.

The Internet's populist offerings — blogs in particular — gave regular folks an unprecedented opportunity to have their say. As I've acknowledged, with so many blogs and bloggers, it's impossible for any single weblog to have a measurable impact. But — as in the Trent Lott, George Allen, and Dan Rather cases — bloggers can come together, sometimes, and bring giants to their knees.

That kind of populism isn't just good for democracy — it *is* democracy.

Google Power!
Google is more than the most powerful brand in the world. It is also the place where people go first — for good or bad — to find out about something. Google has supplanted encyclopedias, libraries, and your parents. It is the font of all accumulated wisdom, whether we like it or not (and, in my view, we shouldn't).

Getting on Google's first-page results — that is, the ten things listed after one does a search — is coveted by many. Entire companies have been founded to help people get their product or name or idea, onto the web search engine's first page. That's because an estimated 95 percent of Google-users don't even go past the first page of results. So one's Google "page rank" is pretty darn important.

Blogs, to the surprise of the likes of the *New York Times* and the big TV networks, have pretty impressive Google page ranks. Bloggers are getting onto Google's coveted page one because bloggers are free and generous "linkers." How come? Well, incoming web links determine a site's spot on a page rank. Blogs attract link exchanges due to some theme or development — and they usually have permanent links from other blogs (I'm linked to by hundreds of bloggers, most of whom I've never even met).

Blogs get all these links because — unlike many regular websites — they offer fresh, regularly updated content. By their readers with daily posts, other bloggers will link to them, and comment on their musings in their own blogs. This mutual linking activity attracts the attention of Google's big computer brain and, as a result, moves bloggers ever upwards in Google search results.

Why does any of it matter? It matters because Google is now giving Joe Blogger equivalency with the aforementioned *New York Times*. Because it is exposing millions of people to blogs. Because it is enabling average, everyday people to have as much of an impact as billionaires and governments and big corporations.

Given how billionaires and governments and big corporations have treated the planet, I'd venture to say that can only be a good thing!

Specialists Are Welcome!

For every point of view, for every idea, there is a blog. Over time, some of these blogs' blogging bloggers — just like journalists who work a beat for a long time — can become awfully knowledgeable about their chosen subject matter.

Here's an example: one blogger I've crossed swords with runs a Toronto-based blog called *Relapsed Catholic*. It's a good name. On it, Kathy Shaidle writes all about, well, Catholic stuff. You may not always agree with her, but you have to acknowledge that she knows Catholicism better than your average, garden-variety pope. As a result, Shaidle gets called by time-pressured media people all the time, looking for a comment or a quote about some news development related to religion. Through her blog, in effect, she has become a specialist — maybe even an expert.

Blogger specialization means blogs are showing up on Google first page searches — but also in quite a few news stories, these days. That may worry some stuffy experts and stodgy professional pundits. But whether they like it or not, there's no disputing the fact that bloggers sometimes have *influence*.

Interactions Are Welcome, Too!

During the Canadian federal election campaign of 2000, the most infamous political website of all was designed by a Halifax firm that produces the CBC-TV comedy *This Hour Has 22 Minutes*. On the site, it was noted that Stockwell Day and his party favoured the use of national referendums to make legislative changes. The pranksters at *22 Minutes* had therefore come up with a novel referendum question: "We demand that the government of Canada force Stockwell Day to change his first name to Doris."

Said the web page: "If you support Stockwell Day's effort to allow citizen-initiated referendums in Canada, be the first on your block to have a referendum of your own! If you want a national referendum on the very important issue below, please join the on-line petition. 22 *Minutes* and Stockwell Day — Putting democracy back in the hands of the people!" By clicking on a button, surfers were given the opportunity to vote for the Doris Day name change; at its peak, Canadians were indicating their support every three seconds. Approximately 1 million votes ended up being cast in favour of the change from Stockwell Day to Doris Day!

The web stunt attracted media attention around the world; one of the top U.S.-based "serious" political website, www.politicsonline.com, highlighted the Day petition in its year-end wrap-up, calling it "wildly successful" and a "neat idea." It was.

Now, lots of bloggers permit *comments* on their posts. Just click and say whatever the hell you want to. Most blogs allow you to do it anonymously, too. Not me.

In our enlightened era, I have noted that calling someone a Nazi, or likening something that is not mass murder to the *shoah*, is now so commonplace that we barely notice. In the Internet demimonde, we bloggers even have a name for it: Godwin's Law. Named for Mike Godwin, the lawyer and Yale fellow who originated the term in 1990, Godwin's Law holds that "As an on-line discussion grows longer, the probability of a comparison involving Nazis or Hitler approaches one."

It happens all the time, and it makes me sick, frankly. So I don't allow comments on my blog. Some blog purists — wearing pyjamas and living in their mother's basement 24/7, as they do — consequently do not believe my website is a *real* blog. Big deal.

It's not because I don't value intelligent feedback, pro or con. I do, I do. I don't have comments because I am way too busy to start policing the orgy of hatred and libel that will inevitably result. Life is too short for that.

What should you do? It's up to you. At one time, blogs were ostensibly about doing whatever the author *wanted* to do, and saying what he or she *wanted* to say (within limits). About being unconventional. Why then, I ask, should I be conventional, and adhere to somebody else's stupid Blog Commandments? Screw that. Blogs are supposed to be against the mainstream — not creating a new one.

End of sermon.

They're Pithy as Heck!
Newspapers take too long to read. Newscasts take too long to sit through.

Blogs don't.

They're Fun!

Why do a blog? You don't get paid for it, you don't get much respect. Sometimes it gets you into trouble.

Well, I can only speak for myself on this one. I've been a diarist since I was eleven years old. I am alleged to have a thousand-word record of every single day since then. I write, badly, because I am compelled to write. But one day — someday soon, or maybe not — I will get tired of my wee website. I do it because I enjoy it; when I stop enjoying it, and notwithstanding the impressive page-view statistics, I will pull the plug. So it goes.

For you, a blog is an excellent way to get yourself heard — to get an idea out there. To get a song heard, or get a poem read. It's a way to promote your invention, or to object to an iniquity. To change someone's mind, maybe. To tell a joke, or get a smile. To defend a friend, or tell the truth (or try to). To be remembered, or remember someone. Or, sometimes, just to get an email from someone, just once, and to learn that something you wrote, late one night, changed someone's life.

And if that ain't a reason to join the citizen media revolution, nothing is.

BLOGS AND THE LIKE CAN BE FUN, certainly. But a lot of people — mainly in the traditional media — continue to regard them as a fad. As something trivial. They may be right, but I don't think so.

In the wake of the terrible massacre at Virginia Tech in April 2007, there were too-familiar debates about gun control, institutional security, and the seemingly bottomless anger of young men. None of it, sadly, was news.

But one thing was indisputably different: the bloody events of that day have shown us all that the citizen journalism revolution is here. It is happening, *right now.*

As the horror unfolded in Blacksburg, Virginia, and as the number of victims rose ever higher, millions of people received updates from traditional news sources, to be sure. But to an unprecedented degree, those media — newspapers, radio, and television networks — were relying upon citizen journalists to supply content. Millions of citizens, meanwhile, were simply ignoring the mainstream media and going directly to citizen journalists.

Through weblogs, through instant messenger, through photo-sharing sites like Flickr, and particularly through social networking sites like Facebook, the mass murder at Virginia Tech was chronicled by average citizens, most of them as young as those who died. Their journalism — as jumbled and as chaotic as it seemed to professional reporters and editors — gave the terrible events of that day an immediacy and a poignancy that the traditional media simply cannot equal.

Within two hours of the first shooting in a campus dormitory at 7:15 a.m. on April 16, 2007, Virginia Tech students were turning to the Internet to reassure family and friends, report developments, and debate why the university's administration did not immediately cancel classes. As one Virginia Tech student wrote on Facebook: "Classes don't start until 8, why couldn't they cancel classes for the day ... *Someone was shot and it turns out they died ... I think that's grounds to cancel class, rather than sending out an email that says use caution, and report anything to police.*" This criticism became the central focus for virtually every story written thereafter.

The role Facebook played in the coverage of the events at Virginia Tech was extraordinary. Created in 2004 by Harvard sophomore Mark Zuckerberg, Facebook quickly became a popular on-line meeting place for college and university students, and reportedly nets its ownership $1 million in advertising revenue weekly. It has nearly 20 million users worldwide (including me) and is one of the top ten most-visited websites.

The social networking site is free for users, the vast majority of whom are college-aged. Those who join Facebook can post profiles about themselves, containing photos, personal interests, private or public messages, and join "groups" based on where one lives, works, or (as we saw at Virginia Tech), studies.

Because Virginia Tech's web server was down after the shootings commenced, and because cellphone networks were jammed, students on other servers turned to Facebook to post details about their status or what was going on around them. One group, "I'm OK at VT," was created simply to inform the outside world that its members were still alive.

Bloggers, too, played an important role in the reporting of the massacre. One Virginia Tech blogger, Bryce Carter, hid in his locked dormitory room and posted details about what was going on around him. On his blog, "Bryce's Journal," Carter offered videos of security cars racing around campus and still photos of police sharpshooters. Knowing the importance of the new technology — although not, arguably, security measures — Virginia Tech's administration posted a podcast of statements from its president.

So what, some might say. Human tragedies often rely upon new communications technologies. During the U.S. Civil War, the telegraph and spy balloons tracked troop movements, and battlefield photos were being wired to newspapers during the Spanish-American War. What's different, however, is not just some newfangled technologies. What is new — what is truly a *revolution* — is the degree to which average citizens now participate in the reporting of the world around them. While few citizen journalists have the training of professional journalists, they more than make up for it in their geographic proximity to events, as well as their ability to report faster, and with no phony pretence of objectivity.

Some traditional media will continue to dismiss the importance of citizen media, naturally. They do that a lot. But the journalist named Jamal Albarghouti would likely have a differing view.

Albarghouti's footage of the shootings — as they happened, capturing the sounds of echoing gunshots — were seen by millions around the globe, mainly on CNN. By suppertime on the day of the killings, Albarghouti was doing live reporting from the Virginia Tech campus with CNN's Wolf Blitzer. But Jamal Albarghouti wasn't actually a journalist. He was a Virginia Tech graduate student, with his own Facebook page.

Virginia Tech will be remembered as a tremendous tragedy, and as the worst gun rampage in U.S. history. But it will also be remembered as the place where citizen media — the Internet, with blogs, podcasts, Facebook, YouTube, and the like — showed, once and for all, how tremendously important they can be in recording, and reporting, history.

The modern media revolution isn't hype. It's real. If you have something to say, the revolution's town square — the Internet — is the best place to say it.

Get Fighting!

"Young man," said the familiar voice on the other end of the phone line. Since he was calling from Russia, the line was hissing a bit. "Young man, I want you to get back in the fight. Don't give up."

I was down, down, down, I admit it. I — the guy who believes you should never, *ever* give up — was certainly considering it. It was early 2002: our weeks-old son had pneumonia; I had been getting a political pounding in the press for weeks; and the Team Martin Kill Machine (as I called it) had been bombarding me with lawsuit threats and anonymous smears, as well as telling my law clients and partners they'd get punished for hiring me. I felt like a human piñata. Oh, and the weather sucked, too.

The voice on the line belonged to my friend Prime Minister Jean Chrétien. He was somewhere in Russia and — as happened whenever he left the country — things were going to complete ratshit. But there he was on the line, in what must have been the middle of the night for him, trying to cheer me up. He had heard that I was fed up with what Paul

Martin and his goons had done to the Liberal Party of Canada, and that I was ready to quit.

"Young man," which is what he always called me whenever he had some advice to pass along, "I know you. You're a fighter, like me. You can't stop fighting. It makes us feel more alive!"

I enjoyed a good political scrap; that much was true. But the fight, circa February 2002, was getting really, really nasty. In January, one of Martin's most fanatical supporters — Toronto-area MP John McKay, the vice-chairman of the Ontario caucus — had defended the restrictions on Liberal Party membership rules. McKay, a socially conservative Liberal type, told the media he didn't want "children and non-citizens" participating. Later on, he got more specific, telling the *Ottawa Citizen* and others that he was referring to "ethnic groups."

"The enfranchisement of those kinds of groups," McKay said, "means that those folks get to choose who the prime minister of Canada is going to be."

"Those kinds of groups." As someone who had been involved in anti-racism campaigns for many years, those kinds of comments — coming from my own political party — depressed the hell out of me. On my website, I questioned whether real Liberals believed such things, and I suggested that the efforts of Martin's unelected advisors to gerrymander party membership rules smacked of racial profiling. No less than Paul Martin himself then held a press conference, flanked by Canadian flags, saying that I was "beneath contempt." On my website, I responded that the feeling was mutual. McKay then told the media that I was "an asshole." One of the more prominent Chrétien-bashers, Michelle Simson, told the *National Post* that I was a "jerk off." The *Post* editorial board then chimed in that I was "Canada's Al Sharpton," and so on, and so on. It was not a happy time, I must admit.

My wife, being a lot more sensible than me, wanted me out. Quit the Liberals. My parents wanted me out, too. My law partners wanted me out. They all pointed out that no one was coming to the defence of those few people who — like me — had publicly objected to the fact that Paul Martin was destroying the Liberal Party of Canada to satisfy his own ambition. Senior New Democrats and Conservatives had called me, saying they wanted me to run their war rooms, even if the Martinite Liberals didn't. And then Jean Chrétien called from Russia.

For every political volunteer — for every corporate leader, for every union activist, for everyone who has ever stepped forward to try to do something that isn't easy to do — there usually comes a moment when you want to pack it in, like I did in February of 2002. When you are feeling isolated, and miserable, and people (even friends) are shunning you. When things just keep getting worse, and you just can't seem to get a break. When the only way out is — it seems — quitting.

Take it from my friend Jean Chrétien, as I did back in 2002: don't quit. Don't stop fighting. *Never stop fighting.*

All of the strategies and tactics discussed in this book — getting a plan, and sticking to it; telling the story that captivates hearts and minds; trying to get your story out through the media or a paid ad campaign; being as creative and as fast as you can possibly be; finding the facts and figures that support the story you're trying to tell; fighting back against unfair scandals and smears; using the latest technology to reach as many pairs of ears and eyes as you can — *all of them* depend upon one crucial element to achieve success: *You.* You and your commitment to fight for your candidate, your campaign, or your cause.

Without a personal commitment to fight for what is right, you're never going to win. And it shouldn't take a midnight phone call from a prime minister visiting Russia to remind you, either. If you read this far in this book, you already know it.

By the end of that phone call, Chrétien had me laughing for the first time in a long time. He told me the story of a politician who had come to see him, seeking his advice. The politician wanted to run for higher office, and wasn't sure if he'd win or not.

Jean Chrétien told him what he tells everyone who asks him that question. "I don't know if you'll win or not," Chrétien told the hopeful campaigner. "But I do know that you'll lose if you don't try."

Do campaigns matter? You won't be surprised to hear me say that they do.

Now, in recent years, those two words — campaigns matter — have become a sort of awkward rallying cry for lunatics like me, who devote too much of their time and effort to political contests. There has been a well-read book bearing that title. There have been more than a dozen international political science conferences put together to answer that question, most of them concluding, with greater or lesser degrees of enthusiasm, that the answer is yes. And most everyone concerned, from respected academics to the consultants who consign themselves to the nasty and brutish (but not always short) world of electoral politics, has repeated the phrase in plenty of books and interviews. Political reporters, especially, have said that yes indeed, campaigns matter — because, mainly, journalists have so much fun writing about them.

But do campaigns *really* matter as much as all those people say? Or are campaigns basically irrelevant to the lives of real people — the ones who sneer or head to the kitchen for a glass of milk when a political spot is broadcast? The ones who say, in increasingly depressing numbers, that they don't ever bother to vote or participate anymore?

Not to put too a fine point on it: if the people we are trying to reach are less and less interested in what we have to say, if they're voting less and less, how can we insist that campaigns matter?

Call me stubborn, and plenty do, but I am one of those who believes that campaigns matter despite (or perhaps because of) well-documented declining rates of voter participation in elections. That said, even I have to concede that the "campaigns matter" claim has a bit of a hollow, defensive ring. It is as if political types secretly worry that the reverse is true. It is as if — and this is even worse — *they* had something to do with the circumstances that led to the disinterest, disaffection, and disenfranchisement that now besets too many campaigns, political and otherwise.

So the doubts stubbornly persist here and there, and especially recently: *do* campaigns really matter?

It all depends on how you define campaigns, I think. If campaigns are designed to inform voters about the choices available to them in democratic contests, if they highlight differences, and if they motivate voters to express themselves on the basis of those differences — then campaigns do, pretty much, what they are supposed to do. Political campaigns may not be the prettiest of dialectical exercises, as even the likes of James Carville or Jean Chrétien would be inclined to admit, but they seem to meet the two basic requirements: information and motivation. War room campaigners try to inform regular folks, and, once informed, regular folks are, hopefully, persuaded to move their way or (at least) to move away from the alternatives.

The do-campaigns-matter question isn't entirely irrelevant — especially coming, as it does, at the conclusion of a book about war rooms, and how to use war room stuff in a non-political context. In recent years, a small but influential number of university professors have asserted that, well, campaigns *don't* really matter at all. People make up their minds about voting choices based on things over which political consultants have no control, they say. For example, some of these professors have developed mathematical models to track changes in personal income, gross domestic product, and so on, and then predicted campaign winners based upon economic results. Not policy, and certainly not hardball campaign strategy.

One of the better known members of the "campaigns don't matter" school is the much-quoted James E. Campbell, at the State University of New York at Buffalo. He's a smart guy. Campbell asserts that, as far as he and like-minded thinkers are concerned, the economy is the answer to every question. Data assembled by Campbell shows the following: since the Second World War, in eight out of the ten presidential elections where the United States has enjoyed annual GDP of at least 2.5 percent, the incumbent has won. The two exceptions, he allows, were Democrat Hubert H. Humphrey in 1968, whose candidacy was battered by the on-going Vietnam War, and the Republicans' Gerald R. Ford in 1976, who was the target of anger for the sins of Watergate and the pardon of Richard Nixon. Until somewhat recently, Campbell was attracting a lot of academic converts, and he was causing much consternation among political consultants. Until Florida.

The definitive rebuttal to Campbell is this: Florida. Florida, Florida, Florida. In 2000, as everyone recalls, the Democrats held the White House, and the GDP was closing in on a whopping 6 percent. Despite that, and, most significantly, because of some pretty good tactical campaigning on the ground, George W. Bush's team defeated the incumbent party's candidate, Al Gore, and thereby captured all of Florida's electoral college votes. Gore was considered smarter and more mature than his rival. But the 2000 presidential campaign *wasn't* all about the economy, stupid (to mangle Carville's line). It was principally about who campaigned better, who fought harder for the prize. Bush did, Gore didn't. Ipso facto, campaigns matter.

I started this book by accepting as a truism that campaigns, and campaign war rooms, should matter to you. Perhaps I shouldn't have done so. Perhaps I should have spent more time arguing for the proposition that the stuff of modern electoral politics are legitimate, and that the way we make important democratic choices is clearly affected by campaigns.

I didn't, and I won't. Sorry. This book's starting point — its starting point long before the weeks-long nail-biter in Florida — is that campaigns count. They matter. It is not even a debatable point anymore. The *methodologies* of campaigns — advertising, opposition research, quick response, the Internet, polling, earned media, stunts, and so on — are therefore all pretty frigging important, as well.

Professor Campbell's statistics are interesting. But there is only one statistic that matters to me in the election campaigns in which I participate. It came to me one morning a few years ago, while I was driving to a campaign office somewhere out west. I was tuned to CBC Radio. As I listened to CBC, the radio host mentioned that, about two decades ago, only about one out of every five households were two-income. By the 1990s, the commentator noted, nearly four out of every five households were two-income.

It would be an overstatement to say that I very nearly drove my car off the road, but not by much. In every campaign I have been involved with since, I have cornered fellow partisans to lecture them about that statistic. Most of the time, they feign interest and go back to whatever they were doing before, wondering who made the decision to hire that strange Kinsella guy.

But it's important! In June 2001, I and some other political consultants gathered in Washington to share trade secrets — and to chat with people like Mark Mellman. Bulky, bearded and brilliant, Mellman has been a pollster to Bill Clinton and Al Gore. And he, too, subscribes to the notion that voters have a lot of things on their minds, but politics isn't one of them. "The voters we are talking to," he says, "are not very interested in what we have to say … It's therefore very important in campaigns to say things over and over again."

Why aren't voters interested? Because, as that two-income statistic suggests, voters are busy. Very busy. During an average day during an average campaign, voters spend far more time contemplating the availability of parking spaces than they do the minutiae of a party's policy platform or the soundness of an organization's accounting principles. "Most of the time, voters don't even have a notional idea of what a candidate stands for," says Mellman. "That's why so many of them vote because of a candidate's image." The lives of voters are preoccupied with too many real-life challenges — getting the kids to school on time, getting the bills paid on time, getting enough time to sleep. For politicians, and the war room warriors who try to get them elected, this represents the biggest challenge of all, not Professor Campbell's economic theories. Given the difficulties of ordinary existence, how do campaigns attract, and hold, the attention of ordinary people?

I hope this book has been about the answers to that question. It has been about doing all that you can do to grab the attention of busy people. It has been about how to get people to choose your side over the other side.

It has been about getting into the fight, and fighting as if everything depends on the outcome. Which, if you are anything like me, it does.

A LITTLE WHILE AGO, I was in Ottawa for my company, which I call Daisy. (Yes, I named it after Tony Schwartz's 1964 ad, because it fit.) I rang up Jean Chrétien and he suggested we go for lunch. Sure, I said.

At lunch, not far from the Sparks Street Mall, where this little war room journey got its start one summer day back in 1992, Chrétien and I sat with his former executive assistant (and my former war room colleague and friend) Bruce Hartley. We all had a lot of laughs. The Paul Martin regime was long gone, replaced by the minority Stephen Harper Conservative government. I told Chrétien that the Harper guys, many of whom I knew well, had an acronym they were all using these days.

"Whenever they face some kind of a dilemma," I told Chrétien and

Hartley, "they say, W.W.C.D."

"What's W.W.C.D.?" Chrétien asked me.

"What Would Chrétien Do!" I said, and we all laughed. It was nice that Chrétien's amazing political skills were being appreciated again — even if by Conservatives. Many of us liked and trusted the Harper Conservatives a lot more than we ever did the Martin cabal. We didn't agree with many of their policies, but they were a lot more respectful than the Martin creeps had ever been. For Chrétien, and for those of us who always stuck by his side, Ottawa had become hospitable again. As if in evidence of that, people would periodically come over to our table to ask for Chrétien's autograph, or to ask him to pose with them for a cellphone picture. It was a lot of fun.

"Hey," Chrétien finally said. "My friend Bill Clinton is in town to give a speech. Have you ever met him? Do you want to meet him?"

Did I? I had never met the former U.S. president. Was he kidding?

He wasn't; Chrétien said he and Hartley would set it up. Later, they called to tell me to meet them at the Westin Hotel. When I arrived, the place was teeming with Ottawa police, the RCMP, and the U.S. Secret Service. I went up to the appointed floor, where a big guy greeted me, a U.S. flag on his lapel. "Hello, Warren," he said, then led me to Clinton's suite.

Hartley and the always-gracious Aline Chrétien were there, along with Chrétien's former photographer and, of course, Jean Chrétien, the guy I still consider to be Canada's best prime minister. There was another bunch of Secret Service types, and, of course, Bill Clinton, the guy who I still consider to be the best president the United States ever had.

"Mr. President," said Chrétien, "this is my friend Warren Kinsella, who ran my war room for me. He did a pretty good job."

Clinton regarded me. "Did he, now?"

"I copied what Carville did for you in 1992, sir," I said to Clinton. "It wasn't very original, but it did the job."

"Well," said Clinton, "when you are running a war room for my friend Jean, that makes it all a lot easier, doesn't it?" Chrétien beamed.

"Yes, Mr. President, that is certainly true," I said. For the briefest of moments, I thought about telling Clinton how I thought war rooms, and war roomers, have plenty to pass on to people who don't even work in politics. How, with smart planning and messaging and advertising — and a willingness to get tough and creative, and use every fact and figure and bit of technology at your disposal — you can beat back scandal and the worst odds, and win. And win big.

But I thought better of it. *Better save it for the book instead*, I thought. So I stood with Aline and Bill and Jean to get my picture taken. And grinned.

Bibliography

Adatto, Kiku. "Sound Bite Democracy: Network Evening News Presidential Campaign Coverage, 1968 and 1988." Research Paper, Shorenstein Barone Center, John F. Kennedy School of Government, Harvard University, 1990.

Ailes, Roger. *You Are the Message: Secrets of the Master Communicators.* Homewood, IL: Dow Jones-Irwin, 1988.

Ansolabehere, Stephen, and Shanto Iyengar. *Going Negative: How Campaign Advertisements Shrink and Polarize the Electorate.* New York: The Free Press, 1995.

Ansolabehere, Stephen, Shanto Iyengar, Adam Simon, and Nicholas Valentino. "Does Attack Advertising Demobilize the Electorate?" *American Political Science Review* 88 (1994): 829–38.

Arterton, F. Christopher. "Campaign Organizations Confront the Media-Political Environment." In *Race for the Presidency*, edited by James D. Barber. New York: Prentice-Hall, 1978.

Asher, Herbert. *Polling and the Public: What Every Citizen Should Know.* Washington, D.C.: Congressional Quarterly Press, 1988.

Atkin, Charles, and Gary Heald. "Effects of Political Advertising." *Public Opinion Quarterly* 40 (Summer 1976): 216–28.

Auletta, Ken. *Three Blind Mice: How the TV Networks Lost Their Way*. New York: Random House, 1991.

Austin, Erica, and Bruce Pinkleton. "Positive and Negative Effects of Political Disaffection on the Less Experienced Voter." *Journal of Broadcasting and Electronic Media* 39 (1995): 215–35.

Bain, George. *Gotcha: How the Media Distort the News*. Toronto: Key Porter Books, 1994.

Bartels, Larry. "Messages Received: The Political Impact of Media Exposure." *American Political Science Review* 87 (1993): 267–85.

Bayer, Michael J., and Joseph Rodota. "Computerized Opposition Research." In *Campaigns and Elections: A Reader in Modern American Politics*, edited by Larry J. Sabato. Glenview, IL: Scott, Foresman and Company, 1989.

Beall, Pat. "Buy Your Own Time." *Campaigns and Elections* (July 1991): 48.

Bennett, James. "Another Tally in '96 Race: Two Months of TV Ads." *New York Times*, November 13, 1996, D20.

Biocca, Frank, ed. *Signs, Codes and Images of Television and Political Advertising*. Vol. 2: Hillsdale, NJ: Lawrence Erlbaum Associates, 1991.

Blaemire, Robert. "Targeting: Before You Start Trying to Persuade, Figure Out Who You're Talking To." *Campaigns and Elections* (October/November 1991).

Blumenthal, Sidney. *The Permanent Campaign: Inside the World of Elite Political Operatives*. Boston: Beacon Press, 1982.

Boorstin, Daniel J. *The Image: A Guide to Pseudo-Events in America*. New York: Atheneum, 1961.

Boyd, Gerald. "Despite Vow to Be 'Gentler,' Bush Stays on Attack." *New York Times*, October 29,1988, 8.

Bozinoff, Lorne, and Peter MacIntosh. "Canadians Oppose Negative Advertising." *Gallup Canada*, November 17,1988.

Broder, David S. "Beware the 'Push-Poll.'" *Washington Post*, October 9, 1994, C7.

Burke, Kenneth. *A Rhetoric of Motives*. New York: Prentice-Hall, 1953.

Cairns, Allan. "An Election to Be Remembered: Canada 1993." *Canadian Public Policy* 20 (1994): 219–34.

Cameron, Stevie. *On the Take: Crime, Corruption and Greed in the Mulroney Years*. Toronto: Macfarlane Walter & Ross, 1994.

Cantril, Albert H. *The Opinion Connection: Polling, Politics and the Press*. Washington, D.C.: Congressional Quarterly Press, 1991.

Cappella, Joseph N., and Kathleen Hall Jamieson. "Broadcast Adwatch Effects: A Field Experiment." *Communication Research* 21, No. 3 (1994): 342–65.

_____. *Spiral of Cynicism: The Press and the Public Good*. New York: Oxford University Press, 1997.

Carey, John. "How News Media Shape Campaigns." *Journal of Communication* 26 (Spring 1976): 50–57.

Carney, Tom. *Negative Political Advertisements in the 1993 Canadian Federal Election: Exploring Their Impact by the Use of Participatory Action Research*. Windsor, ON: Department of Communication Studies, University of Windsor, 1994.

Ceci, Stephen J., and Edward L. Khan. "Jumping on the Bandwagon with the Underdog: The Impact of Attitude Polls and Polling Behaviour." *Public Opinion Quarterly* 46 (1982): 228–42.

Chrétien, Jean. *Straight from the Heart*. Toronto: Key Porter Books, 1985.

Christ, William, Esther Thorson, and Clarke Caywood. "Do Attitudes Toward Political Advertising Affect Information Processing of Televised Political Commercials?" *Journal of Broadcasting and Electronic Media* 38 (1994): 251–70.

Clarkson, Stephen. "Yesterday's Man and His Blue Grits: Backward into the Future." In *The Canadian General Election of 1993*, edited by Alan Frizzell, Jon Pammett, and Anthony Westell. Ottawa: Carleton University Press, 1994.

Coffey, P.J. "A Quantitative Measure of Bias in Reporting of Political News." *Journalism Quarterly* 52 (1975): 551–53.

Combs, James E., and Dan Nimmo. *The New Propaganda: The Dictatorship of Palaver in Contemporary Politics*. New York: Longman Publishing Group, 1993.

Cook, Philip S., Douglas Gomery, and Lawrence W. Lichty, eds. *The Future of News: Television, Newspapers, Wire Services and News Magazines*. Baltimore, MD: Johns Hopkins University Press, 1992.

Corcoran, Paul E. *Political Language and Rhetoric*. Austin: University of Texas Press, 1979.

Crouse, Timothy. *The Boys on the Bus*. New York: Random House, 1972.

Cundy, Donald T. "Image Formation, the Low Involvement Viewer, and Televised Political Advertising." *Political Communication and Persuasion* 7 (1990): 41–49.

Cunningham, Stanley B. "Sorting Out the Ethics of Propaganda." *Communication Studies* 43 (1992): 233–45.

Curran, Tim. "'Attack' Ad May Preview '92 GOP Tactics." *Roll Call*, November 4, 1991, 35.

Davey, Keith. *The Rainmaker: A Passion for Politics*. Toronto: Stoddart, 1986.

De Vries, Walter. "American Campaign Consulting: Trends and Concerns." *PS: Political Science and Politics*, March 1998, 21–25.

Denton, Robert E., Jr. *The Primetime Presidency of Ronald Reagan*. New York: Praeger, 1988.

Denton, Robert E., Jr., and Gary C. Woodward. *The Political Communication in America*. Westport, CN: Praeger, 1998.

Devlin, L. Patrick. "An Analysis of Presidential Television Commercials: 1952–1984." In *New Perspectives on Political Advertising*, edited by Lynda Kaid, Dan Nimmo, and Keith Sanders. Carbondale, IL: South Illinois University Press, 1986.

____. "Contrast in Presidential Campaign Commercials of 1988." *American Behavioural Scientist* 32, No. 4 (March/April 1989): 389–414.

Diamond, Edwin, and Stephen Bates. *The Spot: The Rise of Political Advertising on Television*. Cambridge, MA: MIT Press, 1984.

Dionne, E.J., Jr. *Why Americans Hate Politics*. New York: Simon & Schuster, 1991.

Erikson, Robert S. "The Influence of Newspaper Endorsements in Presidential Elections: The Case of 1964." *American Journal of Political Science* 20 (May 1976): 207–33.

Faber, Ronald J., Albert R. Tims, and Kay G. Schmitt. "Negative Political Advertising and Voting Intent: The Role of Involvement and Alternative Information Sources." *Journal of Advertising* 22 (1993): 67–76.

Fallows, James. *Breaking the News: How the Media Undermine American Democracy*. New York: Pantheon Books, 1996.

Felknor, Bruce L. *Dirty Politics*. New York: Norton, 1966.

Finkel, S., and J. Greer. "A Spot Check: Casting Doubt on the Demobilizing Effect of Attack Advertising." *American Journal of Political Science* 42 (1998): 573–95.

Fleitas, Daniel W. "Bandwagon and Underdog Effects in Minimal Information Elections." *American Political Science Review* 65 (1971): 434–38.

Fletcher, Fred. "Media, Elections and Democracy." *Canadian Journal of Communication* 19 (1994): 131–50.

Fletcher, Fred, and Robert MacDermid. "Reading the Spots: The 1997 Federal Campaign." Paper presented at the annual conference of the Canadian Political Sciences Association, Ottawa, June 1998.

Fox, William J. *Spinwars: Politics and New Media*. Toronto: Key Porter Books, 1999.

Fraser, Graham. *Playing for Keeps: The Making of the Prime Minister, 1988*. Toronto: McClelland & Stewart, 1989.

Friedenberg, Robert V. *Communication Consultants in Political Campaigns: Ballot Box Warriors*. Westport, CT: Praeger, 1997.

Garramone, Gina. "Voter Responses to Negative Political Ads." *Journalism Quarterly* 61 (1984): 250–59.

____. "Effects of Negative Political Advertising: The Roles of Sponsors and Rebuttal." *Journal of Broadcasting and Electronic Media* 29 (1985): 147–59.

Goldwater, Barry. *With No Apologies*. New York: Morrow, 1979.

Graton, Michel. *So What Are the Boys Saying? An Inside Look at Brian Mulroney in Power*. Toronto: McGraw-Hill Ryerson, 1987.

Greenspon, Edward, and Jeff Sallot. "How Campbell Self-Destructed." *Globe and Mail*, October 27, 1993, A1.

Griese, Noel L. "Rosser Reeves and the 1952 Eisenhower TV Spot Blitz." *Journal of Advertising* 4 (1975): 34–38.

Grossman, Laurence K. *The Electric Republic: Reshaping Democracy in the Information Age*. New York: Vintage, 1995.

Hall, J.A. "When Political Campaigns Turn to Slime: Establishing a Virginia Fair Campaign Practices Committee." *Journal of Law and Politics* 7 (1990–91): 353–77.

Hansborough, Mac. "Dial N for Negative: Using Phones to Make Your Attacks Heard but Not Seen." *Campaigns and Elections* 13 (April 1992): 58–61.

Harris, John F. "Va. Republicans Say Democrats Are Slinging a Little Mud in Their Poll Questions." *Washington Post*, August 18, 1993, D1.

Harwood, John, and Daniel Pearl. "In Waning Campaign Hours, Candidates Turn to Phone 'Push-Polling' to Step Up the Attack." *Wall Street Journal*,

November 9, 1994, A24.

Herbert, Christopher J. "Listen Up: A Guide for the Focus Group Observer." *Campaigns and Elections*, (July 1994): 42.

Herbst, Susan. *Numbered Voices: How Opinion Polling Has Shaped American Politics*. Chicago: University of Chicago Press, 1993.

Hertsgaard, Mark. *On Bended Knee: The Press and the Reagan Presidency*. New York: Shocken, 1989.

Hickman, Harrison. "Public Polls and Election Participants." In *Polling and Presidential Election Coverage*, edited by Paul J. Lavrakas and Jack K. Holley. Newbury Park, CA: Sage, 1991.

Hill, Ronald. "An Exploration of Voter Responses to Political Advertisements." *Journal of Advertising* 18 (1989): 14–22.

Hofstadter, Richard. *The Paranoid Style in American Politics and Other Essays*. New York: Knopf, 1965.

Holbrook, T. *Do Campaigns Matter?* Thousand Oaks, CA: Sage, 1996.

Hollitz, John E. "Eisenhower and the Admen: The Television 'Spot' Campaign of 1952." *Wisconsin Magazine of History* 66 (Autumn 1982): 25–39.

Hooper, Michael. "Party and Newspaper Endorsement as Predictors of Voter Choice." *Journalism Quarterly* 46 (Summer 1969): 303–05.

Iyengar, Shanto. *Is Anyone Responsible?* Chicago: University of Chicago Press, 1991.

Iyengar, Shanto, and Donald Kinder. *News that Matters: Television and American Opinion*. Chicago: University of Chicago Press, 1991.

James, Karen, and Paul Hensel. "Negative Advertising: The Malicious Strain of Comparative Advertising." *Journal of Advertising* 20 (1991): 53–69.

Jamieson, Kathleen Hall. *Packaging the Presidency*. New York: Oxford University Press, 1984.

____. *Dirty Politics: Deception, Distraction and Democracy*. New York: Oxford University Press, 1992.

____. "Broadcast Adwatch Effects: A Field Experiment." *Communication Research* 21 (1994): 342–65.

____. *Everything You Think You Know About Politics … And Why You're Wrong*. New York: Basic Books, 2000.

Jamieson, Kathleen Hall, Paul Waldman, and Susan Sherr. "Eliminate the Negative? Categories of Analysis for Political Advertising." In *Crowded Airwaves: Campaign Advertising in Modern Elections*, edited by James A. Thurber, Candice Nelson, and David Dulio. Washington, D.C.: Brookings Institution Press, 2000.

Johnson-Cartee, Karen S., and Gary A. Copeland. *Negative Political Advertising: Coming of Age*. Hillsdale, NJ: Lawrence Erlbaum Associates, 1991.

____. *Inside Political Campaigns: Theory and Practice*. Westport, CT: Praeger, 1997.

Joslyn, Richard A. "Political Advertising and the Meaning of Elections." In *New Perspectives on Political Advertising*, edited by Lynda Kaid, Dan Nimmo, and K.R. Sanders. Carbondale, IL: Southern Illinois University Press, 1986.

Kaid, Lynda Lee. "Political Advertising in the 1992 Campaign." In *The 1992 Presidential Election: A Communication Perspective*, edited by Robert Denton, Jr. Westport, CT: Praeger, 1994.

Kaid, Lynda Lee, and John Boysdon. "An Experimental Study of the Effectiveness of Negative Political Advertisements." *Communication Quarterly* 35 (1987): 193–201.

Kaid Lynda Lee, and Dorothy Davidson. "Elements of Videostyle." In *New Perspectives on Political Advertising*, edited by Lynda Kaid, Dan Nimmo, and Keith Sanders. Carbondale, IL: Southern Illinois University Press, 1986.

Kaid, Lynda Lee, and Anne Johnston. "Negative Versus Positive Television Advertising in U.S. Presidential Campaigns, 1960–1988." *Journal of Communication* 41 (1991): 53–64.

Kaid, Lynda, et al. "Television News and Presidential Campaigns: The Legitimization of Televised Political Advertising." *Social Science Quarterly* 74 (1993): 274–85.

Kaplan, William. *Presumed Guilty: Brian Mulroney, the Airbus Affair and the Government of Canada*. Toronto: McClelland & Stewart, 1998.

Katz, Elihu, Hanna Adoni, and Pnina Parness. "Remembering the News: What the Picture Adds to Recall." *Journalism Quarterly* 54 (Summer 1977): 231–39.

Keesel, John. *Presidential Campaign Politics: Coalition Strategies and Citizen Response*. Chicago: Dorsey, 1988.

Kellner, Douglas. *Television and the Crisis of Democracy*. Boulder, CO: Westview Press, 1995.

Kent, Montague. *30-Second Politics: Political Advertising in the Eighties*. New York: Praeger, 1989.

Kolodny, Robin, and Angela Logan. "Political Consultants and the Extension of Party Goals." *PS: Political Science and Politics* 31, No. 2 (1998): 155–59.

Krasno, Jonathan, S. *Challengers, Competition, and Reelection*. New Haven, CT: Yale University Press, 1994.

Kurtz, Howard. *Spin Cycle: Inside the Clinton Propaganda Machine*. New York: The Free Press, 1998.

Ladd, Everett, and John Benson. "The Growth of News Polls in American Politics." In *Media Polls in American Politics*, edited by Thomas Mann and Gary Orren. Washington, D.C.: Brookings Institution Press, 1992.

Lane, Robert E., and David O. Sears. *Public Opinion*. Englewood Cliffs, NJ: Prentice-Hall, 1964.

Lang, A. "Emotion, Formal Features, and Memory for Televised Political Advertisements." In *Psychological Processes*, edited by F. Biocca. Vol. 1 of *Television and Political Advertising*. Hillsdale, NJ: Lawrence Erlbaum Associates, 1991.

Lau, R.R. "Negativity in Political Perception." *Political Behaviour* 4 (1982): 353–77.

Lee, Robert Mason. *One Hundred Monkeys: The Triumph of Popular Wisdom in Canadian Politics*. Toronto: Macfarlane Walter & Ross, 1989.

Leonard, Thomas C. *The Power of the Press: The Birth of American Political Reporting*. New York: Oxford University Press, 1987.

Lowry, D.T., and J.A. Shidler. "The Soundbites, the Biters, and the Bitten: An Analysis of Network TV News Bias in Campaign '92." *Journalism and Mass Communication Quarterly* 97 (1995): 33–44.

Luntz, Frank. *Candidates, Consultants and Campaigns: The Style and Substance of American Electioneering*. New York: Basil Blackwell, 1988.

____. "Should a Poll Push You to Run?" *Campaigns and Elections* (March 1991).

MacInnis, Craig. "B.C. Premier's Nose out of Joint over Ad." *Globe and Mail*, April 30, 1996, A7.

Marsh, Catherine. "Back on the Bandwagon: The Effects of Opinion Polls on Public Opinion." *British Journal of Political Science* 15 (1984): 51–74.

Martinez, Michael D., and Ted Delegal. "The Irrelevance of Negative Campaigns to Political Trust: Experimental and Survey Results." *Political Communication and Persuasion* 7 (1990): 25–40.

Mason, William M. "The Impact of Endorsements on Voting." *Sociological Methods and Research* 1 (May 1973): 463–95.

Matalin, Mary, and James Carville. *All's Fair: Love, War, and Running for President*. Random House, 1994.

Mauser, Gary. *Political Marketing: An Approach to Campaign Strategy*. New York: Praeger, 1983.

McCombs, Maxwell. "Editorial Endorsements: A Study of Influence." *Journalism Quarterly* 44 (Autumn 1967): 545–48.

McCombs, Maxwell, and Donald Shaw. "The Agenda-Setting Function of Mass Media." *Public Opinion Quarterly* 36 (1972): 176–87.

McGinniss, Joe. *The Selling of the President, 1968.* New York: Trident, 1969.

McGuire, W. "The Myth of Massive Media Impact: Savagings and Salvagings." *Public Communication and Behaviour* 1 (1986): 173–257.

Mehrabian, A. "Effects of Poll Reports on Voter Preferences." *Journal of Social Psychology* 28 (1998): 2119–30.

Mellman, Mark. "Benchmark Basics and Beyond." *Campaigns and Elections* (May 1991).

Merritt, Sharyne. "Negative Political Advertising: Some Empirical Findings." *International Journal of Public Opinion Research* 13 (1984): 27–38.

Meyer, Chris, and Phil Porado. "Hit or Miss: Your Guide to Effective Media Buying." *Campaigns and Elections* (August/September 1990): 38.

Mickelson, Sig. *From Whistle Stop to Sound Bite: Four Decades of Politics and Television.* New York: Praeger, 1989.

Miller, Mark Crispin. "Political Ads: Decoding Hidden Messages." *Columbia Journalism Review* 30 (1992): 36–39.

Mittal, Banwari. "Public Assessment of TV Advertising: Faint Praise and Harsh Criticism." *Journal of Advertising Research* 34 (1994): 35–53.

Moore, David W. *The Superpollsters.* New York: Four Walls Eight Windows, 1992.

Morwitz, V.G., and C. Pluzinski. "Do Polls Reflect Opinions or Do Opinions Reflect Polls? The Impact of Political Polling on Voters' Expectation, Preferences, and Behaviour." *Journal of Consumer Research* 23 (1996): 53–67.

Mueller, Claus. *The Politics of Communication.* New York: Oxford University Press, 1973.

Neel, R.F., Jr. "Campaign Hyperbole: The Advisability of Legislating False

Statements out of Politics." *Journal of Law and Politics* 2 (1985): 405–24.

Nelson, Candice J. "Inside the Beltway: Profiles of Two Political Consultants." *PS: Political Science and Politics* 31, No. 2 (1998): 162–70.

Nieves, Evelyn. "Spelling by Quayle (That's with an E)." *New York Times*, June 17, 1992, A17.

Nimmo, Dan. *The Political Persuaders: The Techniques of Modern Election Campaigns.* Englewood Cliffs, NJ: Prentice-Hall, 1970.

Noonan, Peggy. *What I Saw at the Revolution: A Political Life in the Reagan Era.* New York: Random House, 1990.

Nordlinger, Gary. "Allocating Your Media Dollars: How and When to Use TV, Newspaper and Radio." Paper presented at the annual National Campaign Training Seminar and Trade Show, Washington, D.C., June 17, 1995.

Novazio, Robert. "An Experimental Approach to Bandwagon Research." *Political Opinion Quarterly* 41 (1977): 217–25.

Nugent, J.F. "Positively Negative." *Campaigns and Elections* 7 (1987): 47–49.

O'Sullivan, Patrick, and Seth Geiger. "Does the Watchdog Bite? Newspaper Ad Watch Articles and Political Attack Ads." *Journalism and Mass Communication Quarterly* 74 (1995): 771–85.

Patterson, Thomas, and Robert McClure. *The Unseeing Eye: The Myth of Television Power in National Elections.* New York: Putman, 1976.

Pentony, J.F. "The Effect of Negative Campaigning on Voting, Semantic Differential and Thought Listing." *Journal of Social Behaviour and Personality* 10 (1995): 631–44.

Perlmutter, David D. *The Manship School Guide to Political Communication.* Baton Rouge, LA: Louisiana State University Press, 1999.

Perloff, Richard. *Political Communication.* Mahwah, NJ: Lawrence Earlbaum, 1998.

Perloff, Richard, and Dennis Kinsey. "Political Advertising as Seen by Consultants and Journalists." *Journal of Advertising Research* 32 (1992): 645–55.

Pfau, Michael, and Michael Burgoon. "The Efficacy of Issue and Character Attack Message Strategies in Political Campaign Communication." *Communication Reports* 2 (1989): 53–61.

Pfau, Michael, and Henry C. Kenski. *Attack Politics: Strategy and Defence.* Westport, CT: Praeger, 1990.

Pfau, Michael, and Allan Louden. "Effectiveness of Ad-Watch Formats in Deflecting Political Attack Ads." *Communication Research* 21 (1994): 325–41.

Pinkleton, Bruce. "The Effects of Negative Comparative Political Advertising on Candidate Evaluations and Advertising Evaluations: An Exploration." *Journal of Advertising* 26 (1997): 19–26.

Randolph, Sallie, G. "The Effective Press Release: Key to Free Media." In *Campaigns and Elections: A Reader in Modern American Politics*, edited by Larry J. Sabato. Glenview, IL: Scott, Foresman and Company, 1989.

Reeves, Rosser. *Reality in Advertising.* New York: Knopf, 1961.

Rhee, J.W. "How Polls Drive Campaign Coverage: The Gallup/CNN/*USA Today* Tracking Poll and *USA Today*'s Coverage of the 1992 Presidential Campaign." *Political Communication* 13 (1996): 213–29.

Ridder, Rick. "Do's and Don'ts of Opposition Research." *Campaigns and Elections* 15 (August 1984): 58.

Roddy, Brian, and Gina Garramone. "Appeals and Strategies of Negative Political Advertising." *Journal of Broadcasting and Electronic Media* 32 (1988): 415–27.

Roese, W.J., and G.N. Sande. "Backlash Effects in Attack Politics." *Journal of Applied Social Psychology* 23 (1993): 632–53.

Roll, Charles W., Jr., and Albert H. Cantril. *Polls: Their Use and Misuse in Politics.* New York: Basic Books, 1972.

Romanow, Walter, Michel de Repentigny, Stanley B. Cunningham, Walter C.

Soderlund, Kai Hilderbrandt. *Television Advertising in Canadian Elections: The Attack Mode, 1993*. Waterloo, ON: Wilfrid Laurier University Press, 1999.

Romanow, Walter, Walter Soderlund, and Richard Price. "Negative Political Advertising: An Analysis of Research in Light of Canadian Practices." In *Political Ethics: A Canadian Perspective*, edited by Jane Hiebert. Vol. 12 of *Royal Commission on Electoral Reform and Party Financing Research Studies*. Toronto: Dundurn Press, 1991.

Rosenstiel, Tom. *Strange Bedfellows*. New York: Hyperion Books, 1993.

Sabato, Larry. *The Rise of Political Consultants: New Ways of Winning Elections*. New York: Basic Books, 1981.

_____. *Feeding Frenzy: How Attack Journalism Has Transformed American Politics*. New York: The Free Press, 1991.

Sabato, Larry J., and Glenn R. Simpson. *Dirty Little Secrets: The Persistence of Corruption in American Politics*. New York: The Free Press, 1991.

Safire, William. *Before the Fall*. Garden City, NY: Doubleday, 1975.

Salmon, C.T., L.N. Reid, J. Pokrywczynski, and R.W. Willett. "The Effectiveness of Advocacy Advertising Relative to News Coverage." *Communication Research* 12, No. 4 (October 1985): 546–67.

Scarrow, Howard A., with Steve Borman. "The Effects of Newspaper Endorsements on Election Outcomes: A Case Study." *Public Opinion Quarterly* 43 (Fall 1979): 388–93.

Schwartz, Tony. *The Responsive Cord*. Garden City, NY: Doubleday, 1973.

_____. *Media: The Second God*. New York: Random House, 1981.

Selnow, Gary. *High-Tech Campaigns*. Westport, CT: Praeger, 1994.

Shapiro, Michael, and Robert Rieger. "Comparing Positive and Negative Political Advertising on Radio." *Journalism Quarterly* 69 (1992): 135–45.

Shea, Daniel M. *Campaign Craft: The Strategies, Tactics, and Art of Campaign*

Management. Westport, CT: Praeger, 1996.

Simon, Herbert A. "Bandwagon Effects and the Possibility of Election Predictions." *Public Opinion Quarterly* 18 (1954): 245–53.

Slade White, Joe. "Lessons Learned: Through the Cutter." *Campaigns and Elections* (February 1996): 22.

Soderlund, Walter, Walter Romanow, Donald Briggs, and Ronald H. Wagenberg. *Media and Elections in Canada*. Toronto: Holt, Rinehart and Winston, 1984.

Stewart, Charles. "Voter Perception of Mudslinging in Political Communication." *Central States Speech Journal* 26 (1975): 279–86.

Stoler, Peter. *The War Against the Press*. New York: Dodd and Mead, 1986.

Straffin, Philip D. "The Bandwagon Curve." *American Journal of Political Science* 21 (1977): 695–709.

Taras, David. *The Newsmakers: The Media's Influence on Canadian Politics*. Scarborough, ON: Nelson Canada, 1990.

Thompson, Spring. "TV Time Buying Rules: Feast and Famine." *Campaigns and Elections* (June/July 1993): 9.

Thurber, James A. "The Study of Campaign Consultants: A Subfield in Search of Theory." *PS: Political Science and Politics* 31, No. 2 (1998): 145–49.

Thurber, James A., and Candice J. Nelson. *Campaigns and Elections American Style*. Boulder, CO.: Westview Press, 1995.

_____. *Campaign Warriors: Political Consultants in Elections*. Washington, D.C.: Brookings Institution Press, 2000.

Traugott, Michael. "The Impact of Media Polls on the Public." In *Media Polls in American Politics*, edited by Thomas Mann and Gary Orren. Washington, D.C.: Brookings Institution Press, 1992.

Trent, Judith S., and Robert V. Friedenberg. *Political Campaign Communications: Principles and Practices*. 3rd ed. Westport, CT: Praeger, 1995.

Wagenberg, Ronald, Walter Soderlund, Walter Romanow, and Donald E. Briggs. "Campaigns, Images and Polls: Mass Media Coverage of the 1984 Canadian Election." *Canadian Journal of Political Science* 21 (1988): 117–29.

Weaver, David H., and G. Cleveland Wilhoit. "Journalists — Who Are They, Really?" *Media Studies Journal* (Fall 1992): 63–79.

West, Darrell. *Air Wars: Television Advertising in Election Campaigns, 1952–1992.* 2nd ed. Washington, D.C.: Congressional Quarterly Press, 1997.

White, Theodore H. *The Making of the President, 1968.* New York: Atheneum, 1969.

Whitehead, Thomas. "Annals of Television: The Man from Iron City." *The New Yorker*, September 27, 1969.

Whyte, Kenneth. "The Face That Sank a Thousand Tories." *Saturday Night*, February 1994, 58–60.

Winsor, Hugh. "How Did Tories Behind Attack Ads Miss the Message?" *Globe and Mail*, December 8, 1993, A8.

Wood, Stephen C. "Eisenhower Answers America: A Critical History." Mimeo, Department of Speech Communication, University of Rhode Island, n.d.

____. "Television's First Political Spot Ad Campaign: Eisenhower Answers America." *Presidential Studies Quarterly* (Spring 1990).

Woolstencroft, Peter. "'Doing Politics Differently': The Conservative Party and the Campaign of 1993." In *The Canadian General Election of 1993*, edited by Alan Frizzell, John Pammett, and Anthony Westell. Ottawa: Carleton University Press, 1994.

Young, Susan. "Candidates Make Push-Polling Claims." *Bangor Daily News*, October 27, 1994, A1.

Zhu, J., J.R. Milavsky, and R. Biswas. "Do Televised Debates Affect Image Perception More Than Issue Knowledge?" *Human Communication Research* 20 (1994): 302–33.